The Experimental
World Literacy Programme:
a critical assessment

398
/33

The Experimental World Literacy Programme:
a critical assessment

The Unesco Press   UNDP   1976

Published by the Unesco Press
7 Place de Fontenoy, 75700 Paris
and the United Nations
Development Programme (UNDP)
Composed by Imprimerie Rhône-Alpes, Lyon,
and printed by Journal de Genève (Suisse)

ISBN 92-3-101314-9
French edition: 92-3-201314-2
Spanish edition: 92-3-301314-6

Preface

A decade ago Unesco, the United Nations Development Programme and a number of governments embarked on an unprecedented and occasionally controversial major effort to evolve an effective approach towards overcoming the problem of illiteracy. This joint effort ultimately included technical co-operation with eleven Member States in the implementation and testing of functional literacy activities.

To carry forward the effort of evaluating these activities, UNDP and Unesco pooled their resources and set up an Expert Group to provide the secretariats with guidance. The Expert Group was composed of the following members:

Chairman: James Robbins Kidd (Canada).

Rapporteur: Le Thanh Khoi (Republic of South Viet-Nam).

Members: B. Hammiche (Algeria); A. Lopes Correa (Brazil); A. Rudra (India).

The group met three times during 1974-75. At its last meeting in July 1975, it endorsed this final evaluation report prepared by a joint drafting committee of the two secretariats, and formulated its own recommendations which appear in the Appendix to this report.

In endorsing the report, the Expert Group stated that it reflected very accurately what they deemed the global evaluation should be. The experts also concluded that in the report a remarkable job of synthesizing considerable data and information had been done and that it was refreshing to note that the report bore the imprint of an honest and critical spirit and showed a great respect for cultural pluralism.

The experts recommended that the report should be disseminated widely to all educators and specialists concerned not only with literacy but also with the problems of mutation and transformation of educational structures and systems. They therefore invited the Administrator of UNDP and the Director-General of Unesco to publish the report in the official languages of Unesco.

This evaluation report, the first of its kind jointly issued by UNDP and

Unesco, is a frank and open discussion of what was learned from the eleven projects. It is intended for a wide audience of individuals and groups interested or active in literacy and development in various capacities at the national and international levels. It attempts to trace the successes and failures of the projects, and to generalize in such a way that policy-makers and administrators may have information of value to them in making decisions in the future. Of necessity, certain of the issues covered concern problems broader than literacy. The report should therefore also interest readers involved in such areas as educational innovation, adult and non-formal education, education and rural development and the reform of modes of international co-operation.

The report is the result of close co-operation between our secretariats. We should like to thank particularly Seth Spaulding, Professor of Education and Economic and Social Development, University of Pittsburgh, acting as Consultant to the Administrator of the UNDP and assisted by Gregory Leroy who worked closely with Unesco staff assigned to the task. Many other staff members of UNDP and Unesco provided essential contributions to the final product.

The technical documents referred to in the report which were prepared by the Unesco Literacy Division will be made available in the future by Unesco to those persons mainly interested in research on literacy.

We are confident that the conclusions of the report will provide useful guidance for relating efforts in the field of literacy to broader programmes of integrated development in adult and lifelong education. We are publishing this joint report for the purpose of placing the knowledge acquired during the decade of experimentation at the disposal of governments and institutions engaged in literacy programmes.

AMADOU-MAHTAR M'BOW
Director-General
Unesco

RUDOLPH A. PETERSON
Administrator
UNDP

Contents

*I struggled through the alphabet as if it had been
a bramble bush, getting considerably worried and
scratched by every letter.*

(Charles Dickens, *Great Expectations.*)

Now faith is the substance of things hoped for, the evidence of things not seen.
(Epistle to the Hebrews 11:1.)

Introduction

A fully literate world: such was not the immediate aim—still less the main result—of the Experimental World Literacy Programme. What the programme did attempt was to begin to halt the worsening situation with regard to illiteracy in the world. During the decade 1950-60, although the percentage of adult illiteracy (over age 15) dropped from 44.3 to 39.3, the number of illiterates increased from 700 million to 735 million. Projections made in 1960 predicted, moreover, that the number if not the percentage of adult illiterates would continue to rise.

Awareness of this fact led the General Conference of Unesco to decide at its thirteenth session (1964) to

initiate in 1966 a five-year experimental world literacy programme designed to pave the way for the eventual execution of a world campaign in this field.

This decision was the culmination of a long series of studies and activities devoted by Unesco, since its inception, to the problem of literacy, adult education and what was earlier called fundamental education. It further testified to a growing awareness in the international community of the political, intellectual and economic consequences stemming from the illiteracy of a large proportion of mankind.

The main objective of the experimental programme was to test and demonstrate the economic and social returns of literacy and, more generally, to study the mutual relations and influences which exist or may be established or strengthened between literacy training—particularly among the working population—and development.

A few months later, the Secretary General of the United Nations, when presenting the proposals adopted by the Unesco General Conference to the General Assembly, expressed the hope that the experimental programme would make it possible

to provide valuable information on the relationship of literacy with social and economic development; to ensure that the programme will make a considerable impact on economic development during the Development Decade in the countries where projects will be conducted; and to prepare the way for an eventual World Campaign for the Eradication of Mass Illiteracy [34].[1]

The World Conference of Ministers of Education on the Eradication of Illiteracy met in Tehran in 1965 to consider, in particular, the manner in which national plans for the eradication of illiteracy could more effectively contribute to social and economic progress and to the objectives of the United Nations Development Decade. The conference gave international expression to this change in outlook when it stated in its conclusions that:

Rather than an end in itself, [functional] literacy should be regarded as a way of preparing man for a social, civic and economic role that goes far beyond the limits of rudimentary literacy training consisting merely in the teaching of reading and writing. The very process of learning to read and write should be made an opportunity for acquiring information that can immediately be used to improve living standards; reading and writing should lead not only to elementary general knowledge but to training for work, increased productivity, a greater participation in civil life and a better understanding of the surrounding world, and should ultimately open the way to basic human culture [45].

Guided by these decisions and recommendations, yet without ceasing to give support, within the limits of its resources and in response to requests from Member States, to activities undertaken as part of conventional literacy campaigns, Unesco, the United Nations Development Programme (UNDP) and various national governments have been engaged for the last ten years in conducting a series of pilot projects and micro-experiments.

These took place in a score of countries within the framework of the Experimental World Literacy Programme (EWLP), making use of a network of institutions and regional and subregional centres responsible for assisting national literacy programmes.

For national and international staffs alike, the launching and implementation of EWLP required intense activity including, for example, initial identification missions to some fifty countries, and the organization of training programmes and regional conferences. Perhaps more than in many multilateral aid efforts, EWLP was a dynamic attempt to achieve in a relatively short period measurable progress against a particularly intractable aspect of Third World poverty.

EWLP comprised five major types of activity. The first three types included independent and diversified projects covering one or several experiments or subprojects of four to five years' duration. Among these, nine were carried out with financial assistance from UNDP. Four projects were launched in 1967 (Algeria, Ecuador, Iran, Mali), four in 1968 (Ethiopia, Guinea, Madagascar and the United Republic of Tanzania) and one in 1969 (Sudan).

---

1. Figures in square brackets refer to the bibliography at the end of the book.

Secondly, one project launched in 1971 (Zambia) was undertaken with international assistance financed from funds-in-trusts. A single project, launched in 1968 (Venezuela), was carried out with national financing.

The final two types of activity included pilot projects where functional literacy was a component organically and administratively integrated with a development project which was the responsibility of an institution other than the literacy project *per se*. Thus, two projects carried out with financial assistance from UNDP were launched in 1970 in co-operation with the Food and Agriculture Organization (FAO) (India and Syrian Arab Republic). The fifth type of project was undertaken with bilateral assistance. This type included two projects launched in 1971 with aid from Sweden (Afghanistan and Kenya) and another project undertaken in 1971 with aid from a Swiss foundation (Niger).

The question uppermost in the minds of concerned individuals and groups at the end of such an international programme as EWLP is: What have we learned? A first important lesson is the extreme complexity of the undertaking, in the case of EWLP at least. The degree of complexity encountered was quite unexpected at the programme's outset and daunted a good many participants, instructors and administrators, not to mention analysts and evaluators. The complexity was all the greater since the present generation of specialists in industrialized countries—who were expected to provide much of the expertise for designing, implementing and assessing EWLP—simply does not have personal experience of literacy as a chronic national problem.

EWLP's complexity, however sobering, is also challenging. The programme had certain tangible and immediate results. Over 120,000[1] men and women were made functionally literate according to the notion of 'functionality' as interpreted by EWLP. In the process numerous obstacles were encountered and it was the various ways in which the programme came to terms (or otherwise) with these obstacles that posed the greatest challenges and offered future literacy action the richest lessons.

It is only natural that these lessons be drawn and converted into guidelines for future action, first and foremost, in and by the countries that participated in EWLP. Nevertheless, an important reason for the provision of assistance to national EWLP projects by the United Nations system was the hope that broader lessons would emerge and be of use for the international community as a whole.

The present report attempts to set out just such lessons. It is based essentially on the experience of countries that received assistance from UNDP and Unesco under EWLP: Algeria, Ecuador, Ethiopia, Guinea, India,[2] Iran, Madagascar, Mali, Sudan, Syrian Arab Republic,[2] United Republic of Tanzania. Some of these countries have already reoriented their literacy efforts in the light of their participation in the programme. Other

1. This figure is the estimated result of projects in five EWLP countries on which data are available.
2. Projects also aided by FAO.

countries in turn may find in this report valuable guidelines for future action. Since the programme was a major international effort and therefore more than the sum of its individual parts, certain of the lessons suggested here may also have implications for multilateral and even bilateral co-operation in the education field and beyond.

The data have been drawn primarily from the following national and international sources:

Project files at UNDP and Unesco headquarters (these included interim and final project reports by chief technical advisers and evaluation specialists; periodic reports of UNDP resident representatives; reports of UNDP-Unesco joint evaluation missions; financial statements on projects).

Preliminary drafts of the technical reports on various aspects of EWLP prepared by the Evaluation and Research Unit attached to Unesco's Literacy Division.

Reports and research documents from universities and governmental and non-governmental institutes and organizations, and studies carried out by individuals.

Interviews with a variety of specialists at different levels who were involved with aspects of the Experimental World Literacy Programme.

The report synthesises information from the various sources and uses material considered most significant in the context of all data available to the authors. Much of the background documentation used is not available in published form and thus does not appear in the bibliography. Those published items directly referred to in the report do appear in the bibliography. A more extensive general bibliography of the Experimental World Literacy Programme is available from Unesco's Literacy Division.

This report approaches EWLP in two ways. First, it analyses EWLP vertically, with a series of project profiles. That is, each project is described and analysed so as to elicit particularly salient information in the following areas, as appropriate: time perspective; policy and objectives; participants; administration and organization; teachers and other personnel; curriculum and methods; teaching materials; costs; and evaluation and research. Each profile ends with a summary which attempts to single out some of the major lessons learned from that project.

Secondly, all projects are analysed—and lessons drawn from them—horizontally. That is, global lessons are sought under the following four headings: Why EWLP?; The wherewithal; Doing the job; The results. Particularly in these chapters a certain paradox appears. On the one hand, problems encountered by EWLP resulted from its innovative aims and character. But on the other, at least some of its limits were imposed by the fact that its implementation depended on traditional forms of technical assistance. From this contradiction emerged, happily, not only problems but also numerous positive guidelines for the future.

This report attempts to make a genuinely honest assessment. Indeed, because it seeks to derive lessons for the future, it may tend on occasion to focus on what went wrong with EWLP rather than what went right. In this way it heeds a warning sounded in 1972 by Unesco's International Commission on the Development of Education in its report *Learning to Be*. Speaking in the name of those concerned with literacy, the commission stressed the need for frankness, so as to avoid the reproach that 'we are succumbing to demagogy in this particularly delicate field of social action' [10].

Thus no claim is made for quantitatively airtight argumentation. The report does not hold up a single 'model' of literacy action for replication or even adaptation. Nor does it defend any single approach to literacy. Rather, it strives to offer information and ideas that could be of use nationally and internationally, in projects ranging from micro-experiments to mass campaigns. In this pluralistic and self-critical spirit, the report asks more questions than it even begins to answer.

The point, then, is to encourage rather than avoid debate, to stoke up rather than damp down even unorthodox thinking about the various subjects covered here. It has been felt that this would be the most useful—and perhaps most readable—manner in which to make known the issues raised by EWLP. If these issues have a rather uneven quality about them, this is because the programme's implementors were understandably more concerned with doing than with recording. As a result, *post facto* information available was of varying reliability. This made an essentially qualitative approach the only—if not necessarily the best—way to interpret the results.

Part I
Country profiles

In order to place Part II of this report in perspective, it is essential to have some notion of how each project functioned in its national context. Although there was a kind of guiding philosophy in the programme, this was translated into action in different ways in each country.

A number of the generalizations in Part II do not apply to all projects with equal strength. The implementation of most projects did not fully correspond in all respects with certain statistical and qualitative norms. These variations can only be understood through a brief overview of each project.

The profiles are presented in alphabetical order by country. Each is a synthesis of information collected from various sources. As far as possible, an attempt was made to locate original sources. UNDP regional bureaux provided access to the complete project files (which generally included periodic and final reports from experts and chief technical advisers), UNDP resident representative reports relating to the projects, UNDP/Unesco evaluation mission reports, and sizeable quantities of financial data. Unesco files yielded similar data. Programme officers and administrators of both organizations gave their views on first drafts, and these were included, where relevant, in final drafts. Members of the Unesco Literacy Division's Evaluation Unit provided comments and some quantitative data which improved the profiles. In some cases where this unit's data seemed to differ from information available from other sources, such differences are noted.

The profiles are essentially qualitative, and they attempt to look at relevant aspects of each project in terms of how the project functioned and in terms of what can be learnt from the unique aspects of each project. Each project speaks for itself.

Algeria

Time perspective

Algeria became independent in 1962 and in 1963 launched a mass volunteer literacy campaign, to be operated through the various labour organizations and through the Ministry of Youth and Sports. By 1965, it was realized that this campaign was not successful, and a request for funding of a functional literacy project was submitted through Unesco to UNDP in 1965. It was reviewed by the Governing Council of the Special Fund in January 1966 and operations were started in early 1967.

The first phase of the project lasted five years (1967-71). Policy and goals were reoriented in 1971 and an amendment to the plan was signed on 27 August 1972. The project ended on 28 February 1974.

Policy and objectives

Project policy in Algeria was influenced by the national economic policy of emphasizing worker-managed collectives, co-operatives and State-owned business enterprises. The government repeatedly stressed the need for literate workers to make the economic and ideological system work. The government called for energetic mobilization of all adults within a revolutionary climate that stimulates and supports the involvement of each citizen. The national political party stressed that it was the stimulus for this action which should be the first national duty.

The goal of raising mass consciousness clearly conflicted with the selective, intensive, experimental nature of the functional literacy project, as modelled by Unesco. For the first five years of the project, the principal objective was to assist the government and the National Literacy Centre to experiment in the functional literacy programme in three distinct target zones: (a) the autonomous agricultural region of Staoueli (about 20 kilometres from Algiers); (b) the industrial zone of Arzew (about 40 kilometres from Oran); and (c) the industrial and agricultural zones of Annaba (north-east of Algiers).

In the second phase which was approved in 1972, the objectives were modified and instead of working in these three subprojects, it was foreseen that the project would contribute to the objective of the four-year plan (1970-73) whereby 1 million workers were to be made literate, the project covering 40,000 farmers and 15,000 industrial workers. Thus, the conflict between the experimental project and the national effort was resolved. The project would no longer have a geographical (selective) emphasis, but would concentrate on certain sectors within the national plan.

The objective of the functional literacy concept as applied in Algeria was to teach not only reading, writing and arithmetic *per se* but to integrate them with general professional and technical training of industrial and agricultural workers and their families. The programmes in the agricultural sectors were primarily concerned with training for self-management (socio-economic education with some specific professional content). In the industrial sector, two distinct approaches were tested: first, a common content for all industrial enterprises covered, which was designed to create among workers an awareness and understanding of technological subjects; second, tailor-made programmes designed for specific industrial enterprises.

The goal of functional literacy as applied in Algeria was to change attitudes and create an awareness and motivation favourable to increased productivity, and to improve standards of living and the integration of individual efforts with national development. Thus, the project attempted to link the teaching of literacy with the economic and social development objectives of the country.

A new national policy was announced in 1974 which stressed the notion of lifelong education, and implied that functional literacy was to be integrated into a variety of other in- and out-of-school educational efforts. Current (1974) policy is to place responsibility and control within workers groups for the design of their own agricultural development and literacy education plan.

Participants

It is estimated that there are some 6 million illiterates in Algeria, about 75 per cent of the population. During the first five years of the project, sixty-five functional literacy groups were established (1,200 participants) in the agricultural sector and fifty-eight groups (about 1,500 workers) in the industrial sector. A large extension of activity took place beginning with the second phase of 1972 and enrolment soon increased to 26,000 participants in the agricultural sector and 6,000 in the industrial sector. By September 1973 (near the end of the project), it was estimated that enrolment had risen to 39,912 in the agricultural sector and 13,954 in the industrial sector. In addition, it is estimated that there was an enrolment of 374,960 from 1970 to 1974 in the government's national programme not included in the project. Thus, the project directly affected less than 1 per cent of the illiterates in Algeria, although the national programme affected another 5 per cent during the last four years of project operation and undoubtedly benefited from the experimental project's activities.

The literacy participants were relatively homogeneous in terms of level of knowledge, despite variances in age. Inscription was obligatory for foremen in agriculture and recommended for workers in both sectors.

The project reported a 30 per cent dropout rate in the first cycle, and a 21 per cent dropout in the second cycle. Thus, only one in every two entering the programme finished the second cycle, which implies about fifth-grade reading ability and somewhat less ability in writing and calculation, plus whatever technical and functional content may be provided during the programme (see evaluation section, below). Among those who did not drop out, attendance rates averaged 67 per cent in the first cycle and 71 per cent in the second cycle.

Administration and organization

The pilot project was under the authority of the Ministry of Primary and Secondary Education. This ministry ensured the liaison between the various technical ministries which were interested in functional literacy as well as between the government and Unesco. The National Literacy Centre played the role of central technical, co-ordinating and organizing agency, with full responsibility for the operational activities of the project. The two consultative committees foreseen in the plan of operations did not function in any important fashion during the life of the project. It proved possible, however, to interest some local agricultural and industrial bodies in undertaking the organization and execution of functional literacy courses. The national centre co-ordinated the activities of these local units and provided the requisite technical assistance.

The lack of effective co-ordination between the various ministries, however, impeded the extension of the work, and the early centralization and control of what was done by the National Literacy Centre further impeded efficiency. Later modifications of the plan of operation (the 1972-73 phase) eliminated the emphasis on geographic regions and placed emphasis on sectors, leading to greater decentralization and to greater involvement at the local level. This mode of operation was consistent with a Council of Ministers decree of 13 May 1971, which indicated that each public institution must include a permanent structure for literacy instruction. This decree further indicated that recruitment and pay of literacy teachers should be in local hands, and that each institution must provide meeting space and other requirements.

The role of the National Literacy Centre, where the project was based, has now been limited to the provision of appropriate functional literacy materials, supervisors and advisers, and the training of teachers. The central political party and other organizations assist the centre in the preparation of materials and other activities. The Assemblée Populaire Communale is responsible at the local level for motivating local groups to undertake functional literacy activities, and each of the national and local self-managed organizations is charged with training its own workers, using centre materials.

Early project reports pointed out the difficulty of getting ministries other than the Ministry of Education interested in the functional literacy project. The national development plan stressed industrial development requiring little use of mass labour and many of these enterprises could see small point in spending time and effort on classes which would not directly affect their production targets. At the same time, most of the planning was done by a small group in the National Literacy Centre with no technical committees to help in the work. With the integration of educational objectives in each sectoral plan, and with the official designation of the National Literacy Centre as co-ordinating agency (1972) a number of these difficulties were gradually overcome.

Teachers and other personnel

The majority of literacy instructors came from the same background as the participants. These instructors were usually supervisors and foremen in the agricultural and industrial sectors, although some elementary-school teachers prepared to give six hours a week to the work were also used. They were given a training of three to four weeks. As a rule the practical demonstrations were given by personnel directly familiar with the work and not by the literacy instructors.

About two-thirds of the instructors had primary-school education and the rest were below this level, with the exception of a small number, about 5 per cent, who had completed secondary education.

Three types of instructors were utilized in the project: one was the part-time instructor, a type which was abandoned after the first phase of the project; the second was an instructor engaged on a permanent basis by the project and paid by it. Towards the end of the project, thirdly, instructors were more frequently recruited from among participants' fellow workers. A total of 1,557 instructors were trained by the project: 1,232 for the agricultural sector and 325 for the industrial.

The training was carried out in decentralized locations, for example at centres for professional agricultural training in the case of teachers working in agricultural areas. A number of follow-up sessions were held, sometimes as often as once every two or three months.

The Unesco team also trained a number of counterparts at the National Literacy Centre in the production and testing of educational materials. Regional supervisors were also trained.

Curriculum and methods

For the agricultural programmes the target populations were chosen in relation to ongoing agricultural development projects (from 1967 to 1971 the irrigation network of Bou Namoussa-Willaya d'Annaba; region of Algiers-Sahel). During this phase, a single programme dealing with self-management in socialized agriculture was applied.

In 1972 some modifications were made in keeping with the objectives of the national development plan. While the programmes destined for farmers having crops requiring water were maintained (in continuation of the first phase of the project), new programmes covering additional crops were developed. During this period three specific programmes were applied, one to crops benefiting directly from the irrigation system, one to crops near the irrigation system, and one to wheat growing in unirrigated areas outside this region.

The industrial programmes during the 1967-71 phase of the project, were directed at workers in key industries (oil and gas, petrochemical and steel, etc.). One common programme was designed to provide the illiterate workers with general training to be followed by a more specific programme in the second stage. This second stage, however, was never elaborated.

During the second phase of the project, the industrial objectives of the four-year plan led to the selection of target populations in large national enterprises engaged in mining, meat and food processing as well as building materials. The programme developed for the first phase was gradually replaced after 1973 by tailor-made programmes, including three covering the above-mentioned industries.

These programmes were designed to bring the newly literate adult to a level enabling him to use his acquired knowledge and facilitate his eventual participation in vocational training. In order to reach this level, an average of twenty-two months were required (a range from twenty-two to twenty-four months per programme structured over three stages at the rate of four sessions of $1\frac{1}{2}$ hours each per week).

In both sectors the same pedagogic approach was followed, beginning with the introduction of a theme of professional interest presented through posters or films and followed by group discussions of possible solutions to the problems. The actual learning of reading, writing and arithmetic was integrated with these discussions and corresponded to the problem situations under review. For the agricultural sector this could mean a discussion of various plant diseases, harvesting, irrigation, the introduction of new techniques and the improvement of techniques already acquired. For the industrial programmes, actual parts of machines and tools were utilized in the discussion. The main themes of the common industrial programme prepared during the first phase of the project included an introduction to technological knowledge, social education, general education and knowledge related to industrial development.

Teaching materials

Literacy teaching was begun through the presentation of a key sentence, followed by an analysis of its constituent parts and an eventual synthesis at the end of the session. For the agricultural programme, 304 Arabic words were covered in the first stage and 876 in the second stage. For the single industrial programme, 580 words were covered in the first stage.

During the first phase of the project, the didactic material was similar for the two programmes. There was an increased diversification after 1973. The following types of material were produced:

1. Instruction sheets, based on sequences of twelve sessions, destined for teachers (professional content, reading, writing and arithmetics).
2. Literacy materials for the participants.
3. Posters covering the themes under discussion as well as literacy.
4. Specially prepared material for new literates.
5. Films on specific professional themes.

The audio-visual means were utilized before, during and after training programmes. Special films were also prepared.

In summary, preparation and production of project materials got off to a very slow start. By the end of the fourth operational year of the project (end of 1970), only one programme had been produced for the agricultural sector, while six were in preparation for the industrial sector but none finished. There was little integration of literacy instruction in the early technicel materials. Additional materials were prepared during the second phase of the project, and many of these showed a distinct improvement over the earlier ones.

Costs

The costs of the Algerian project were difficult to assess because of the decentralized nature of the programme, with costs spread between various organisms. The instructors were paid by local groups and by the various government enterprises and collectives, while the teaching materials were partially subsidized by the State through its support of the National Literacy Centre, which also trained teachers and provided various forms of supervision. The budget of the National Literacy Centre in 1974 was approximately 3 per cent of the budget of the Ministry of Primary and Secondary Education.

Estimates on planned and actual cost of the project (as supplied by the Unesco Literacy Division's Evaluation Unit) are shown below:

| | Funding source | | Total |
	UNDP	Government	
Actual expenditure (U.S.$)	1,009,500	4,793,100	5,797,600
Planned expenditure[1] (U.S.$)	1,216,300	5,070,600	6,287,000
Percentage of planned expenditure actually used	83	94	92

1. Plan of operation.

Based on these estimates, the total cost per participant was $71 ($60 if research costs are deducted) and per final participant (those who took, but did not necessarily pass, the final examination), $98.63 ($83.27 if research costs are deducted). These figures appear on the high side, compared to some other projects, and may be partially explained by delays in implementation during the early phase of the project.

Evaluation and research

The slow implementation of this project meant that most evaluation activities were devoted to programme support. A number of context studies on potential target populations have helped in the planning of operations and the design of more suitable instructional programmes. During the various phases of the project, different information systems were developed to follow the educational process and to control the statistical turnover of participants (attendance registers, tests and observation guides).

Most studies undertaken in the project were designed to help improve ongoing functional literacy activities. They dealt with questions of motivation, technical problems encountered in work situations, absenteeism from work, and surveys of the socio-economic conditions of families.

With the accelerated momentum of the project in the second phase (1972-73), somewhat more evaluation data was generated. An achievement study of 600 adults finishing the first cycle of the programme showed that, on the average, adults achieved somewhere between first- and second-grade (elementary school) ability in language, writing, reading and mathematics. A comparable study of 350 adults finishing the second cycle showed that they achieved, on the average, an ability level of somewhere between the fourth- and fifth-grade level in all skills, although they tended to do somewhat better in mathematics and reading than in writing. The younger students did slightly better than the older students.

The evaluation of the work-related portion of the training is somewhat less conclusive. In 1972, a baseline survey was designed to collect data on a sampling of adults in the agricultural sectors. The thirty-two page questionnaire was in French, and administered by students of an agricultural technical institute who spent two weeks in the field, surveying about 100 agricultural collectives (*domaines autogérés*).

A second questionnaire, this time in Arabic, was designed in 1973 and administered in roughly the same areas by the National Literacy Centre. Some of the questions were roughly comparable to some of those in the earlier questionnaire, but many tended to be more open-ended than on the earlier form.

The results of the two surveys are difficult to compare. The populations surveyed, although in roughly the same geographical areas, were not necessarily the same. The questionnaires used different questions, while one was in French and the second in Arabic. Finally, the questionnaires tended to ask opinion and information questions, with only a few questions related to actual practice of the adults in their personal, community and productive life. Those questions which did deal with the latter points were often phrased in such a way that the validity of the response may be open to question.

Examples of such questions include one in the second survey which asks adults who have participated in literacy courses which part of the course has been most useful: reading, writing, mathematics; the socio-economic part; the technical part? To give import to a semi-literate's response to such an abstract question is simply not serious.

A similar question asks adults what radio and television programmes they listen to: 'recreational, cultural, informational, technical and professio-nal?' This is a valid area of concern, but their listening habits cannot be identified by asking them to classify their habits in an abstract conceptual category system that is meaningful only to the researchers. Even university graduates would have difficulty responding to such a question in any way that would produce valid responses.

At best, there is some indication in the before-and-after results of the questionnaire that the participants in literacy classes gained some information on how collectives are managed and on members' expected participative role. About the same proportion of those surveyed in the first and second questionnaire say that they go to collective meetings. Those responding in the second survey say that they read more and sign more documents than those surveyed earlier. The individuals in the 'after' group tend to indicate that they are more likely to be candidates for leadership posts in the collectives than individuals in the 'before' group. But there are no data to indicate that actual behaviour is what they say it is on the questionnaire.

Several questions on the second questionnaire asked about the need to introduce new methods of cultivation. About three-quarters of the respondents answered 'yes' and suggested things that needed improvement. Slightly fewer (not statistically significant) of those replying to the earlier questionnaire felt that new practices were necessary. In the follow-up questionnaire it appeared that hostility towards production norms of the collective had increased.

Summary

The early phases of the Algerian project suffered because of a lack of agreement between the national authorities and the international experts concerning the basic nature of the project. The international experts wished to conduct an experiment in limited geographical areas while the government was committed to a programme of mass education designed to prepare citizens for full participation in its new socio-economic programme.

Once the government's policy was accepted, the project became viable. Certain productive sectors were accepted as priority areas of concern, but the project became national and was so conducted for the latter half of the project.

Although there was high-level policy support for the project, there was some slippage between policy and implementation. For example, various ministries were not convinced of the utility of functional literacy in their sectors, given the limited resources available. In later stages of the project, priorities relating to functional literacy and appropriate resources were inserted into the development plans of each sector. However, co-ordination between ministries was never fully effective.

A strategy gradually evolved through which content and materials were established at the national level, through the National Literacy Centre, which was also responsible for training of supervisors and teachers. Responsibility for actual conduct of classes was delegated to local authorities, both in the political and productive sectors. This decentralization had obvious theoretical advantages, but made control of what actually took place somewhat difficult. Additionally, although it had the advantage of absorbing many of the costs of the programme at the local level, it made it difficult to accurately estimate the cost of the programme.

Teachers, at least towards the end of the project, tended to be from the same community as the illiterates and themselves had limited formal education and technical skills. Thus, the effectiveness of the technical side of the training, and perhaps the literacy skills element, was somewhat restricted by the limited skills of the instructors. Furthermore, the literacy materials did not effectively integrate the technical element with the literacy skills aspects.

The Algerian project was one of the few among the experimental projects that made a serious attempt at evaluation. However, the evaluation studies suffered from a lack of continuity and sophistication and are, at best, inconclusive as to the effects and/or benefits of the project. Although it is clear that those illiterates who stay with the programme for two years achieve about fourth- or fifth-grade reading, writing and mathematical skills, there is only scant information concerning their use of these skills, no information on their retention of them, and little information (mostly opinion surveying) about their acquisition of new behaviours and utilization of new technical skills which affect their personal lives or productive patterns.

Common sense, however, suggests that functional literacy, no matter how it is defined, must be important in a country which has opted for a national economic policy based on collectives, co-operatives, and worker-run enterprises. Thus, if the Algerian authorities have acquired skills in the preparation of literacy and basic education materials and in the conduct of adult education activities through the project, it can reasonably be concluded that the project has contributed to the long-term goals of the country.

Ecuador

Time perspective

In 1966 the Government of Ecuador submitted to UNDP a request for assistance in carrying out an experimental Work-Oriented Adult Literacy Project, with Unesco as the Executing Agency. The request was approved by the Governing Council in January 1967. In April 1967, the original Plan of Operation was signed. Field operations began shortly thereafter, and continued for approximately five years. A single phase of the project was carried out. During 1971 and 1972 the government considered the extension of the project and a request for a second phase of two years' duration was submitted to UNDP (September 1972). However, the request was not included in the country-programme proposal (the approved country-programme foresaw UNDP and Unesco assistance to functional literacy during the period 1973-76, but not as an extension of the pilot project). By May 1973, after the termination of the WOALP, a UNDP memo noted that 'we understand that the government is not carrying on a continuing literacy programme of any proportions'.

The national literacy effort appears to have discarded the idea of differentiated programmes and is drawing on Paulo Freire methodology rather than EWLP doctrine.

Policy and objectives

The general objective of the programme was to assist the government in organizing and implementing a work-oriented adult literacy pilot project to develop new techniques and materials, to improve the country's adult education and literacy programme and to demonstrate, in measurable and practical terms, the impact of functional literacy on economic development.

The project was to be co-ordinated with the agrarian reform

programmes and with agricultural, vocational and industrial training, and the promotion of co-operatives; its chief objectives[1] included :
1. Training national personnel in functional literacy techniques.
2. Achieving work-oriented elementary skills in reading, writing, and arithmetic.
3. Promoting the socio-economic orientation of the worker.
4. Developing gradual use of the means of mass communication.
5. Promoting active participation of adults in civic, social and economic organizations.
6. Promoting sanitary practices.
7. Contributing towards the improvement of working skills with a view to increased productivity, improvement of consumption habits and better salaries.

Programme policy emphasized the articulation of literacy training and training in agricultural and technical skills. Functional literacy was designed to be supportive and subsidiary to wider social/economic development efforts, particularly in the area of agrarian reform. A revision in the original Plan of Operation placed great emphasis on enhancing the 'social awareness and participation' of the participants (see objectives 3 and 5 above).

Due to the difficult problems which hampered the implementation of the country's development plans, the link which should have existed between these plans and the functional literacy programme became weaker than had been foreseen at the beginning. For example, the agrarian reform was not implemented at Milagro as programmed; the expansion of an industrial park in Cuenca, foreseen in the country's industrial development plan, did not materialize. In the last years of the project (1971-72) a closer link between the literacy programme and agricultural programmes, industrial and handicrafts training programmes, and co-operatives development was established. It is clear that throughout the programme government support at the national level was weak at best (some reports and memoranda imply that it was virtually absent).

Participants

Three pilot areas, one in Cuenca in the southern Sierra industrial zone, one in Milagro on the coast near Guayaquil, and one in Pesillo in the northern Sierra, were selected for operations. The last two areas are agricultural, Pesillo being a former hacienda with some 2,000 inhabitants being reorganized under agrarian reform. Enrolment targets were 15,900 in Milagro, 15,000 in Cuenca and 2,000 in Pesillo. These targets were successively scaled down to 6,560, 7,520 and 1,120 respectively, as the

1. The project's objectives were originally considerably broader than these, reflecting a more comprehensive programme of adult education. The development of the project is well documented in Seth Spaulding, 'The Unesco World Literacy Program—A New Strategy that may Work', *Adult Education*, Vol. XVI, No. 2, Winter 1966, p. 70-84, Washington, D.C., Adult Education Association of the United States of America.

project got under way. The final report shows 17,410 'effective enrolments', and 8,715 enrollees completing a cycle of training.[1]

The project in general covered a population of small producers and independent workers, among whom existed a certain co-operative organization based upon commercialization or trading. There was a grouping effort in order to sell better on the local or national market. The tools used were quite diversified, ranging from traditional to modern.

Rather more women participated than men. The large number of women was due to the programme in home economics, which was well accepted by the population in the three pilot zones. The groups of participants were homogeneous only as to language (Spanish), and very heterogeneous as to age. Some homogeneity existed as to:

1. Socio-professional status.
2. Level of knowledge at the start of the programme (illiteracy and semi-literacy).
3. Level of technical knowledge.
4. Sex (some classes were mixed, others were not).
5. Origin of trainees (same community, same district, same workshop or industry).

Not all trainees were actively involved in work related to development. Some were unemployed due (at least in one subproject area) to the drop in the sale of Panama hats.

Administration and organization

The project was under the general responsibility of the Ministry of Education which acted through the Director of the Department of Adult Education and the National Co-ordinator of the project. The National Co-ordinator was to ensure liaison with other national ministries and organizations concerned in the project. A regional office of the project, under the direct responsibility of zone administrators, existed in each pilot zone.

A large National Co-ordinating Committee existed under the chairmanship of the Minister of Education. This committee included representatives of several national and regional development agencies, high officials of the ministries directly related to the project (education, agriculture, industry and commerce), the Junta Nacional de Planificacion y Coordiacion, and international appointees in a non-voting capacity (UNDP, Unesco, FAO, ILO). The full committee met only exceptionally. Supporting services were provided to a certain extent by the Ministry of Agriculture, the Centro de Reconversion Economica de las Provincias Australes, and the Instituto Ecuatoriano de Reforma Agraria y Colonización. Some bilateral aid was forthcoming from the United States and the Federal Republic of Germany. The Roman Catholic Church gave its support in certain

1. Unesco Evaluation Unit final figures indicate 17,722 'effective enrolments' and 9,988 completing a training cycle.

communities. The local authorities in Cuenca and Milagro also gave their support in terms of land, buildings, etc.

Teachers and other personnel

The literacy instructors, a majority of whom were employed on a part-time basis, presented the following features: nearly two-thirds of the instructors were used only for literacy instruction and were not in charge of vocational training and practical demonstrations. Some were in charge only of demonstrations and vocational training, while a few taught both literacy and vocational skills.

Almost 30 per cent of the instructors employed had not completed secondary school. Fifty per cent of the literacy instructors were primary school teachers, 25 per cent were 'supervisors' (agricultural extension personnel, etc.), 9 per cent came from the same socio-professional background as the trainees, and the remaining 12 per cent were not categorized. The great majority of the literacy instructors were selected by the project staff ; a few were appointed by the Ministry of Education and by other co-operating agencies. The criteria for selection were primarily a candidate's professional status and his level of education (based on titles, certificates, etc.). The training of literacy instructors was apparently the responsibility of the National Co-ordinator (see above 'Administration and Organization'); however, the Plan of Operation and project reports do not go into further detail on the nature of instructor training.

Major problems involving the recruitment and training of literacy instructors were experienced. A great majority of instructors were paid a nominal wage (U.S.$15-20 monthly). Many of those who were recruited remained with the project only until they secured more lucrative employment, and consequently the attrition rate was high (close to 50 per cent at times). Teacher turnover exceeded the capacity to train new recruits, and as a result many literacy instructors were placed in the field without adequate training.

Largely due to the government's inability to release promised funds, the number of personnel working with the project lagged far behind the original plans. In 1970, after three years of operation, only 52 per cent of the promised staff had been recruited, thus forcing a drastic reduction in the hoped-for number of participants.

As with other projects, the Unesco team trained a number of counterparts in the production and testing of educational materials as well as various kinds of supervisory personnel.

Curriculum, methods and materials

Four distinct types of training programme were employed: agricultural, handicrafts and small industries, home economics, and co-operative education.

It appears that classes succeded only partially in integrating literacy instruction with instruction in vocational/technical areas. Sometimes complete integration was realized, sometimes there was none at all.

The teaching of reading utilized several different methods, including analytical, global and mixed. The official national language (Spanish) served as the medium of literacy instruction.

During the first phase of the project, the materials employed in each distinct type of programme were essentially undifferentiated. Only in the second phase (chiefly after 1970) were diversified, programme-specific primers and other materials developed. These generally utilized a 'key word' approach to reading instruction. Key words and sentences were drawn from the particular technical vocabulary and environmental context around which a programme had been built. Writing was closely integrated with reading exercises. Mathematics were a part of each sequence of the programme, the problems being related to programme content.

The preparation of materials was a joint enterprise of the specialists in different fields (agriculture, industry and handicrafts, home economics, etc.), who initiated such preparation for each programme, and the literacy specialists of the project, who were responsible for the methodologic and didactic aspects which had to be taken into account. A 'production unit', fully equipped, produced the required quantity of the material, which can be summarized as follows:

1. Materials for literacy instructors: six guides (e.g. literacy teaching in rural areas, in home economics, in community workshops, etc.); several brochures dealing with agricultural extension in general and the main crops in Ecuador.
2. Materials for the trainees: twelve primers (one general, eleven diversified); posters; audio-visual materials; and a twice-weekly television programme in Cuenca.
3. Follow-up materials for neo-literates: approximately twenty brochures and leaflets on specific subjects related to the project; filmstrips, slides, etc.; a monthly newspaper, and a yearly almanac.

Costs

The Interagency Mission Report (1970) indicated that the financial contribution of the government was, at that time, running well behind the annual government contribution specified in the Plan of Operation. Lack of funds, the report noted, had dramatically reduced the ability of the project to train national counterparts, and had limited the ability of the various staff experts to travel from one field site to another to assess the actual operation of the programmes. For the total duration of the project (through 1972), only 62 per cent of the planned government expenditure was actually utilized, as shown below (figures supplied by the Unesco Literacy Division, Evaluation Unit):

	Funding source		Total
	UNDP	Government	
Actual expenditure (U.S.$)	1,193,800	1,071,400	2,275,200
Planned expenditure[1] (U.S.$)	1,156,400	1,739,800	2,896,200
Percentage of planned expenditure actually used	103	62	78

1. Plan of Operation, April 1967.

Project cost per enrollee is estimated at $69.83 and per final participant (those who took, but did not necessarily pass, the final examination) at $122.55. Both figures include preparatory and operational costs and indicate a high degree of participant wastage. Approximately 40 per cent of all costs were estimated to be for research and evaluation activities.

Evaluation

During the first two and a half years of the project, evaluation activities were somewhat detached from actual operations. This was, in great part, due to the fact that the preparatory phase foreseen in the Plan of Operation was not carried out and field activities were begun immediately. This meant that the objectives of these programmes could not be specified in advance, and were often very general and not operationalized.

In the individual programme areas, baseline studies were carried out to establish benchmarks on existing socio-economic conditions, aspirations, level of knowledge, and literacy skills. These surveys were amplified through studies at the regional and national levels. The evaluation plan foresaw interim surveys for each succeeding year, but this plan had to be modified. Nevertheless, some interim surveys were conducted, and they indicate that the migration of participants to the cities was high. They also revealed the need to redefine some of the indicators in use to ensure greater relevance in terms of programme content.

In 1970, as a result of an attempt at more precise definition of indicators and corresponding instrumentation to measure achievement of operational objectives, three new surveys were carried out in the programme zones covering all new registrants at the first and second phases. In addition, a comprehensive information system was set up which provided statistical turnover information on all participants. Reasons for high turnover, however, were not reported.

Final measurements were conducted in June 1972, in respect of about seventy of the participants who had been surveyed in 1970. The final report of the programme was recognized as being very subjective. It attempted to highlight the few successes of the programme and to obscure its many failures. Its conclusions (demonstrating the programme's success) rest on shaky assumptions and methods, and are inconclusive at best. More objective assessments agree that the programme, in general, failed to meet its objectives and goals. On the other hand, an incomplete final report of the evaluation expert implies that the functional literacy process did exercise a favourable influence on participants in helping them move toward a more autonomous approach in seeking solutions to their learning problems and towards an improved level of living.

Summary

The major shortcoming of the project was the lack of government financial and logistical support. The relative failure of the project to meet its objectives can be traced ultimately to insufficient funds. The most graphic demonstraction of this was the project's inability to recruit and maintain a skilled teaching staff and other professional personnel at competitive salaries. High staff turnover resulted in a strain on the training machinery which ultimately diluted the quality of the project's teachers, and forced the enrolment of participants to be cut.

A second obvious shortcoming was the failure to implement the 'functional literacy' concept in the manner foreseen. This problem appears to be partly attributable to the failure of the government to establish close links between the project and wider development efforts, and partly to high-level misunderstanding of the concept itself (the literacy and vocational components of the project were frequently viewed as parallel, but not integrally related activities). This conceptual confusion in turn was exacerbated by the dearth of funds which precluded the possibility of training an instructional staff skilled in both literacy and vocational-instructional techniques.

A third area in which difficulties arose was that of evaluation. It would appear that concern for actual teaching overshadowed important early stages of evaluation, including evaluation which might have facilitated teaching. The evaluation sector seems to have been characterized by a lack of foresight and planning and was not well integrated into the other sectors of the project.

A final source of difficulty apparently lay in the fact that many of the participants were either unemployed or engaged in work not related to the vocational components of the subprojects. This may have contributed to the project's relatively low level of participant enrolment.

Ethiopia

Time perspective

In April 1967, an Inter-Agency (UNDP-FAO-ILO-Unesco) Preparatory Assistance Mission went to Ethiopia to reformulate a government request for UNDP assistance. The revised request involved provision for assistance in the establishment of a Work-Oriented Adult Literacy Project (WOALP) to be linked to economic and social development. It was submitted by the government to UNDP on 3 August 1967. The project was aprroved by the Governing Council (fifth session) in January 1968, and the Plan of Operation was signed on 31 August 1968. The first literacy experts arrived in August/September 1968, and the project became operational in October. The duration of the project was to be five years, from mid-1968 to mid-1973. The first fourteen months of the project were 'preparatory', and actual operation in the field commenced when the first series of functional literacy classes was initiated in the Abela and Areka areas of the Wolamo/ Sodo subproject in December 1969 and January 1970.

Policy and objectives

The general purpose of the project was to assist the Government of Ethiopia in organizing, implementing and evaluating a work-oriented adult literacy project closely linked with rural development in particular, as well as industrial/vocational training. The project was also to train national counterparts, supervisors, and trainers of literacy teachers in the new approach and techniques of functional literacy. The specific objectives of the project were:
1. To teach basic reading, writing and arthmetic, emphasizing the current vocabularies of agricultural and industrial practice.
2. To plan and carry out experiments bearing on curricula, teaching methods, materials, forms of organization, supervision and administration and co-ordination.

3. To integrate educational, social and economic activities so as to achieve overall development through co-ordination of training with practical development work being carried on by public and private bodies.
4. To evaluate the various aspects of the project and its effect on economic and social development, so that it might serve as an example for other parts of the country or for other nations.

The experimental approach (objective 2) was never fully operationalized, due in part to the lack of enthusiasm of early Unesco project personnel, and to a failure to communicate to the government the true meaning of an experimental approach. Instead, an approach known as 'action research' was adopted. Under this programme, a particular method was decided upon and tried. It was then modified and tried again and again, as often as necessary to obtain the best form and combination.

The programme employed the concept of 'functional literacy', whereby selected target illiterates were to be taught basic reading, writing and arithmetic, by emphasizing the current vocabularies of agricultural and industrial practice. Literacy training was to be supported by, and closely linked with, agricultural extension, farmer training services, assistance to cottage industries, family living education, industrial vocational training, industrial safety and hygiene. The extent to which links were established between literacy training and these other development activities varied considerably from one subproject to the next, depending partly on the nature of the subproject and partly on factors ouside the programme's control; however, in each subproject, a preliminary study was conducted to determine the development needs of local target populations (based largely on interviews with heads of families in rural areas—a somewhat limited approach to the definition of development needs) and an attempt was made to incorporate these needs into the functional literacy programme.

When WOALP began, a national development plan had already been established. The Plan of Operation for each subproject corresponded to an appropriate regional plan, which in turn was part of the national plan. WOALP was thus designed to contribute both to the economic and social well-being of the individual participant, and to the previously articulated development aims of the region and of the nation as a whole. Following from these dual goals, each subproject developed a set of commonly shared methods and materials and curriculum content, while simultaneously employing methods, materials and content suited to the unique cultural, economic and social needs of the local participant communities.

The Ethiopian WOALP was one of the few which appeared to receive continuous high-level governmental support throughout its duration, and which received a degree of inter-ministerial attention as an integrated element in development efforts.

Participants

The main emphasis of WOALP was on developing the rural sector; accordingly, three of the four subprojects conducted were implemented in rural areas. Baseline surveys indicated a 14 and 17 per cent literacy rate in two of these areas. These were not areas in which Amharic (the language of functional literacy) was widely spoken, the major language (over 60 per cent) being Galigna. The literacy and speaking rates of Amharic in the larger towns of these areas was predictably higher. In two of the three rural target areas, agricultural development was being assisted by external agencies operating through the Ethiopian Government. In areas with government-supported agricultural development programmes, it appeared that the population enrolled in the functional literacy programme was definitely more involved in development work than in other areas where literacy was not closely integrated with structured development efforts. The same generalization can be made for the fourth subproject, which was conducted in the industrial sector. About 97 per cent of the workers undergoing functional literacy training in this project spoke Amharic. The most successful of the industrial-sector WOALP subprojects took place at the Bahr Dar textile mill, where a truly co-operative and management-supportive atmosphere obtained and, in general, it can be said that the fortune of the various industrial-sector subprojects depended largely upon the attitude of management, and the degree of management support. However, in at least one industrial subproject—a brewery—problems in arousing and maintaining worker-motivation derived from the simplicity of the job itself, which made vocational training irrelevant.

Administration and organization

WOALP functioned under the Ministry of Education and Fine Arts. Until 1971, the central co-ordinating body for the project was a National Advisory Committee (NAC) which met infrequently. The NAC consisted of representative of eleven ministries, plus representatives from several external agencies, the Church, the university, etc. The body was apparently too large, and its views too divergent, to administer the programme effectively at the highest level. Subsequently, the NAC was replaced by an Executive Committee, a smaller body whose members were more directly concerned with the operation of the programme. Central administration was thus improved. Most administration and co-ordination, however, took place at the subproject level. Having attained a relative degree of autonomy, WOALP was able to co-ordinate its efforts in two rural areas with local agricultural development agencies. The actual literacy classes were supervised in the field by trained, largely full-time individuals whose responsibility lay primarily at the subproject level.

WOALP is one of a number of literacy programmes operating in Ethiopia. It was more centralized than many of the others, in spite of a certain degree of local control. Little effort at co-ordination between WOALP and other literacy efforts was observed. WOALP, in fact, employed methods and materials which were quite different from those employed by other programmes, and soon alienated the proponents of the

Ministry of Education's own literacy programme. Finally, a fundamental organizational problem was the need to procure both competent literacy instructors and skilled, innovative agricultural and industrial personnel, and somehow to link the two into harmonious functional literacy packages.

Teachers and other personnel

The main characteristics of literacy instructors employed by WOALP were that :
1. They were used part time.
2. Males were employed in all programmes except family education programmes where women were employed.
3. The majority of the literacy instructors were not in charge of the technical training of participants; this was handled by a separate cadre of technical instructors, and co-ordination between the two groups appears to have been limited.
4. Technical training personnel tended to be drawn from various government services (i.e. agricultural extension) or on-the-job technicians.
5. There is some discrepancy regarding the socio-professional origins of the instructional staff, but most were students of at least Standard 6 or 7. Others were professional teachers. Each literacy teacher received fifteen days of training in the 'global method' (see below), while it appears that their technical-training counterparts—drawn from local extension agents and others with requisite technical skills—received far less briefing about the teaching of adults and WOALP in general, if they received any at all. The selection of literacy instructors was made on the basis of ability to teach and stimulate students; prospective instructors were given an examination. Initial training consisted of both lectures and demonstrations, and refresher training courses were offered. An evaluation of a sample of functional literacy instructors revealed that most were dedicated, confident and utilized the skills in which they had been trained. Many had problems preparing and implementing lesson plans, but this can be attributed largely to external factors (lack of written materials, slowness of learners, presence of newcomers, etc.). Most of the instructors indicated a desire for better initial training, and more opportunities for remedial training after field teaching actually commenced.

Curriculum and methods

WOALP literacy instruction (not including technical instruction) was divided into three sequential stages. The first presented the skills of basic literacy and numeracy. The second was called a 'language programme', based primarily upon the reading of books designed to increase the students' reading skills and vocabulary. The third, or 'follow-up' stage, was to consist in the provision of a travelling 'suitcase' library transported from village to village, with students being visited by a teacher about once a month. The agricultural programmes for the different zones had common elements, as well as elements specific to each zone. The programmes for 'family living' and 'cottage industries' were completely diversified, while the programme for industrial vocational training was common at the literacy stage, and diversified at the post-literacy follow-up stage. All subprojects had a component of 'co-operative eduction'.

The three-stage programme was to provide a standard of literacy high enough to ensure permanent gains and was to take two years. A major problem, however, was poor time utilization. In some subprojects, up to nineteen months were needed to complete the first stage alone. By 1972, only about 1,700 students had successfully finished the first stage, whereas the originally plained figure was 73,000 new literates having completed the whole programme by 1973. Slow progress was accompanied by high wastage: approximately one-eighth of those enrolling in the first stage actually entered the third stage. High wastage and slow progress combined to hinder the programme's goal of adequately testing and improving new materials before the programme's termination in 1973.

The language of instruction throughout the programme was Amharic, which was not the first language of a substantial proportion (a majority, in some subprojects) of the participants. WOALP—and other parallel programmes—did not distinguish between Amharic and non-Amharic speaker-learners. A logical assumption would seem to be that non-Amharic speakers could benefit from a different set of methods and materials; however, it appears that WOALP did not solve the issue, and this factor probably contributed significantly to the slow progress of many participants and to the high dropout rates.

Teaching materials

The literacy materials—primers and others—were developed from baseline data gathered in a survey conducted before the establishment of each subproject. Key concepts familiar to local populations made up the bulk of the initial (first stage) literacy materials. All materials were related to 'centres of interest', such as soil conservation, row planting, etc. The programme produced and utilized a substantial number of audio-visual materials, including wall-newspapers, posters, photographic materials, films, slides, tapes, etc. The programme operated a private radio transmitter, and offered radio topics in at least one subproject which were related to farming and community life. Some materials, as noted, were specific to each programme, while others were of a more universal nature, and incorporated into all subprojects.

The 'technical training' side of the programme, of course, utilized whatever facilities were available and relevant for demonstration purposes. This was somewhat easier in industrial settings, particularly where there was managerial support, than in some of the rural subprojects, where facilities had to be improvised. A problem encountered in the use of agricultural demonstration plots was that the local agricultural cycle did not always coincide with the material being covered in the curriculum. Furthermore, functional literacy classes were run independently of agricultural development programmes, resulting in something of a gap between theory and practice.

Classes were held in local schools, factories and even homes, and it does not appear that finding an appropriate class site constituted a major problem. In places, participants even constructed their own class site facilities.

There was a great variation between the kind of materials employed by WOALP and those employed by other Ethiopian literacy programmes. There is no indication in Unesco materials that a systematic comparative assessment has been conducted to determine which sets of materials are most effective, most cost-efficient, etc. Such a comparative study would seem to be indicated in future projects.

Costs

Actual and planned expenditures as reported by the Unesco Literacy Division's Evaluation Unit, were as shown below:

	Funding source		Total
	UNDP	Government	
Actual expenses (U.S.$)	1,812,000	1,661,700	3,473,700
Planned expenditure[1] (U.S.$)	1,507,100	2,206,000	3,713,100
Percentage of planned expenditure actually utilized	120	75	94

1. Plan of Operation, July 1968.

UNDP exceeded its planned contribution by 20 per cent, while the government failed to meet its commitment by 25 per cent. *Per capita* costs are estimated at $54.43 per participant and $92.15 per final participant (those who took, but did not necessarily pass the final examination). About 30 per cent of this cost was for research and evaluation components of the project. *Per capita* costs were higher than *per capita* costs for other literacy programmes operating in the country simultaneously with WOALP. The comparatively high cost of WOALP may be justified in terms of knowledge gained from the materials and methods tested and developed in the projects.

However, even this form of cost-justification can be questioned, given the failure of the project to develop a true 'experimental' character, and the fact that in most instances the project was terminated before the third stage could be completed.

Subproject *per capita* cost data indicate that the industrial-vocational subproject at Wonji/Shoa Sugar Estate involved the smallest difference between per-participant and per-'graduate' costs. Predictably, *per capita* costs were greatly reduced as the number of participants increased.

Calculation of costs in the final evaluation report conformed to a formula established by Unesco early in the project. This formula, however, appears to omit a number of important cost considerations, including costs to participants and (with one exception) a cost-benefit analysis which would give some idea of the degree to which the relatively high costs of functional literacy were being absorbed by increased productivity on the job, more efficient 'investment-oriented' money management attitudes, etc. Again, a series of follow-up 'tracer' studies would be required to answer cost-benefit questions of this sort.

Evaluation

WOALP's evaluation programme was 'written into' its original set of objectives and Plan of Operation. Evaluation was comprehensive in nature, covering the duration of the programme and including the following:
1. Studies for programme support, including several national and regional baseline studies to help facilitate programme (and subproject) planning.
2. Process studies-observation of functional literacy classes in operation to provide immediate feedback to field personnel and central organizers.
3. 'Change studies'—the core of the evaluation—which included baseline, interim and terminal studies of participants' performance on predetermined critical change variables. In addition, a cross-sectional study which attempted to determine the relationship between functional literacy and socio-economic development was conducted in one subproject.
4. A series of studies not necessarily related to participant behaviour change; these were carried out by the evaluation section of the programme in co-operation with other specific sections of WOALP.

The baseline surveys generated a series of recommendations for programme and subproject implementation, only a portion of which seem to have been accepted for use in planning. Process studies appear to have been short (one to two day site visits) and rather general in terms of the kinds of information and feedback generated. The change-in-participant studies were more standardized and rigorous, and featured comparisons between participants and non-participants (matched samples) with respect to a number of important dimensions of change. There appears to have been some change in the format of the data gathering instruments (interviews and questionnaires) between the initial baseline surveys and the interim studies; in some subprojects, baseline surveys were not completed, or were conducted after the project had been in operation some months. There appears to have been only scattered use of long-term measurements to ascertain participant behaviour change. Such measurements might have confirmed or refuted the results gleaned from interviews and questionnaires. In addition, there were no long-term studies of actual use by participants of literacy and new productive skills over a period of several years. Such studies would seem to be of crucial importance in a literacy scheme linked closely to socio-economic development, as was WOALP. The evaluation report treats most subprojects individually, with little attempt to develop recommendations and conclusions on the relative efficacy of the subprojects, based upon a comparison between them. This failure to develop intra-programme comparisons is an important omission, since a major feature of WOALP was its 'tailoring' of methods, materials, etc., to individual subprojects.

Although the reliability of the data generated by the evaluation process must be considered questionable, as they were often derived from methods and instruments which themselves were unorthodox and suspect, there does appear to be an indication that a number of positive changes occured in participant behaviour as a result of the programme. These changes were noted in terms of participation in co-operatives, adoption of health and dietary practices and attitudes towards development.

Summary

The Ethiopian WOALP received high-level government support but suffered from a number of logistical, organizational and technical deficiencies. Although there were mechanisms for co-ordination at the policy level, operational co-ordination in the field left something to be desired, with many of the functional literacy classes lacking resources for practical field-work in conjunction with agricultural development activities. In industrial enterprises, on the other hand, practical work appeared to be more integrated into the vocational setting.

Baseline surveys were limited. For example, development needs were defined in the industrial sector primarily by examining work requirements of relevant jobs. Such needs were defined in rural areas by interviewing heads of household—a useful contribution, but of limited value when used as the sole source of information.

A number of innovative methods and materials were developed, and there was some field testing and revision of approaches. However, there are few generalizable data on what worked well and what worked poorly. Furthermore, the experts do not appear to have fully communicated to the government the experimental nature of the project and the need to conduct rigorous research and evaluation activities.

Language problems of participants were ignored, and the same materials were used both with participants whose native tongue was the national language and those whose native tongue was not the national language.

As with other projects where the experimental programme was set up parallel to existing literacy programmes, some confusion and conflict developed. It is unclear what positive effect, if any, the innovative approaches pioneered in the project may have had on the various other efforts in the country.

Finally, evaluation efforts were inconclusive, largely because of inadequacy of evaluation methodology, inadequate baseline data, and inadequate interim studies. Available data indicate significant changes of socio-economic behaviour among new literates with regard to participation in co-operatives, health and nutritional practices. Attitudes towards development also seem to have changed significantly.

Guinea

Time perspective

A Unesco functional literacy planning mission visited Guinea in November 1965, and a request for UNDP funding was submitted the same year. The Plan of Operation was signed on 28 October 1968. Authority to commence operations was given on 25 November 1968.

Two national literacy campaigns had been attempted prior to the start of the UNDP/Unesco programme, one in 1968 and one in 1969. These campaigns were subsequent to a statement by the Head of State on 13 April 1967, which criticized the Unesco approach and indicated that the party must mobilize the masses through a very simple technique of making available a literacy manual. This statement suggested that all illiterates take the manual to someone literate in order to get help in learning how to read and write. With the failure of these campaigns, the government elected to accept the UNDP/Unesco plan.

The first chief technical adviser arrived in June 1968, and stayed until July 1970; he was replaced by a second who remained until UNDP/Unesco assistance was prematurely terminated at the end of 1971, at the request of the government. Thus, the operational period of the project lasted from the end of 1968 to the end of 1971, or approximately three years. Despite its decision not to continue the functional literacy project, the government embarked, in 1972, on a systematic five-year nation-wide literacy programme.

Policy and objectives

The UNDP/Unesco Plan of Operation set as its goal the establishment of a selective and intensive functional literacy project for: (a) 3,500 illiterate and newly-literate workers in the industrial enterprises of Conakry, covering the meat and vegetable processing plants of Manou and the sawmills of Sérédou; and for (b) 75,000 illiterate farmers living in the three regions of the country (lower Guinea, middle Guinea and the forest region) and covering various crops such as rice, coffee, quinquina, horticulture, animal husbandry and forestry.

From the signing of the Plan of Operation until 11 March 1971 (some seventeen months), the UNDP/Unesco-supported programme was considered as separate from the national campaign and up to that time had initiated nine literacy classes. By government decision, there was no distinction between the functional literacy programme and the national campaign after this date and until the UNDP/Unesco project terminated in December 1971.

Thus, a conflict which had plagued the project since its inception in 1965 was resolved. The government had consistently objected to the notion that there should be selective experimental literacy programmes, and proposed a massive national campaign linked to 'consciousness-raising' of all the people in economic, social and political spheres.

This policy was consistent with public declarations of the Head of State who, on several occasions, emphasized the need for mass education to create a 'mystique of production', to 'form the man of today through development of his social, political and cultural capabilities', thus raising individual and collective productivity. A circular sent to all federal bureaux, regional directors of education and regional directors of rural development on 15 April 1971 indicated that 80 per cent of all workers (rural and urban) were in need of in-service training and literacy, and that in-service education 'must not be considered by those in education, rural development, industry, commerce, etc., as something added and therefore marginal. It is on the contrary. . . one of the fundamental needs'.

The approach led to three trends which affected the project. The first was to emphasize a mass approach to literacy and in-service training; the second was to stress the involvement of the Secretaire d'Etat à l'Idéologie in the orientation of the content and the organization of the programme; and the third was to stress the involvement in the work of ministries and departments other than the Ministry of Education.

Participants

The original goal of the project was to reach some 3,500 illiterates and semi-literates in an industrial area around Conakry and 75,000 illiterate farmers in three rural regions. With the abandonment of any distinction between the experimental project and the national campaign (in March 1971), the goal was expanded to include the 80 per cent of the population considered under-educated for the purposes of achieving the revolutionary goals of the country and of the party in power.

During the short intensive period of 1971, forty-three classes were opened, seven in Conakry and thirty-six in lower Guinea, although no precise information as to the number of participants is available. But in order to prepare for a large extension programme designed to serve some

100,000 people, the main activities of the project in 1971 were directed to the training of instructors.

Beginning in 1973 (after the termination of the UNDP/Unesco project), the government embarked on a five-year literacy programme, and indicated that no active board member of government enterprises would be allowed to continue unless literate.

Administration and organization

The National Literacy Service was established under the general supervision of the Ministry of Education and of the Ministry of Ideology (SEITA) in 1968. In October 1971 (virtually at the end of the UNDP/Unesco project), three units were created within the National Literacy Service: the methodological unit; the planning, evaluation and documentation unit; and the operational unit.

A planning meeting in January 1970, recommended that a production team be appointed at the office of each regional director of education. This team, to produce instructional material for the region, was to consist of an expert on rural economy or artisan work, an expert in education, one in health and one in public works. In addition, mobile teams were to visit the field when needed. It appears that this structure was never fully established and that most of the production was done from the central office, although there was some field input and supervision through appropriate units of the national party. Since 1972 (after termination of the project), it appears that full responsibility has been entrusted to all State enterprises for the conduct of literacy and basic adult education among their respective workers, with advice and materials being furnished by the National Literacy Service.

Teachers and other personnel

Instructors were selected in accordance with the political requirements of education in Guinea. All instructors worked on a voluntary basis and were chosen by the political and administrative organs of the government. Eighty instructors were trained in 1970 in five training sections and 123 were trained in 1971. Training was extended to about forty-five foremen in various industrial enterprises. The Unesco team, in addition, trained specialists in the central production of materials and in overall planning and administration.

Curriculum and methods

The methods and techniques applied have evolved in accordance with the changing objectives of the project. In 1971, a decentralized approach was implemented and the instructional programmes were prepared in collaboration with the political administration and technical services concerned in the industrial and agricultural target zones. These programmes were prepared in the national languages of each zone. The general principle of 'intensive training' (*surformation-alphabetisation*) called for the combination of an intensive study of socio-economic problems of general interest as well as a diversified study of specific problems tied to economic production.

Content and methodology were developed through operational seminars that made possible the combining of several operational goals in one process: baseline studies necessary to understand the local context; analysis of content and elaboration of teaching materials; active participation by various community groups as well as literacy class members.

Nineteen differentiated programmes were developed by the project, of which eleven were in the industrial sector and eight in the agricultural. These programmes were based on the concept of group discussions which provided the workers with an opportunity to acquire a group spirit as well as an awareness of the relationship between their personal professional interests and the development of the country.

The acquisition of literacy was closely tied to professional training and practical demonstrations in factories or in the fields. The basic theme of the programme was a specific agricultural or industrial problem.

Stages of thirty weekly sessions each (one and a half hours of theoretical work per session, the practical and demonstration activities varying in duration) covered technical and scientific components, socio-economic and civic information as well as literacy *per se*. Only the first stage could be applied in 1971.

Beginning with the problem areas, literacy teaching followed a logical sequence of group discussions, observations and practical demonstrations leading to the presentation of a key word, the learning of new words, the memorization of a new element, reading and finally writing. For example, the learning of arithmetic corresponded to practical problems associated with the professional work of the participants (rice culture) and involved the ability to determine the percentage of seeds planted which would actually grow (computation of percentages) and the learning of numbers both in terms of writing and of visual memory.

Teaching materials

Didactic materials destined for the instructors were prepared for each of the specific programmes and included a pedagogic guide and technical information on the subject matters to be covered. All materials were prepared in the language of the participants which included several national languages. Illustrations accompanied this guide as well as photographic posters and stencil reproductions. The participants received the corresponding booklets with illustrations. The normal didactic instruments were utilized, such as blackboard, booklets, etc. Some efforts were undertaken to utilize mass media, particularly in relation to follow-up work for new literates which led to the production of five booklets in the national languages. Special radio programmes were also organized.

Costs

The Unesco Literacy Division's Evaluation Unit estimates the project costs as:

	Funding source		Total
	UNDP	Government	
Actual expenditure (U.S.$)	756,000	229,500	985,500
Planned expenditure[1] (U.S.$)	1,192,100	1,236,000	2,428,100
Percentage of planned expenditure actually spent	63	18	40

1. Plan of Operation, 1968.

Unesco estimates the per-participant cost of the programme at about $208, about 46 per cent of this being for the research and evaluation phases of the project. Since the project closed prematurely, it can be assumed that these costs would have been lower had the project continued long enough to increase enrolments.

Even so, the costs seem astronomical considering the fact that all instructors were volunteers. One can only assume that large sums were spent on the preparation and distribution of teaching materials and on administrative and supervisory tasks.

Evaluation and research

There has been little formal evaluation study of the programme. An international expert started some evaluation work in early 1969, including problem surveys in factories, training of a national evaluation specialist, preparation of attendance registers and construction of tests. The work was, however, halted after the premature departure of this specialist. A consultant in evaluation visited the project in late 1970 and formulated a number of recommendations concerning evaluation and research. It appears that these recommendations were not carried out. A further difficulty was that the government did not accept the appointment of a new evaluation specialist despite earlier approval of his candidature. In practical terms this meant that no evolution was actually carried out in this project during its short operational phase. However, in the preparation of educational materials, the results of context studies and problem surveys conducted by the national specialists were taken into account.

The Head of State, in a circular dated 15 July 1971, suggested that systematic and continuous evaluation of results be obtained, not only in training but in production. He later (on 22 November 1971, at the end of UNDP/Unesco involvement) set 1976 as the target date for the achievement of mass literacy and a significant increase in productivity. By then, he expected that productivity of rice would be raised from an average of 800 kilograms per hectare to 3 tonnes per hectare.

Summary

Although it is virtually impossible to evaluate the effect of UNDP/Unesco action in this project, one can reasonably conclude that:

1. The selective approach to functional literacy was not acceptable to the government. The authorities were committed to a mass approach.
2. The functional approach, combining basic productive skills training with reading, writing and mathematics training, was found acceptable by the government, with the proviso that ideological instruction be included, as well.
3. The specialists and instructors trained by the Unesco team should be useful in the mass approach selected by the government.
4. The decentralized approach as regards planning the content of programmes so as to meet local needs, and as regards the conduct of training relevant to each region, shows promise if there is some continuity, which appeared to be lacking in efforts prior to 1971.
5. Although collaboration was expected from all sectors and government enterprises and industries, this was not as intense as might have been desired. As with most programmes which imply the need for inter-institutional collaboration, new mechanisms must be found to assure that such collaboration is effective.
6. As with many literacy programmes, there was no provision for establishing a national service to produce reading and follow-up material for the new literates, nor for the creation of a national library or information system. Thus, it may be that people are being made literate but will have little to read.
7. Finally, the project shows the futility of any attempt by an international agency to impose an approach on a country which wishes to do something else. Much of the early difficulties of the project revolved around the Unesco effort to develop a model project along the intensive, selective lines of what was then Unesco dogma. Although the government wished assistance in a mass basic adult education programme with a literacy component, they did not wish to participate in an experimental pilot project activity.

India

Time perspective

A joint Unesco/FAO mission visited India in 1966 to assist the government in preparing the project. In 1968, a Unesco/FAO/UNDP mission assisted the government in evaluating and revising the project for a $2\frac{1}{2}$ year period. A formal Plan of Operation was signed on 4 December 1969, and the project became operational on 12 December. The project had been approved for a first phase of $2\frac{1}{2}$ years, with the provision that it would be evaluated during the last six months so as to determine the desirability of mounting a second phase. In March 1972, a joint Unesco/FAO/UNDP mission visited India and recommended continuation of the project until the end of the fourth five-year development plan on 31 March 1974. UNDP thereupon extended phase 1 until December 1972. The second phase began on 1 January 1973, and continued until March 1974.

Policy and objectives

Functional literacy in India was but one component—really a supportive element—of a wider and more immediate goal, that of increasing food production. India's high rate of population increase, its lower-than-expected rate of economic growth, and continuing food shortages, led the government to formulate a dynamic plan for increasing food grain production. The programme is popularly known as the 'green revolution'.

For this, 100 districts were selected in the country, covering 32 million acres. The areas selected were among the most potentially productive in India, fully suitable for double and triple cropping. These districts were to receive official supplies of high yielding varieties of seed, as well as insecticides and fertilizers, in an effort to realize vast food production increases. It was vital that the 5 million farm families living in these areas should understand the need for change, and should apply modern methods of agriculture. This necessitated a large and comprehensive farmers' training programme, of which functional literacy became a part.

The principal objective of the scheme was thus to provide a well organized functional literacy programme for illiterate farmers in the 'High Yielding Varieties Programme' (HYVP) districts, which would enable them to obtain both literacy and strategic agricultural skills and information of immediate use to themselves and to HYVP.

The Indian functional literacy project was theoretically designed to be immediately functional. That is, the project was intended to help in achieving specific operational food production goals. Literacy training was designed to impart skills which would make possible the successful implementation of the High Yielding Varieties Programme. The Indian project (along with the project in the Syrian Arab Republic) was therefore unique in EWLP in that literacy efforts by the Ministry of Education were organized in direct collaboration with another ministry (agriculture) and in order to assist that ministry in high priority development work. Actual implementation of this policy was retarded by a number of organizational and administrative problems (see below), coupled with fluctuating, but generally low-to-moderate, government interest in the project's success. The consequence of such problems was a rather traditional approach to literacy instruction, running more or less parallel to certain work-oriented educational activities under the FAO part of the project.

Participants

The principal groups were illiterate/semi-literate farmers living in the High Yielding Varieties Programme districts at the time. Each district was responsible for implementing sixty functional literacy classes, and each class averaged thirty participants. Villages selected for the establishment of classes were chosen on the basis partly of local interest and partly the existence of an 'educational infrastructure'.

In many cases, classes enrolled non-farmers, or children under the age of 14, simply to fill out their ranks. Neither of these groups was considered appropriate by the organizers. Additionally, in some cases the participants in the functional literacy classes were not the same as those participating in the agricultural component of the programme. This is an important example of a widespread lack of co-ordination between the literacy and agricultural components of the programme at all administrative levels (see below).

In 1972, the system of reporting functional literacy class enrollees collapsed, chiefly due to the failure of the Ministry of Education to exercise proper supervision. At that time, estimates of current enrolment ranged from 110,000 to 125,000 participants, while approximately 108,000 had successfully passed the literacy test since 1969. Total beneficiaries of the functional literacy project were expected (in 1972) to reach 180,000 by 1974, but a subsequent government document (1974) indicated that more than 300,000 farmers had so far benefited from the programme. Neither of these estimates indicate the standards used to determine who has benefited.

Administration and organization

The nature of this programme required close working co-ordination between three ministries (education, agriculture, and information and broadcasting) at several administrative levels (national, state, district, block and village). India being a federally organized nation, 'vertical' co-ordination (e.g. between states and districts) was also called for in order to facilitate the local implementation of national policy decisions. Perhaps the most evident shortcoming of the entire project was the failure to establish this horizontal and vertical co-ordination effectively. While an Interministerial Committee for Co-ordination existed to promulgate programme policy at the national level, and while counterpart co-ordination committees at the state, district, block and local levels also existed, actual programme implementation tended to be accomplished through traditional intraministerial channels. At the district level and below, co-ordination committees were frequently not operational, and there was little dynamic leadership at the national level which might have induced greater effort and participation by state and district leaders.

Throughout its duration, the functional literacy component of the total programme lagged behind the agricultural (farmer training) component, and was never really well integrated with it. This may have been due to any or all of the following factors:

1. The rapid expansion of the programme between 1960 and 1971 which imposed a great strain on the recruiting and training of literacy instructors and supervisors.
2. The slow flow of funds between national and state governments, and later between states and districts.
3. The high percentage of national, state and district officers (particularly the last) appointed to the programme on a part-time basis only.
4. The inadequate provision of basic literacy materials, the dearth of appropriate follow-up materials, and the obsolescence of much of the content of the literacy materials employed.

Clearly, the vast scope of the programme, far greater in terms of enrolment and geographical area than most other EWLP projects, could not have been handled smoothly by the administrative structure outlined in the Plan of Operation, and while some of these administrative shortcomings were eventually redressed, the project was nearing termination when most of the remedial measures were actually implemented.

Teachers and other personnel

Functional literacy classes were conducted by part-time instructors. Most of these were primary-school teachers drawn from the local areas where the functional literacy classes were conducted. The training of these instructors was the responsibility of the district, but rapid programme expansion frequently diluted the quality of training. Each district appointed either six part-time or two full-time supervisors, who were responsible for the sixty or so functional literacy instructors. Supervision, in turn, was initially the responsibility of the District Education Officer, who as a rule could devote only a token percentage of his time to overseeing the functional literacy project. In 1972-73, therefore, his responsibility was shifted to a full-time literacy project officer. District-level project officers were responsible to the state ministries of education. At national level, the principal officer of the Directorate of Adult Education (a branch of the Ministry of Education) was in charge.

Several major difficulties relating to personnel were:

1. The high rate of personnel 'turnover' at all administrative levels.
2. The chronic lack of full-time (and fully committed) personnel at all administrative levels.
3. The simple lack of strategic personnel in some districts.
4. The inadequacy of the training for those personnel who were involved at all levels. The training problem was compounded by the need to recruit agricultural teacher-counterparts to the functional literacy instructors, since the latter were primarily non-agriculturalists. In practice, instructors in the agricultural component of the programme were drawn from many sources, ranging from professional agricultural extension workers to successful local farmers. Each of the four above-mentioned problem areas contributed to the sluggishness of implementation of the project in new districts, and to the relatively low motivation for the programme exhibited at all administrative levels. Furthermore, many teachers, despite the functional content of the teaching materials, tended to pursue traditional academic methodology, stressing traditional literacy skills.

Curriculum, methods and materials

The National Directorate of Adult Education was responsible for the elaboration of content and methods, and the provision of teaching materials. The new orientation in the concept of adult literacy implied far-reaching changes in curriculum, materials and methods. This was achieved mainly through the organization of workshops and seminars of literacy writers at national and regional levels. During 1972 as many as seven workshops were organized to study the reading requirements of farmers, methods of ascertaining such requirements, approaches to integrating literacy with aspects of agricultural development, etc. The participants in these workshops were assisted by a Unesco specialist in functional literacy materials preparation.

The Directorate of Adult Education conducted an evaluation of previously prepared primers and instructional materials. In 1971, the National Workshop on Functional Literacy recommended that the curriculum should be problem-oriented and based on a survey conducted with the help of agricultural extension personnel. A pilot study in the Jaipur District helped elaborate the new curriculum, methodology and instructional materials. Curriculum development proceeded as follows: (a) a survey was made among farmers and extension workers of problems encountered in farming; (b) the problems were classified and arranged in order of priority; (c) a sequence of remedial measures was prepared with the help of agricultural specialists; (d) the sequences were aligned with the calendar of agricultural operation; (e) a syllabus was drafted which indicated the innovative working tasks ; and (f) the complex working tasks were broken down into primary working operations and a suitable inventory of knowledge and skills was developed for each task. Functional literacy methods were devised to ensure an effective transfer of this inventory of knowledge and skills to the farmer-student. The functional literacy methods decided upon included the spoken word, visual non-verbal communication and verbal communication. At the earliest stages of instruction, greater reliance was placed upon verbal messages and demonstrations. Generally, brief phrases and progressive language structures were then presented, broken up into words, syllables and letters and new structures were built with the help of the phrases learned. The extent and complexity of written texts gradually increased. This technique of literacy instruction is described as analyticosynthetic. The phonetic structure of most Indian languages lends itself to the method which has been in use in India since 1948.

The following types of materials were employed for the nine languages in which literacy was imparted: (a) a literacy primer supported by posters and supplementary reading materials; (b) a workbook containing exercises for the practice of reading and writing; (c) a workbook containing exercises in arithmetic; and (d) a guidebook for instructors.

Throughout the last years of the project, materials were tested and improved so as to promote integration with the agricultural component of the programme. There was a constant need to provide neo-literates with sufficient and appropriate follow-up materials, and to revise materials in order to keep them technically up to date and in line with the agricultural inputs which students were receiving. In spite of efforts in these directions, some districts continued to employ traditional materials which were inappropriate to the goals of functional literacy. Materials were localized to meet differing agricultural needs. However, since nine languages were being employed for functional literacy training, a major problem was getting Hindi-language materials translated, tested and revised to meet local conditions in non-Hindi speaking areas.

Costs

Little can be said about costs; cost figures provided by Unesco's Literacy Division, EWLP Evaluation Unit, for this particular project (unlike most of the other EWLP projects) are sketchy and of little value.

Although the Farmer's Training and Functional Literacy Project was declared an international project in 1969, financial responsibility for its execution fell almost exclusively on the Indian Government (of a total of $4,308,000 in actual project expenditures, UNDP contributed $143,800).

The government allocated far more money to the project than was actually spent. A total of 20 million rupees was allotted to functional literacy during the fourth five-year development (1969-74), but only 7.5 million rupees were utilized. The failure to employ available resources to the full can be largely attributed to the administrative entanglements and consequent slowness of implementation noted above.

Evaluation and research

A provision for project evaluation was written into the original Plan of Operation, the first time that this had been done in respect of the Indian literacy programmes. Evaluation was to be the responsibility of national authorities. UNDP budgeting provided for an international evaluation expert for both the functional literacy and agricultural components: however, FAO was reluctant to appoint an evaluation expert for its component, so that only the former post was filled; the expert who was eventually assigned noted that his work included many duties other than field evaluation. Because of the lack of a co-ordinated evaluation infrastructure, the expert became a kind of evaluation administrator, facilitator and co-ordinator. A field evaluation manual for India was developed early in the programme, but the approaches suggested in it were never fully implemented.

The tremendous scope of the project made comprehensive evaluation of all participating districts and villages a practical impossibility; thus, evaluation tended to be 'spotty'—with more than ten evaluative or quasi-evaluative studies being carried out in sample districts or villages between 1967 and 1974. The rapid expansion of the project, and the demands for quick feedback, precluded the systematic use of longitudinal studies employing baseline surveys and interim and terminal evaluation. Only in Jaipur District were such systematic longitudinal methods employed. Most evaluation utilized a *post-facto* design, employing control groups where this was possible.

Evaluations were conducted by several different ministries and other organizations, only some of which were directly involved in the implementation of the project. It is not known to what extent the studies of these sundry organizations were centrally co-ordinated and flowed from centrally defined evaluative needs. However, a number of factors point to the conclusion that specific evaluation strategy and criteria evolved only after the project had been in existence for several years. As late as January 1973, the resident representative's semi-annual report noted that preparation of the guidelines on evaluation of farmers' training and functional literacy presenting the strategy approach, methodology and organization of evaluation to be utilized by policy-makers, administrators, and practitioners had been completed. On this same general theme, a 1972 memorandum expressed reservations about the viability of a government proposal to extend the project, in view of the lack of proper evaluation.

The final report of the UNDP evaluation specialist indicated that evaluation, throughout his tenure in India, was constantly 'on the defensive', beset with bureaucratic problems (attrition of evaluation personnel, poor qualifications of lower-level evaluation team members, low prestige/priority of evaluation, etc.).

In terms of the findings of the various evaluation studies, there was a general indication of positive results on nearly all fronts of the project— acquisition of literacy and numeracy skills, improvement in knowledge of new agricultural practice, attitudinal change, behavioural change (utilization of newly-learned agricultural skills), and improvement in the standard of living, although differences were found among the various subprojects and programmes. The results were sufficiently favourable for Unesco and UNDP to recommend continuation of the project.

Summary

The 'federal' nature of India's political system largely dictated, the kind of project administrative structure which was possible. Since the additional 'layers' of bureaucracy created by the existence of states and districts tended to work against effective 'vertical' communication, and to hinder the implementation of national policy at local levels, a reasonable research and development priority item for UNDP/Unesco might be the exploration of administrative models which could facilitate the achievement of project goals in 'federal', multi-level bureaucracies such as India.

Evaluation data (not complete for all subprojects, and open to methodological criticism in some cases) does indicate that the project had significant overall effect on participant behaviour. There is no way in which this effect can be analysed, however, in terms of cost/benefit per participant because of the lack of adequate financial data.

Finally, the gap between theory and practice in respect of the integration of literacy training with vocational skills training is evident. The literacy programmes, in part because of the use of instructors not competent in vocational areas, and in part because of organizational and administrative problems, were essentially traditional.

Iran

Time perspective

A request for an experimental work-oriented adult literacy project was approved by the Governing Council of the UNDP Special Fund in January 1966, and authorization to commence operations was given in May 1967. The original duration of the project was to be four years, but an extension was granted in 1971 until July 1972. Following the end-of-project-review mission in May 1972, certain posts were extended to permit the preparation of a final report on the project's experimental activities and to assist the Iranian Government in setting up a National Centre for Adult Education and Training.

Following initial project authorization in 1967, more than two years of study, research and experimentation were needed to solve some difficult organizational problems (particularly in the Ministry of National Education, which was the project's sponsor), to obtain the collaboration of ministries (all initially unenthusiastic), to overcome, at least in part, methodological difficulties and, finally, to formulate and implement five general programmes relating to agriculture, industry, and the advancement of women. Beginning late in 1969, an additional twenty-eight programmes were begun and their elaboration and testing proceeded until the end of the project. The long preparatory phase of the project represented one of the more intense efforts, among EWLP projects, to prepare a viable operational support structure which would enable the experiment to reach its goals.

Policy and objectives

The immediate goal of the project was to assist the government in carrying out an experiment in work-oriented adult literacy in two pilot areas (Esfahan and Dezful). The ultimate aim was to enhance the social and economic development of these areas (both of which had been identified as potential high-growth regions) by upgrading the literacy and numeracy skills of the productive inhabitants. The essential assumption of the project was that there is an integral link between literacy and the improvement of technical skills leading to increased productivity and social development. Further, it was assumed that functional literacy training, which links literacy and vocational skill training, would facilitate the student's learning in a way which would not be accomplished by literacy and vocational instruction offered separately.

This assumption was important, since it conflicted with some of the notions then underlying the national campaign, and caused some friction in the pre-operational phase between advocates of the two literacy efforts. This friction, in turn, resulted in compromise, affecting the concept of functional literacy as it evolved in Iran and at the same time affecting the national campaign, which, in one way or another, increasingly adopted approaches developed within the experimental project.

A fundamental principle of functional literacy implies that the target populations should be part of development projects, that the objectives of these projects can be translated into educational terms and educational processes (teaching materials) and finally, that the organization in charge of these development projects should participate in the implementation of the literacy programmes. However, the integration of functional literacy with the economic and social development structures and plans was not fully realized in Iran, particularly in the initial year of the operational phase of the programme.

The first generation of five functional literacy programmes developed before 1969 did not correspond to clear-cut socio-economic objectives and could not meet specific needs of individuals nor of industrial or agricultural concerns. The twenty-eight programmes started in 1969 were based on a more precise formulation of the principles for the elaboration of functional literacy programmes. These principles called for the identification of 'programme areas' conceived as economic activities in which illiteracy was a bottleneck and in which technical upgrading and literacy could be helpful in reaching social and economic development objectives.

Government policy towards the experimental project was supportive from the beginning. Iran, of course, had hosted the World Conference of Ministers of Education on the Eradication of Illiteracy at Tehran in 1965 and was one of the first countries to request UNDP/Unesco collaboration in beginning a project. Iran considered the project as a vehicle for providing a new work-oriented literacy approach, with tested and validated methods, which would be integrated into the national campaign after having been refined through an experimental phase. Towards the end of the project, this was in fact done through the creation of a National Centre for Adult Education and Training (as a part of the fifth development plan, 1973-78) to service all literacy needs of the country.

The high-level policy support, however, was not always operationalized through effective collaboration between the various ministries, development agencies and government bureaucracy in general. Most of these agencies, at least during much of the project period, remained negative, sceptical or at best indifferent to the project.

Participants

The project was established in two zones, chosen for the following reasons:
1. They seemed to correspond to typical change situations in Iranian society.
2. The experience acquired could thus be applied later to other geographic areas in Iran.
3. In each of the areas, economic development was on the verge of making great advances, but illiteracy was hindering further growth.

The two project zones which were selected on the basis of these criteria were the Greater Dez irrigation project (near the town of Dezful), and the city of Esfahan and the semi-agricultural area around it. The Dezful area was primarily agricultural, and undergoing a period of rapid change due to the construction of an irrigation dam. It was felt that the Dezful subproject could be a model for up to fourteen other areas in Khuzestan Province where similar irrigation projects were being implemented. Esfahan was chosen because it has a dense concentration of traditional craft industries and textile workshops which were in the process of modernization. Additionally, a large metallurgical complex was being constructed, the town's population was growing rapidly, other industries were beginning to proliferate, and the surrounding semi-agricultural area supplied foodstuffs to the city and provided some of the labour for the industrial complex.

It was originally estimated that 80,000 inhabitants in these zones would participate in the project. The number of actual participants (i.e. the total enrolled—far fewer actually completed courses) was estimated towards the end of the project at a maximum of 66,000. However, a year later a survey reported a total enrolment of 94,365, with 79,059 at Esfahan and 15,306 at Dezful.

One reason for the low rate of participation in the Dezful area was the decision by the government to expropriate peasant lands in the irrigated areas in order to turn these lands over to agro-industrial groups. Following this decision, all literacy activity in the irrigated zones of Dezful ceased.

Six general economic sectors were represented in the various specialized classes which the project developed. They included: mining (4 per cent of total enrolment), agriculture (28 per cent), industry (15 per cent), handicrafts (9 per cent), home economics (health, nutrition, etc.) (43 per cent), and civics (4 per cent). The large home economics component of the project involved only women, and the total of women enrolled in the entire project thus slightly outnumbered the men.

Although one essential component of the functional literacy method is to tailor literacy to specific occupational concerns, it is notable that the vast majority of participants in the project were actually enrolled in general, as opposed to occupation-specific, subprogrammes. Highest enrolment was realized in the home economics programme, and in Esfahan's general agricultural programme. An overwhelming 85 per cent of the participants were enrolled in programmes of a general nature such as these.

One of the project's principal objectives was to match literacy instruction and vocational instruction appropriate to a specific geographical/economic area and a specific occupational group. However, the project did not achieve complete age and occupational homogeneity in the subprogrammes, except in institutional setting where the participants were more or less a captive audience. In subprogrammes not affected by institutional factors, not only were large numbers of children enrolled (up to 40 per cent in the women's programmes), but there was also considerable crossing of occupational boundaries (industrial workers enrolled in agricultural programmes, etc.). As regards the broad economic sectoral affiliation of participants by programme, most participants in Dezful were not enrolled in agriculture programmes and most participants in Esfahan were not enrolled in industrial programmes. Hence, in terms of the project's original explicit objective of concentrating on agriculture in Dezful and industry in Esfahan, the project was unsuccessful.

Attempts to build programmes tailored to very specific occupations were further upset by the government's transfer, in October 1970, of all literacy activities in the Province of Esfahan (two-thirds the size of Italy) to the functional literacy project, so as to avoid competition and waste of resources. This administrative move opened the project to much public pressure, and it was no longer free to discriminate between villages and districts according to whether they conformed to some prior plan of literacy in human resources development. The great increases in enrolment which the project experienced after 1970 indicated that there was, indeed, a large demand for literacy instruction.

Community studies carried out by the project noted that the heterogeneity of participants was partly due to the fact that employment patterns are changing rapidly in Esfahan, and an industrial worker will often continue farming during the agricultural season or may even own a small piece of agricultural property. Similarly, these studies show that children as young as 7 or 8 often begin working, perhaps in a rug factory or on the farm, and even marry at 13. Thus, they may, in sociological and economic terms, be functioning as adults.

None the less, the studies further demonstrate the impossibility of truly diversifying a functional literacy curriculum into many specialized programmes that will attract only people interested in that particular content. Employment patterns do change rapidly, so it does not make sense to limit enrolment in one specialized course to those actually in that occupation at the time. The course may be of value to someone entering the occupation at a later date, or someone who is a member of a family which has members in that occupation. And if younger children are interested and can follow the material, it may be an excellent functional substitute for the primary schooling they have missed.

Class attendance and dropout data is somewhat ambivalent. Classroom attendance among those who remained in the programme was unusually high, ranging, according to several estimates,[1] from 75 to 90 per cent. In the rural areas, class attendance varied seasonally, with agricultural work cycles.

In terms of individual class sessions, students, on the average, were present for only 43 per cent of the class period, thus necessitating much repeating of instructions and lessons on the part of literacy teachers.

There was considerable wastage in terms of dropout rates as the course progressed. An estimated 40-50 per cent of the original enrolment actually completed the three-stage course, while an even smaller percentage (35 per cent) actually took the final examination.

Administration and organization

WOALP was administered by the Ministry of Education, but maintained a considerable degree of administrative autonomy throughout its duration. The project was headed by a national director, who, for the greater part of the project's life, worked part-time. The national director was changed three times during the project, twice during a one-year period. Regional directors served as key administrators in the two experimental zones.

Project headquarters were in Tehran, but after 1970 there was considerable delegation of authority to the regional centre at Estahan, so as to improve administrative efficiency.

An advisory committee, provided for in the original Plan of Operation, existed on paper, but met only once in the first three years of the project. This committee, which was to serve a mainly co-ordinating function, failed in its task of establishing effective interministerial co-operation and communication. Lack of interministerial co-ordination, in turn, led to a less than adequate integration of literacy instruction with vocational instruction and the economic sector in general.

Throughout the project's duration, it was beset by various setbacks in the implementation of planned social and economic development projects, thus creating confusion and lack of certainty with regard to what directions the vocational side of the functional literacy instruction should take.

Major problems were associated with internal administration, at both the central and field levels. Unesco had a difficult time co-ordinating the travel, and identifying the specific duties, of the international expert staff. Regional directors and their subsidiary colleagues were often absent, and for

1. Sources for the dropout and attendance data cited in this, and subsequent paragraphs, include: M. Bazan, 'Evaluating an Experimental Functional Literacy Project: The Esfahan Experience' [4], and John Smyth, 'Costs Effectiveness Report on the Work-Oriented Adult Literacy Pilot Project in Iran: Synopsis' [41]; while the Bazen report deals with a single subproject and the Smyth report presents figures for the country as a whole, the data presented in both reports are mutually reinforcing.

the first three years of the project, administrative malaise was common-place. Beginning in 1970, however, incompetent personnel were removed on several occasions and the administrative situation at all levels improved.

Following this period, the Unesco team cohered into an efficient, collaborative group which in many ways demonstrated how a group of research and development specialists can work together to innovate, try out the innovations and gather data on them so as to make them understandable to others. The Iran project is the best-documented of all of the eleven experimental efforts, with a number of volumes available on the various aspects of the project and numerous articles summarizing aspects of the work by various members of the Unesco team.

An organizational need which was pointed out in several project reports was for some sort of follow-up programme to help new literates maintain their skills and avoid relapses into illiteracy. Such a follow-up stage was never implemented. Curiously, such activity was not part of the plan of operations of this project nor of any of the other ten experimental projects sponsored by UNDP and Unesco, even though the need for such materials in order to make the literacy training worthwhile is mentioned in virtually all project reports. It is even more curious considering the historic interest of Unesco and its outstanding projects in this area from the early 1950s until the commencement of the experimental functional literacy work in the mid-1960s, when practically all Unesco activity in the preparation of reading materials for new literates was dropped.

Teachers and other personnel

The administrative problems associated with high-level expatriate and country personnel have been documented in the preceding section. A central problem with country staff was that they were part-time employees for the most part, with pressing responsibilities and priorities elsewhere.

The majority of the literacy instructors working at the field level were primary-school teachers. The instructors, on the average, had achieved a higher degree of formal schooling (virtually 100 per cent having reached the ninth grade, and almost 80 per cent having achieved the twelfth grade) than was the case in other EWLP country projects. Additionally, the teaching force averaged 5.5 years of professional experience in education.

Instructor training was accomplished by teams of trainers who themselves were trained by the project staff. By 1970, a clear training policy was being established, after much experimentation. This involved an intensive training period of two to three weeks, followed by weekly or monthly in-service training sessions. These in-service sessions were particularly innovative, since they were based upon the teacher's guide and designed to prepare teachers directly for the following week's lesson.

An ongoing problem faced by the project was the weakness of the vocational component of the literacy instruction, due not to lack of functional teaching material but to weaknesses in the training of literacy instructors in vocational skills, and occasionally the lack of such essentiel vocational-instruction supports as agricultural demonstration plots.

Expansion after 1970, especially in Esfahan, placed a great strain on the training of literacy instructors, and frequently resulted in a drastic reduction in the length of initial training (to one week), and a corresponding diminution of instructor quality. This situation was partially remedied by the development of semi-programmed instructional materials, which to some extent reduced the instructional role of the literacy teachers. Another method of upgrading instructor quality which appeared to work was the 'efficiency instructor payment' scheme, whereby an instructor's stipend was pro-rated with the quality of his work, as measured by various criteria. Finally, periodic in-service training was arranged for all teachers, and this was felt by project staff to be more efficient than long initial periods of training.

A major problem in this project (as in others which used non-technical personnel to teach both literacy and technical skills) was that most of the functional literacy instructors were recruited from the ranks of school teachers. Most had no technical skills in the functional areas of the curriculum. Thus, unless the teaching materials were constructed to stand more or less on their own, the quality of the technical content in the classes would suffer.

Curriculum and methods

For the first two years of the project (1967-69), a series of operational and conceptual difficulties precluded the development of a curriculum and methodology which had internal coherence and which could be said to meet the objectives of the project. From 1970 onwards, however, data from field studies identified factors which might be related to bottlenecks in the implementation of development plans in Esfahan and Dezful. These bottlenecks led to the construction of twenty-eight differentiated programmes designed to serve adults with different occupational interests. The new generation of programmes were conceived of as 'programme areas' in which illiteracy was a bottleneck and in which technical upgrading and literacy could be helpful in reaching social and economic development objectives.

The programmes thus developed were related to the agricultural sector (intended primarily for the Dezful area) and the industrial sector (primarily for workers in the steel and textile industries in Esfahan). In addition, there were two programmes primarily for women which emphasized family planning, home economics, child care and related matters, and two which related to handicrafts.

After the programme areas had been identified, field studies were undertaken, using various techniques, including guided group discussions, structured interviews, direct observation, etc., to collect information useful in constructing the programmes. In fact, a kind of continuous feedback system was developed, which was useful in re-structuring and improving the programmes based on actual experience in the field.

The first five programmes consisted of three stages of seven to eight months' duration, but later programmes were reduced to two stages. Each stage was divided into sequences or units, and each sequence into lessons. Ultimately, twenty-eight such programmes were developed.

The aim was to integrate reading, writing and numeracy skills with technical and vocational training. In fact, there was some evidence that numeracy skills were much more effectively retained when introduced logically, when needed as a part of the technical information being taught, rather than in the traditional sequence of counting followed by addition, subtraction, multiplication and division.

Contrary to the practice in some of the other functional literacy projects, where separate instructors were used for the technical and the literacy components of the programme, it was assumed in Iran that the technical/vocational and the literacy skills would be taught in the same class and by the same instructor. Thus, integration of curriculum content in one set of materials was possible.

By 1969, however, it was realized that this was easier said than done. Although there had been much general discussion concerning the nature of functional literacy, there was in fact no agreed set of pedagogical practices known to be effective in this kind of activity. Thus, a major portion of the time and effort of the research staff was devoted to pedagogical experiments designed to assist in developing content and methodology appropriate to the goals of the project and to the environment of the pilot areas.

The teaching manuals and materials suggested the allocation of a certain amount of time to each aspect of the lesson. Studies showed that, in practice, instructors devoted about 73 per cent of the allocated time to literacy instruction and only 27 per cent of available time to the vocational component. Less than the recommended time was given to science and social science components, perhaps because of the preference or training of the teachers used (largely elementary-school teachers).

Teachers' manuals recommended extensive use of group discussion, but classroom observation revealed little use of this method, with barely 6 per cent of the classes observed using group discussion effectively.

Achievement tests of adults using pre-1969 materials were disappointing, and the teaching materials were restructured to better integrate the materials being taught and to introduce arithmetic not in a traditional and scholastic format but linked to the themes under discussion. This produced dramatically better results.

The holding power of the classes varied, with high dropout rates early in the course and substantial dropouts between the first and second (and third, when this was part of the programme) stages. About 40 per cent of those beginning the course finished and most of these had acquired reading, writing and numeracy skills equivalent to a sixth-grade elementary-school child. However, most participants fared relatively poorly in the acquisition of technical and vocational knowledge. This may be, in part, because most of the teachers were not technicians, but were drawn from the elementary-school teaching cadre. It may also have been because of the large number of enrollees in the general agricultural and women's curriculum who had no specific interest in the technical content.

One estimate, based on studies of adaptation of farming innovations by participants, indicates that perhaps 30 per cent of the farming practices advocated in the courses were adopted. In general, changes that are costly, either in money or in time, or which are intended to increase productivity in the long term rather than the short term, are resisted.

Teaching materials

Instructional materials consisted of an instructor's guide, primer, work sheets for group or individual activities (writing, counting, graphic designs) and, for some topics, posters. A variety of audio-visual aids were purchased for the project, but few were ever used for instructional purposes, though some were used in promotional efforts.

Each programme consisted of two (and occasionally three) stages of twenty-four sequences each. About 300 hours of classroom activity were required to complete a two-stage programme.

A production centre at the project headquarters at Esfahan reproduced and distributed the material. This centre also distributed the various test and evaluation instruments.

Costs

According to the Unesco Literacy Division's Evaluation Unit, the total costs of the Iran project were as shown below:

	Funding source		Total
	UNDP	Government	
Actual expenditure (U.S.$)	1,683,300	4,268,900	5,952,200
Planned expenditure[1] (U.S.$)	1,693,913	1,677,446	3,371,359
Percentage of planned expenditure actually spent	99	254	176

1. Plan of Operation, 1970.

This is one of the few projects in which the government exceeded its original commitment by a sizeable amount. However, the above figure apparently includes costs in kind since final accounting by UNDP shows that allocations from the Planning Ministry in Iran totalled only $2,715,000, including preliminary expense prior to the start of the project in 1967.

The Iranian contribution was largely used for operational expenses (90 per cent) while a small portion (about 10 per cent) was used for capital investment (construction of Esfahan headquarters building, purchase of equipment, etc.). Operational expenses included salaries, full and part time (61 per cent), supplies, including paper for printing (5 per cent), and miscellaneous, including travel, rent etc. (24 per cent).

During the 1970-71 operating year, according to the Smyth cost-effectiveness report cited above [41], the operating cost to the Government of Iran per participant was $17.00, and $31.00 per participant completing one stage. Dropout rates of 40 per cent per stage pushed the cost to the government per functional literate even higher. Smyth estimates the cost of a participant completing two stages to have been about $74.00 [41].

According to the Unesco Literacy Division's Evaluation Unit, average *per capita* and per graduate costs for the entire programme were $48.75 and $99.60 respectively.[1] These figures, however, include research cost of about 23 per cent of the total, and these were largely covered by UNDP expenditures. Thus, Unesco calculates cost to the government of a successful graduate at about $76.00, not including research costs, and per participant at $37.33, not including research. The discrepancy in the estimated per participant costs during 1970-71 of $17.00 (by Unesco's Iran cost expert) and overall programme average of $37.33 (by Unesco's Evaluation Unit) are not so easily explained.

In any case, the figure of something less than $80.00 per successful graduate compares favourably with the approximate cost in Iran of $183.00 to bring one primary-school student to a similar level of literacy attainment. And it may reasonably be assumed that the *per capita* cost would fall somewhat further with increased enrolments in the future.

Since expenditures prior to June 1970 were used primarily to develop the pedagogy and machinery which became fully operational only during 1970-71, these expenses must be considered as primarily research and development costs necessary for the implementation of the project. In essence, it took three years of research and development and planning at a total cost of $2.4 million ($1.1 million, UNDP; $1.3 million, Government of Iran) before the pedagogical and organizational infrastructure was developed to the point of being able to operationalize the programme.

Only modest *per capita* savings could be effected by mass extension of the programme since most of the expenditure was for teachers' and supervisors' salaries. Assuming that the pedagogy and materials developed in the project are adopted by the national literacy programme, however, the research and development costs would appear to be minimal compared to the total annual cost of running the national campaign (estimated at about ten times the cost of the pilot project).

1. Iran cost figures are of those who successfully passed the final examination, whereas most other case study figures are those of participants who presented themselves at the final examination, not necessarily passing it.

Evaluation and research

Mr Bazany, an evaluation expert on the project, has succinctly pointed out the problems in evaluating the Iran project:

Originally, the evaluational process was conceived in classic terms. . . . Implicit in this conception of evaluation was the assumption that functional literacy was premised upon an elaborated and empirically confirmed theory from which a set of verifiable hypotheses might be deduced. . . . The facts of the matter were sharply at variance with such optimistic assumptions. Functional literacy considered as an instructional theory was little more than a loose agglomeration of assumptions and inference; supported by unsystematic findings and a considerable element of faith. There was no defined methodology for integrating professional training, literacy and other develop-oriented activities into an organized educational process. Moreover, the very nature of regional development plans was known only in very vague terms, if at all. Thus, neither the meaning nor nature of a proper integration of such activities with literacy and training could be anticipated.

In such circumstances, it was necessary to approach the problem of evaluation from a quite different point of view [4].

The new approach basically assumed that the evaluation team's first task was to assist the operational arm in research and development activities designed to identify project objectives and subojectives, in the try-out and revision of various approaches and methodologies for the preparation of instructors, and in the preparation of teaching content, methods and materials. As this research and development proceeded, certain evaluative data were accumulated which give some picture of the effectiveness and cost of the various methodologies in the aggregate.

Results of the various studies are now available in nine volumes. These nine volumes report on five distinct categories of research and evaluation activities:

1. Studies related to the definition of operational objectives which served as guidelines for the preparation and implementation of the instructional programmes.
2. Studies related to the selection of suitable localities and instructors and to the creation of an information system which provided continuous feedback information useful for the organization and supervision of each of the courses.
3. Studies and evaluations of the teaching-learning process through the application of tests, special studies, comparative research studies, etc.
4. Studies on the socio-economic effects of the acquired knowledge observed in changes of behaviour, adoption of recommended practices, utilization of literacy, community participation, attitudes towards the education of children, etc.
5. Studies related to the costs and benefits of a satisfactory literacy method through the use of standards which serve to assess the financial viability of the method.

A number of the results of the research and evaluation scheme are reported on in the appropriate sections, above. In summary:

1. It was found that there are effective approaches for combining technical vocational and literacy skills content in one set of training materials, and that mathematics can best be taught in conjunction with technical skills. However, achievement in literacy skills was markedly higher than achievement in technical and vocational areas, raising the question of whether or not economically productive skills of use in the short range can be taught effectively through such a programme, using primary-school teachers with little technical training. This does not mean that the literacy skills may not be more meaningful to the participants in the long run when taught in the context of technical vocational information, but there are no long-range data available to assess this hypothesis.

2. One reason that the technical-vocational material may not have been maintained at a high level is because of the impossibility of controlling the enrolment in each of the twenty-eight specialized programmes. By far the larger enrolment was in the more general agricultural and home economics programmes, and the occupational background of those attending varied widely. There was also great variance in the background of those in the more specialized programmes, except within the textile and steel industries. Large numbers of children were enrolled in many of the programmes whose occupational status was as yet undefined. Finally, the instructors were usually primary-school teachers without any technical ability in the occupational areas being taught (this appears to have been the case in many of the EWLP projects whose technical/ vocational components were regarded as weak and/or not integrally linked to the literacy component of the project).

3. The studies on adoption of new practices by those attending literacy classes were disappointing. According to the project's evaluation specialist, only about one-third of recommended new practices were adopted in those cases studied, and these were practices requiring little expenditure of time and effort and little expendtiture of funds. The Unesco Literacy Division's Evaluation Unit, on the other hand, reports that of the relatively few verifiable changes in economic practice observed in experimental villages, nearly 90 per cent appeared to have been directly or indirectly influenced by the literacy classes. Including attitudinal and social effects, along with economic practice, about 85 per cent of observed changes were related to the literacy classes. These figures relate to data retained after discarding information considered unreliable in the unit.

4. Dropout rates were high—probably as high as 60 per cent by the end of the two-cycle programme. However, the cost of successful 'graduates' was substantially less (about half the cost of training a primary-school pupil to the level of fifth-grade reading and writing ability— approximately the level achieved by the literacy programme 'graduates').

5. Many of the pedagogical and organizational innovations of the programme merit study and possible adaptation in other countries.

Summary

The Iran project was unique in the amount of time and effort put into the development and testing of teaching materials and methods. It was also unique in the extensive documentation on all aspects of the project.

It was, in fact, probably the most publicised of all the eleven projects sponsored by UNDP/Unesco under the experimental functional literacy programme. Experts and their counterparts from other projects were sent there to see the project, various articles and reports were published about it, the Iranian Head of State took a personal interest in it, and it led, directly, to the establishment in Tehran of the National Adult Education and Training Centre.

It was not a project without problems, nor can it be said to have established an organizational pattern that should be emulated elsewhere. Certainly, the methods for planning and testing the educational materials were well conceived and merit examination as a process perhaps appropriate to other countries. The project was also reasonably successful in attracting large numbers of adults and children to literacy classes. Project evaluation shows that the classes had a positive effect on adults, both in literacy training and in skills and attitudes related to social and economic spheres of activity.

However, the project was less than successful in matching specific technical components of the training to the adults who presumably could use it. Further, the use of primary-school teachers with little technical background limited the quality of technical training that could be expected in the classes.

High dropout rates in this well-supported and well-prepared project show the futility of assuming that any literacy programme can attract and hold all people to the point where illiteracy can be eliminated solely through literacy classes. With a 40 per cent average dropout rate for each of the two stages of the programme, even if the programme were extended to cover all adult illiterates in Iran, the majority would drop out before they had become literate.

For all of the high-level policy support for the projects, many development organizations and industries in Iran remained sceptical of the programme and offered little collaboration or support. This phenomenon was not peculiar to the Iran project. In fact, only in certain countries where adult functional literacy and technical training was made the responsibility of development enterprises themselves, with technical training offered by technicians (and often the literacy training, as well) were the interests of some of those in charge of development enterprises truly engaged.

In essence, Iran has provided some methodological lessons of interest, but the conceptual, organizational and motivational problems remain to be solved by each country. Perhaps Iran has shown how to set up a process for continuously studying, evaluating and assessing—and that may be the first step towards the answers being sought.

Madagascar

Time perspective

The Malagasy Government participated actively in the 1965 World Conference of Ministers of Education on the Eradication of Illiteracy held in Tehran, and shortly thereafter invited a Unesco team to recommend a programme of functional literacy in Madagascar. This mission (April-May 1966) recommended functional literacy activities in three district areas (Farafangana, Tulear and Befandriana). Each area represented a specific and difficult problem of social and economic development. A first request was submitted to UNDP in March 1967, but further adjustments were necessary and, while preliminary operations were authorized in June 1968, the Plan of Operation (eighth version) was only signed in June 1970. In the meantime, the first phase of operations was started in 1969 in the region of Farafangana and in 1970 in the region of Tulear. The project came to a premature close in December 1971, following numerous difficulties (it was originally scheduled to end in October 1973) and at the request of the government, which accepted the recommendation of a special review mission.

Policy and objectives

The objectives of the project were as follows:
1. To assist the government to identify problems and needs of the adult illiterate population in the three selected regions.
2. To explore possible solutions and development activities which could help to increase production and raise the standard of living in these regions.
3. To spread information on necessary modern techniques and prepare those responsible for development projects in the target zones to participate in literacy operations. It was hoped to reach 50,000 people involved in rice, cotton and coffee growing.
The objectives of the project corresponded to a concept of functional literacy

which required a close link with concrete development activities in association with rural extension. Despite some variations over time, the government maintained a conception of education which emphasized a global approach to changing attitudes and behaviour prior to dealing with technical content.

The principal policy problem at the inception of the project revolved around the reluctance of the Institut de Recherche et d'Application des Méthodes de Développement (IRAMD), the spiritual father in Madagascar of *animation rurale,* to accept the functional literacy project as something that could be separated from the overall programme of *animation rurale.* In the Malagasy sense *animation rurale* consists of 'enlightening' action based on training local leaders with a view to making the rural population more aware and establishing 'dialogues' between the community and local authorities. Information on rural problems and development priorities was given orally and literacy was not considered necessary. Co-operation was requested (but not always obtained) from the agricultural and extension services of other ministries.

The functional literacy project was, according to the Plan of Operation, to be set up as a self-contained project within a literacy service running parallel with *animation rurale.* This policy caused a three-way conflict: the UNDP/Unesco project was within, but separate from, the national literacy service, and the national literacy service itself was in some competition with the national rural extension programme. Finally, the government wished a national literacy scheme with a relatively simple structure, while Unesco insisted on selective projects in limited geographical areas and a relatively sophisticated and costly infrastructure.

These various cross-curents contributed to the impossibility of agreeing on a Plan of Operation until after eight versions had been drafted, and to the early closing of the project, after which the programme was integrated with the rural extension programme and the literacy effort became entirely national.

Participants

The original Plan of Operation set as its goal the training of 51,000 adult illiterates in three subprojects. Serious operational difficulties were encountered, due in part to lack of agreement as to how to organize the projects and in part to the inadequate supply of instructors and the need to utilize voluntary teachers. Only a few thousand persons participated in the project on a regular basis.

In Farafangana there were 50 participants in 1969 and 1,022 in January 1970, spread over 15 literacy centres, which were increased to 80 in July 1970 and 402 in January 1971. In the Tulear subproject, 389 participants were enrolled in 12 centres. At the end of 1970 there were 362 participants and in 1971, 465. In the Befandriana subproject classes were opened in March 1971, with 1,891 participants, and 15 instructors as well as 19 voluntary teachers, in 31 centres. These results contrast sharply with the target of the Plan of Operation which was to train 51,000 adult illiterates in the three subprojects.

Because of the premature closing of the project there are only limited data on the background of participants, on retention and dropout rates and on participant's achievements, and no data of the effect of the classes on the productive behaviour of the new literates.

Administration and organization

A General Commission for Rural Extension and Civic Service was attached to the office of the Vice-President. This commission underwent some changes and finally becamse the Secretariat of State in charge of *animation rurale* and co-operation. After the closing of the project the operations were transferred to the Ministry of Internal Affairs. The project had some financial and technical autonomy but was attached as of 1970 to the national literacy service. The personnel reponsible for the execution of the subprojects were located in the three areas of the project but decentralization proved difficult because all decisions were taken only in Tananarive and their execution was strictly controlled by the national director. Field-work on the part of the international personnel was not encouraged.

In March 1970 study seminars were organized in all of the three regions of the project. The transfer of literacy activities to local development bodies was discussed and the principle of collective responsibility defined. The integration of a project with ongoing rural extension work, which was considered fundamental to all activities, encountered difficulties in the implementation phase due to differences in intepretation of this integration and varying views concerning the respective interest of each service. During the implementation of the project, there was a clear tendency to extend functional literacy to a national level rather than to maintain it in a distinct project framework. This policy has in fact been adopted by the government since the closing of the project through the introduction of project methods and techniques into the national literacy programme.

Logistical problems also hampered early development of the project. The experimental zones had very different population constraints, numbers ranging from 500,000 in one zone to 15,000 in another. They were dispersed, geographically, and none nearer than 800 kilometres to the project office. Within the development zones, the district headquarters were at some distance from the areas where the functional literacy activities were to have evolved. Finally, the experimental zones were very isolated from a cultural point of view, with no stimuli for literacy; by and large, there was no written material available in the areas, whether newspapers, magazines or books.

A system was established for the production of material, although some (deemed inadequate by project staff) was produced by the rural extension service for use in the pilot projects. Only at the end of the project, after delivery of a printing press, did the project begin to produce materials for participants and for teachers.

In general, it must be concluded that the organization and administration of the project was inadequate, in part due to the insistence of Unesco on an experimental, selective, intensive functional literacy scheme in limited geographical regions, while the government wished a national scheme integrated with all development enterprises. This caused continuing conflict between national counterparts and Unesco experts together with conflicts between national services and led to early closing of the project.

Teachers and other personnel

Two types of instructors were foreseen: professional personnel recruited from among young members of the *service civique* (a kind of paramilitary service engaged in educational and agricultural operations) and voluntary teachers recruited on the spot. The concept of rural development and literacy was based on community action which was responsible for the organization of classes and instruction. Teams of literate farmers and persons who had received some rural extension training were to be used by the project since they had proved their effectiveness in the national programme. But the lack of qualified personnel in the subproject areas was a fundamental problem and only eighty-nine instructors underwent training in all the subprojects. Of these only twenty-two remained through the life of the project. Part of the problem was that the *service civique* personnel had limited time to spare because of other priority para-military activities.

The average age of the instructors was between 20 and 22 with a relatively high level of education and eighteen months of experience in the *service civique*. A few former literacy workers were also taken over by the project and on the whole proved effective, although a number had to continue to undertake responsibilities within the national literacy programme.

Few volunteer instructors were recruited, in part because there were few literate adults in project areas of activity. In contrast, the national literacy programme operated in some zones where there were already sufficient literate adults to provide volunteer instructors.

The quality of the training methods for literacy instructors stands in contrast to the limited quantitative impact which so few instructors could have had. Careful provisions were conceived for a better understanding of rural groups' specific needs and cultural patterns, and a sharp emphasis was placed on practical knowledge and concrete social experience.

The project trained a number of supervisors, but these had many tasks (dissemination of agricultural techniques, new work methods, in-service teacher and extension-worker training, etc.) and most spent only one year in the field, having been loaned by the *service civique* to work on literacy activities as part of their para-military service.

There was little effective training of national supervisory, educational materials production, and evaluation staff. The counterpart idea did not work well, with few people at the proper level being attached to the Unesco experts. The evaluation expert worked more or less on his own, carrying out studies of some value in providing general background information to project staff, but making no attempt to integrate his work into the efforts of others or to answer the critical questions that needed to be resolved as the project proceeded. Part of the problem was that the evaluation specialist received instructions directly from Unesco Headquarters and these instructions were not always realistic in the local context.

One evaluation specialist underwent a nine-month training programme abroad but did not return to the project. A month-long mobile study group of all project staff, under the direction of the methods and materials experts, was useful in examining first-hand local problems. The national director made short visits to Paris and to Iran in order to attend evaluation meetings while some of the local project officers participated in a literacy operational seminar in Tunisia. Other training fellowships provided for in the plan of operations were never utilized.

There was some reluctance to help on the part of resource people in project areas, apart from offering occasional advice on pedagogical or technical matters.

Curriculum and methods

Already in 1968 (in preparatory work authorized prior to the signing of the UNDP/Unesco Plan of Operation) a functional literacy methodology in the national language was being experimented and tested in a context of operational seminars. The *milieu* of the target area was studied by literacy officers and prospective teachers. Problems had been studied at the individual level in collaboration with technical specialists. The problems of integrating literacy with *animation rurale* were discussed with these officials. A semi-global approach to literacy teaching was adopted which was based on the introduction, through a key sentence, of a social theme of interest within a discussion group (for example, hygiene, child care, home economics, improvement of crops, marketing, saving). Didactic materials were prepared, utilizing as much local material as possible and these were tested by the pilot project when it officially began in 1970, with some necessary adaptations corresponding to the conditions of the subproject areas.

The elaboration of instructional programmes was preceded by in-depth baseline surveys which were utilized as a programme input. All elements of the programmes were integrated in order to use reading, writing and arithmetic as the means for transmitting the technical content. Programmes were to some extent organized in collaboration with technical services attached to development operations, and the officials in charge of literacy played the dual role of supervisors and instructors, as well as being internal evaluators. The instructors participated in the preparation of programmes, particularly in the Farafangana subproject, as well as their continuing adaptation.

The educational process was started through group discussion during which the participants analysed the technical problems and jointly reviewed possible solutions. These solutions were grouped into key sentences which then helped in the learning of literacy. The sentences were broken down into their constituent parts and then transformed into words once the letters had been learned. Mathematical concepts were introduced in much the same way.

Teaching materials

The main didactic instruments were technical and pedagogic sheets and posters (*fiches techniques-pédagogiques*). Posters represented problems with their respective solutions and served as the basis for discussion during the sessions. A special poster was prepared to illustrate the conclusions which these discussions reached. The technical and pedagogic sheets provided guidance on how to maintain the interest of the participants and provided indications on desirable solutions.

There was no really effective machinery for obtaining suggestions from the various technical services as regards the content of teaching materials, and no infrastructure was established for the printing and distribution of the material. Only a small amount of material prepared (largely by the international staff) was ever reproduced for distribution, even after the arrival of a printing press towards the end of the project.

Some of the materials were not distributed because of the absence of government authorization (for example, in the case of the manual for supervisors). Other materials prepared outside the project by the rural extension service, but distributed to participants in the project, were judged by project staff to be too difficult, using words and language not suitable for the rural semi-literate audience.

During the two preparatory years of the project, the government failed to provide either counterpart staff for the expert in the preparation of teaching texts (only a junior artist was assigned to him) or the expert in audio-visual aids (for whom there was never any sort of counterpart). This situation improved during the final eighteen months of the project after the Plan of Operation was signed by the government.

Costs

Total cost of the project, according to the Unesco Literacy Division's Evaluation Unit, was as shown in the table opposite.

Unesco estimates the cost per participant at $111.90, and per final participant (taking the final examination) at $125.80, both figures, including research and evaluation costs, amounting to about 38 per cent of the total.

There is little point in attempting to further analyse costs since the project was stopped in mid-stream and no one can estimate what the true costs might have been had the project been completed.

	Funding source		Total
	UNDP	Government	
Actual expenditure (U.S.$)	558,500	366,100	924,600
Planned expenditure[1] (U.S.$)	876,000	1,239,200	2,115,200
Percentage of planned expenditure actually spent	63	29	44

1. Plan of Operation, July 1970.

Evaluation and research

Evaluation activities in this project provided guidance for the planning and elaboration of functional literacy programmes (particularly for the Farafangana region) through baseline studies and special surveys on the motivations and perceptions of the illiterate population. Although extensive preparations were undertaken through the construction of tests, training of personnel and the conducting of baseline surveys at the individual and community level for the purpose of establishing benchmarks, the premature closing of the experimental project prevented completion of an evaluation report.

Studies were undertaken on the literacy levels of prospective participants and their motivation in joining functional literacy groups. Studies were also conducted on the quantitative and qualitative results obtained at the end of the first stage in one subproject. Most of the efforts were directed, however, to the preparation of baseline surveys in Befandriana and Farafangana.

As mentioned above (under 'Administration and Organization'), evaluation and research was undertaken by the evaluation expert more or less independently of the rest of the project staff. Thus, although some of the baseline material was of general use to project personnel, little material related specifically to project needs. Most studies were never completed, either because they were interrupted by national authorities (as in the case of the vocabulary studies of words used by farmers) or because of the early termination of the project.

Summary

At best, one can conclude from this project that there is no one model of functional literacy that is acceptable to all countries and in all contexts. From the beginning, there were different conceptions on the part of Unesco, UNDP and the government as to what was needed to introduce functional literacy. Although the government resisted the idea of a discrete, experimental project, limited to three geographical areas, it finally agreed to the plan, only to continue to resist its implementation in a number of direct and indirect ways until the project was prematurely terminated. The government subsequently reverted to its original idea of the incorporation of functional literacy activities within its *animation rurale* programme on a national scale.

The project raises the question of whether traditional modes of technical assistance are appropriate in cases where the government is reluctant to accept the usual formula of experts, equipment and fellowships. The Madagascar officials did not, it appears, really want a group of full-time experts to take the lead in developing a programme and in working with local groups at all levels. It may be asked whether another formula for helping Malagasy officials to do the job they had in mind might not have been possible. Such a formula could perhaps have better met both the needs of indigenous personnel and specific Malagasy management techniques. At the same time, it could conceivably have provided other countries with useful pointers.

Mali

Time perspective

Mali became independent in 1960 and immediately began a mass literacy effort which, by 1965, had 600 literacy centres operating throughout the country. Although there were a number of local languages (four major languages plus a number of variants and minor languages), literacy classes were in French, essentially a foreign language for the participants. Precise figures are not available but it would seem that these early literacy efforts to teach French as a foreign language were not notably successful.

A Unesco planning mission visited Mali in 1965 to assist the government in the preparation of a functional literacy project. A request by the government was submitted to the Special Fund and approved by the Governing Council in January 1966. Preparatory work started in 1966. By January 1967, nine experts were already working in the project although the signing took place only in February 1967. Successive adjustments extended project operations until the end of 1972.

French bilateral assistance continued to be provided to the functional literacy programme until 1974, and United States bilateral assistance has been provided for 1975-76 to pick up certain costs of functional literacy activities (including an extensive evaluation) in the rural areas of Mali. Other bilateral and multilateral donors have also expressed interest in the programme.

Policy and objectives

The Plan of Operation stated two main objectives:
1. To reinforce the National Centre for Literacy Material Production, making it possible to reach 100,000 illiterate rice and cotton farmers in the region of Segou and 10,000 illiterate workers in the industrial and commercial enterprises of the State.
2. To explore and test the most suitable methods and techniques for the training of illiterate farmers and workers with a view to improving their productivity and raising their standard of living.

It was agreed from the start that the project would be national in scope, although certain methods and materials would be developed and tested in pilot areas where the government had development enterprises under way in rice, cotton and groundnut (peanut) production. It was further agreed that the programme would no longer teach French as a foreign language, but would teach illiterates in their own language, or in whatever national language was a lingua franca of the region in which the illiterates lived.

Literacy and language policy has received careful attention from the Mali Council of Ministers. In 1967, the council passed a decree giving official status to a new language transcription system which used the same alphabet for transcribing the four national languages selected for functional literacy programming (Mande, Peul, Tamasheq and Songhai). Following this decree, vocabulary and transcription work concentrated on Mande and its variants, Bambara, Malinke and Diula, because of the wide use of the variants in cotton and rice-growing regions and of Bambara in groundnut production areas. Paradoxically, French was used in industrial programmes, which seems to have affected results adversely.

This policy led to the creation in 1973 (after the termination of UNDP/Unesco assistance) of the Institut National d'Alphabetisation Fonctionnelle et de Linguistique, whose function is not only to watch over and backstop functional adult literacy work but also to look at possible fundamental reforms of all education in order to give Malian youth (many not in school) an education for life in the context of their national culture and in their own national languages. The institute is to have three units: functional literacy; applied linguistics; and experimentation related to basic education.

Since there was never any division between the functional literacy project and the national programme, there was no confusion as regards policy such as existed in many of the other experimental projects. In fact, the government early decided that the functional literacy programme would be the only national programme, and the assistance provided from UNDP/Unesco was used to strengthen a national commitment.

A related policy decision by the Ministry of Production was to integrate functional literacy into development projects, with the administrators of the rice, cotton and groundnut schemes to be responsible for encouraging literacy in their programmes. This policy, however, was resisted at the beginning of the project by those responsible for the cotton programme, which was already well established with French assistance. The administrators of this programme could not see the importance of literacy and did not co-operate for the first few years of the project. The rice and groundnut projects, however, were beginning at about the same time as the functional literacy operation and those in charge more readily accepted the literacy programmes as an integral part of the projects.

Participants

The collection of precise data on participants was difficult early in the project due to the problem of the setting up a comprehensive information system. This system was finally operational (using alternate sources of data) in May 1970. About 2,000 literacy centres were opened between the beginning of the project (1967) and 1972, with about forty participants enrolled per centre. It is estimated that some 83,000 illiterate adults were reached by the project, of whom about 50,000 completed a literacy programme. The number of centres and the enrolment fluctuated in accordance with the agricultural calendar, according to a survey in early 1972, which showed that only 55 per cent of the reported centres were actually operating. Participants were distributed in the agricultural sector as follows: cotton, 60 per cent; groundnuts, 30 per cent; Niger river development project (Office du Niger), 7 per cent; rice, 3 per cent.

A special programme for women was prepared during 1970-72 and was implemented in several pilot centres. The dominant demographic group in all but the programme for women was the young male adult between 15 and 25 years of age. Many of these participants migrated to the city for a period of about four months between February and May to earn some money from sale of crops. This, in turn, led to the slowing down of literacy activities.

The linguistic homogeneity of groups was high, with the exception of the Segou region where the participation of the Bobo group required special programme adjustment (in most other groups, Bambara or a variant was used by the participants). The centres, which were opened by local communities and industrial enterprises, did not attract groups of participants which were homogeneous as to sex or age. In the preparation of content and material, the project had assumed that the technical and educational level of the participants was roughly the same in all cases and, although precise data are not available, there undoubtedly were exceptions to this generalization.

Administration and organization

At the national level, the project was integrated into the fundamental education and literacy service and, as of 1969, into the General Directorate for Fundamental Education and Literacy, under the authority of the Minister of National Education, Youth and Sports. The functional literacy service was headed on the national side by a national director responsible for the national centre for the production and diffusion of literacy material. The actual operations were subdivided into seven regions each headed by a director. A special literacy committee was usually set up at the grass-roots level and, towards the end of the project, numerous local development organizations agreed to finance and take over the operation of future functional literacy activities.

Functional literacy was viewed as a means of transmitting vocational knowledge and skills, technical, scientific and socio-economic information, as well as guidance related to health and industrial security. The need to develop effective literacy programmes in the national language was taken into account. While the socio-economic aspect was always the pre-dominant objective, the development of an instructional system capable of teaching a large number of adults in different languages was noted by the authorities as one of the key results of the project. This is reflected by the decision of the national authorities to create the National Institute for Functional Literacy and Applied Linguistics after the closing of the project.

Through practical experience, an approach was evolved which initiated the educational process through the presentation of a selected problem (chosen after conducting baseline surveys and problem studies) which then served as the central didactic unit. Starting in 1969, 'functionality' was achieved by introducing a programme for groundnut growers which not only presented the problems encountered as pedagogic vehicles but was able to present the learning process itself as a means of solving this type of problem.

This notion was ultimately accepted by the various development ministries in Mali, ensuring the taking over of literacy activities by development structures themselves. The technical services concerned, however, became involved in the actual execution of literacy programmes only after they had been able to observe the first practical results obtained in other areas of the country. Subsequently, diversified, inexpensive and decentralized literacy activities, which could be carried out by community-based organizations or production enterprises, were developed and accepted by the responsible officials. For example, it was possible to link up functional literacy with the following development operations:

1. Five rural development organizations concerned respectively with: groundnuts; rice; cotton; tomatoes; Niger river development (Office du Niger).
2. Five State enterprises concerned respectively with: electrical power; transport; matches; tobacco; textiles.

The project covered 81 districts (out of 250) and 14 administrative units (out of 42). At the conclusion of the project, it was estimated that 2,000 literacy centres were in operation. Because of the fact that some centres would open for a time and then close, and because of inadequate reporting procedures, it was impossible to establish an accurate figure.

In any case, the project only scratched the surface in terms of the country as a whole. Ninety per cent of the population was illiterate when the project began, with the 10 per cent literate population largely in urban areas. Only one child in five received an elementary education. Although elementary education spaces have trebled in the last ten years (and continue to grow), the population growth rate has increased illiteracy figures by some 50,000 per year in the 15-year age group and above. To deal with these illiterates, some 1,200 new literacy classes would have to be initiated each year, some three or four each day. It was in recognition of this fact that the government increasingly assumed that literacy instruction should be decentralized and come under the direct supervision of those locally responsible for the various development enterprises, rather than that a self-contained national literacy network should be superimposed on existing national and local development project structures.

Teachers and other personnel

About 2,000 instructors were trained by the project personnel (95 per cent men and 5 per cent women). Over 90 per cent of these were of the same professional and demographic background as the participants, 6 per cent were professional foremen and 1 per cent were primary-school teachers. Ninety per cent of the instructors had not finished primary school. The selection was made by the local community or the production unit in accordance with their status in social and educational terms. A training session of three to five days was organized for the selected instructors during which they were introduced to the different materials prepared. The regional literacy directors were responsible for their training and supervision. These training sessions usually involved development activities. Instructors were also introduced to the use of mass media as a support device in the educational process. They were directly supervised by specially trained supervisory personnel.

There is some question as to whether or not the short training period for instructors (many of them only semi-literate themselves) was sufficient. In addition, training materials were limited in scope and may need to be improved in the future.

A number of specialists in linguistics and in the preparation of educational materials were also trained by the international experts. These specialists constituted the staff of the Institute for Functional Literacy and Linguistics, created in 1973.

Some forty-five Zone Alphabétisation Fuctionelle (ZAF) heads, under the National Literacy Service, supervised up to fifty literacy centres each at the end of the project, often travelling on motor cycles provided by the programme. These supervisors worked under the direction of the seven regional directors.

Until the end of the project, both participants and volunteer instructors received varying amounts of World Food Programme commodities as incentives for participation. These commodities were presented to participants and instructors in a small ceremony at each literacy centre.

Curriculum and methods

At the more general level, zones were selected by the Planning Ministry. Subsequently, the literacy project, and usually its evaluation unit, undertook special studies. The officials responsible for development activities were involved in this process and their participation in the execution of the programmes was considered essential. The linkage between literacy and agricultural extension was recognized as an essential component of all agricultural programmes. Greater difficulty was encountered in applying the 'extension' concept to industrial programmes.

Once a specific target population had been identified, a special work team was set up, usually consisting of: (a) an illustrator or photographer who could produce the problem-oriented posters; (b) a specialist in vocational training (industrial or agricultural) who was in charge of maintaining close contact with the technical services of the target area; (c) a programme specialist and, if possible, an evaluator. This team visited the agricultural or industrial enterprise, surveyed the production process and identified possible bottlenecks. Both the supervisory personnel and the illiterate workers were involved in this survey of the operations and problems encountered. An educational programme, usually covering two years, was designed to encourage study of these problems on a priority basis. For each socio-economic group a differentiated programme was prepared.

Teaching materials

The actual production of materials was entrusted to a National Production Centre which prepared the technical sheets necessary for the instructional programme. The programme was structured into two stages each corresponding to a full year of instruction. Each stage was subdivided into twenty sequences for the agricultural programme and thirty-eight for the industrial programme, although the latter was task- rather than problem-oriented. Each sequence had the same structure. It usually covered one week of instruction and was centred on one specific professional problem which the above-mentioned survey had retained. But in practice a particular problem area might be covered over several sequences.

The practical and professional content was presented by the extension workers in the agricultural areas or by the technical services personnel within the factory. This practical demonstration was then utilized in the presentation of the literacy materials.

Whenever the literacy instructor was required to present a practical demonstration he would have benefited from materials specially prepared for this purpose. The technical information not only touched upon specific economic subjects but also included social, hygiene and nutritional topics. The basic principle of the pedagogical approach used was to introduce and reinforce knowledge directly related to the daily lives of the participants. This process was then followed by literacy skills training *per se*.

The literacy materials, in turn, were prepared in the context of the technical and professional content of the programmes. A key sentence was presented on each subject under discussion. Each sentence was accompanied by a pictorial presentation which tied in with previously learnt technical content. The sentence was then broken down into its various parts and used to reconstitute new words in accordance with the learning process. Such integration of technical content with reading and writing skills was not always achieved in the teaching of arithmetic, however, although there was full integration of mathematics content with technical content in the groundnut programme.

A key innovation introduced by functional literacy in Mali was the link with practical demonstration and extension work. Starting from a concrete situation, the problem was translated into a more abstract form through various media, the first step being the preparation of a 'problem poster'. Each problem poster was accompanied by a technical sheet which was later expanded to include, in addition to technical information, methodological guidance for the instructors. Photographic representation of the problem was used, since field testing seemed to indicate that this was more effective than drawing. Separate instructor material was prepared for each element of the curriculum but in accordance with an overall programme design.

The materials for the second stage were usually of a general character dealing with economic and civic problems such as the role of production in agriculture, the nature of public services, investments, savings, etc. The second stage followed a less restricted pattern since the participants were already familiar with the basic literacy skills. In addition to the extensive literacy material and complementary technical booklets, the project also prepared some films and an important number of radio programmes. An agricultural calendar was prepared for distribution to literacy centres. This gave advice (related to each region) as to appropriate agricultural practices for each season. Finally, a nationally distributed newspaper, *Kibaru,* was created, at first distributed free to participants in the literacy classes only, but later sold successfully to all villagers interested. This newspaper has continued to grow and it has recently been recommended that it should have regional pages as well as material relevant to all regions.

Distribution problems plagued the project and no one was ever sure that the right materials reached the right centres. These problems, of course, were a function of the limited communications infrastructure in the country.

Costs

Total costs of the project, as reported by the Unesco Literacy Division's Evaluation Unit, were as shown below:

	Funding source		Total
	UNDP	Government	
Actual expenditure (U.S.$)	1,400,700	1,099,600	2,500,300
Planned expenditure[1] (U.S.$)	1,176,500	3,070,600	4,248,100
Percentage of planned expenditure actually spent	119	36	59

1. Plan of Operation, December 1966.

The actual expenditure of the government appears low when compared with original estimates, but this may be due to several factors. As noted earlier in this case study, the government stressed local volunteer participation in the construction of literacy facilities and in the staffing of the programme. Although incentives were used to attract both volunteer teachers and participants (in the form of World Food Programme commodities), the cost of these foodstuffs was not included in the cost figures. Thus, if contributions in kind are included, the total cost would be somewhat higher, and the government contribution substantially higher.

Based on identifiable cash-flow expenditures reported in the table above, the cost per enrolled participant was about $13.58 and per final participant (taking the final examination) about $34.63, of which Unesco estimates about half was used for research and evaluation purposes and the remainder for operational expense. These figures more or less agree with estimates in final project reports that it cost approximately $30.00 to bring an illiterate through the second cycle to a point where he had about fifth-grade reading ability and somewhat less writing and mathematical ability, plus elements of functional training. The annual Gross National Product of Mali was estimated, at the conclusion of the project, at $50.00 *per capita*. Assuming that it takes about half of that to bring an illiterate to successful completion of a literacy course, it would take nearly half a year's GNP to bring the 90 per cent of the population now illiterate to a minimal level of literacy skills. Assuming the continued use of volunteer teachers and locally constructed literacy centres at no cash cost to the government, the major expenditure would seem to be for supervisory staff and for the preparation, testing and distribution of teaching materials. Budgets for the preparation of such material (although rising) consisted at the project's end of less than 1 per cent of the education budget of the country.

Finally, in a country where illiteracy is as high as 90 per cent, there is great need for the provision of reading materials (such as the newspaper *Kibaru*, mentioned above) in areas where people are becoming literate. Such expenditure would be in addition to the minimal costs noted above.

Mali is one of the few projects which encountered a degree of success in using volunteer teachers. However, even in Mali, there was minimal compensation in the form of World Food Programme foodstuffs and even this was discontinued at the end of the project. One wonders if the volunteer policy can be maintained, should the programme be expanded in the future, with no compensation at all for the teachers.

Evaluation and research

The Evaluation Unit of the Mali project encountered difficulties which hindered its work and make it unlikely that any comprehensive evaluation report will be forthcoming from this project. Among the most significant difficulties were inadequate material conditions (transportation, offices, assistants, etc.), lack of counterpart personnel, gaps of some six months between the departure and arrival of each of the three international evaluation specialists, and the slow implementation of operations.

Furthermore some resistance to evaluation occurred at the local level since, in a setting of voluntary action, it often appeared as an unwanted control. An additional burden, familiar to other projects, was the need to meet certain external standards of the Experimental World Literacy Programme which the local authorities were never able to entirely comprehend.

During the 1967-68 period, studies were carried out on the demographic, economic and social problems in the target zones. One of these surveys led project officials to choose cotton production over rice production as an initial sphere of activity. During this phase, the Evaluation Unit participated in the preparation of some of the programmes. Several efforts were made to institute an information system on enrolments but this support service never functioned properly for various logistical reasons.

Starting with the 1969 classes, an important baseline survey was conducted covering a sample of sixty-four villages (thirty-two experimental and thirty-two controlled villages). Each group was divided into subcategories according to the size of the community (large or small), the part played by cotton growing (important or not important) as well as the linguistic characteristics. Specially trained personnel conducted field-work covering ten families in each village, utilizing an extensive interview schedule and an observation sheet. Already during the analysis of collected data, difficulties arose due to fluctuations in literacy centres (new centres were opened in the control area and centres were closed in the experimental area). The analysis of the baseline data took one year (only one international expert was working on this task). Slow implementation of literacy activities made it impossible to conduct the interim surveys as foreseen in the summer of 1971. Even a year later, the number of the centres which had actually completed their programmes was too small to permit a valid survey. Nevertheless, a survey of the population of certain villages not served by literacy centres shed light on non-literacy factors involved in changes in socio-economic behaviour. These data would be useful as controls in future studies of changes in villages where literacy classes have been undertaken.

A special study was conducted in an industrial setting on the learning level reached by the participants of a first-stage programme. This permitted the reorganization of the programme, the constitution of more homogeneous groups, and the more careful selection of additional workers for further vocational training related to the enterprise's needs. Efforts were also made to prepare studies on the average unit cost of a final participant in Mali, ultimately estimated at $30.

A 1974 World Bank mission attempted to assess the impact of the project on the basis of such indicators as were available nearly two years after the conclusion of UNDP/Unesco assistance, especially in the area of groundnut production. This mission found that, despite withdrawal of Unesco, UNDP and World Food Programme support, the functional literacy programme was still operational. Activities within the Operation Groundnuts project, according to an opinion survey, were especially appreciated for their community character, their linkages with daily life, and their use of local languages. However, logistical problems continued to be encountered and a new reorganization of functional literacy activities was under way at that time, preparatory to further French, United States and Canadian bilateral assistance, and World Bank collaboration. Some 450 new centres are to be added between 1974 and 1976.

Although the World Bank mission reports that a rigorous evaluation of the impact of functional literacy in Mali is not possible, there is some information that is helpful in making judgements concerning the programme. A French-sponsored evaluation survey in early 1974 found that the large majority of participants in literacy classes were farmers of 15 to 50 years of age and that they participated for what they saw as utilitarian, cultural and sociological (prestige) reasons. The volunteers (*animateurs*) also participated for a variety of reasons, and the production units in charge of groundnut enterprises found the literate villagers more productive in that they were able to understand extension ideas and could better understand marketing procedures. Many who were involved in the programme felt that the government did not give enough priority to it, and many asked that the teachers be paid for their services and that the literacy centres be better equipped.

This World Bank report notes that productivity has consistently increased in areas served by functional literacy programmes, but is cautious in suggesting that functional literacy can be said to be the causal factor. Unfortunately, evaluative studies undertaken by the Unesco team were never completed, and although there were good baseline data, follow-up studies were carried out only in certain villages where literacy work had not been undertaken. Obviously, such 'practice-oriented' studies should be encouraged in the future.

Summary

The Mali project took the most sophisticated approach of all of the eleven experimental world literacy projects *vis-à-vis* the problem of teaching in national languages used by participants in various regions. The national centre charged with literacy administration became, in fact, a language policy and linguistic research centre as well as a centre charged with the preparation of literacy materials and methods. This linguistic work should have a long-term impact on educational policies and programmes in the future.

The Mali project was also particularly successful in integrating functional literacy into national development schemes, in large part by placing operational responsibility for local literacy activities squarely in the hands of development enterprises. The task of the national centre was to stimulate, co-ordinate, provide teaching materials, train staff and generally encourage the work. Thus, expenditures of cash were kept at a minimum since many operational costs were absorbed within the day-to-day operations of local development enterprises.

None the less, this delegation of responsibility to local enterprises and groups without major additional resources being made available has caused many local groups to conclude that the government does not give high enough priority to the programme.

Logistical problems plagued the project. Poor communication systems precluded the gathering of accurate data on the subprojects and prevented efficient distribution of teaching materials. High turnover of instructors and even of classes caused breaks in continuity in individual groups and probably contributed to the high drop-out rate.

Studies on the socio-economic impact of the project are inconclusive, but recent (1975) information indicates that literacy activities are expanding and that they receive good grass-roots support, both among participants and among local organizations and productive enterprises. The general impression is that behaviours of participants reflect more receptivity to change and to participation in development activities as a result of having been involved in the functional literacy programmes.

Cost per participant seemed to be among the lowest of the various country projects, in part because of the use of volunteers as literacy instructors, and in part because of the integration of the programme into the infrastructure of the various local production enterprises. It may be wondered whether these hidden costs can be absorbed if the programme expands to enrol more than a token number of the 90 per cent of the adult population considered functionally illiterate in Mali.

Finally, the project demonstrated some concern for follow-up and supplemental reading material in the form of a national newspaper and agricultural calendars. In a country which includes large regions of traditionally illiterate people, such activity must be intensified if new literates are to have something to read. Mali, at least, appears to have recognized this problem to a greater extent than some other countries which undertook to develop experimental functional literacy programmes.

Sudan

Time perspective

In January 1966, the Government of Sudan made a formal request to UNDP for assistance in setting up an adult literacy project. The request was accepted and a Plan of Operation signed in February 1969. Authorization to commence operations was given in April 1969, but project implementation was postponed for several months due to the delay in arrival of the international experts.

The project was shorter in duration than most other EWLP projects, its first phase ending in mid-1972. A one-year extension of phase I was granted (to June 1973) in order to complete the experimental phases in the subprojects then in operation.

In spite of positive recommendations by the inter-agency evaluation mission (December 1971) and independent assessments by Unesco (1972), the project was officially terminated in March 1973, without extension into a second phase.

It might be added that the government did request a functional literacy expert to assist in the literacy training of 6,000 police officers and 6,000 others who were to be engaged in agricultural schemes. These requests were turned down by UNDP (July 1973), as they did not meet UNDP assistance criteria. It also appears that UNDP believed that a sufficiently sound infrastructure had been created during phase I of the project for the government to carry it on without further UNDP assistance.

Policy and objectives

The project's main purpose was to introduce the functional literacy method into the Sudan—to link literacy training activities with rural development as well as industrial-vocational training. The project's specific objectives included:

1. Setting up the basic infrastructure of the functional literacy scheme.
2. Teaching the illiterate adults in project zones basic reading, writing and arithmetic, emphasizing the csrrent vocabularies of agricultural and industrial practice.
3. Planning and carrying out experiments bearing on curricula, teaching methods, materials, forms of organization, supervision, administration and co-ordination.
4. Integrating educational, social and economic activities so as to achieve overall development through co-ordination of work with various public and private bodies.
5. Evaluating the various aspects of the project and its effect on development.
6. Stimulating and functionally orienting adult literacy in areas not covered by the two experimental subprojects.

These objectives lent the design of the project a certain ambivalence; for, while some of them emphasize the selectivity and experimental character of the project, others hold out prospects for a massive impact in eradicating illiteracy in the country.

This ambivalence was reflected in project implementation. On the one hand, the international experts concentrated heavily on the experimental aspects. They dealt in a sophisticated manner with the technical feasibility of the method. However, they (and in particular, the project manager) also promoted the method as 'the' solution to Sudan's illiteracy problems, as if it was a foregone conclusion that the concept had proven its efficacy in all circumstances.

The government, in turn, saw more in fuctional literacy than a circumscribed experiment, and during the lifetime of the project adopted several far-reaching implementation measures. Among other steps taken, a law was passed compelling employers to provide their employees with functional literacy training. The law was not fully enforced, but showed the anxiety of the government to use method as a means of eradicating illiteracy in a relatively short time.

Government policy, as implied above, was, and remains, extremely supportive of the total eradication of illiteracy in Sudan. From its inception, WOALP was viewed as being a first step in a much broader campaign, which campaign was, in fact, launched in 1974 under the title 'Four millions to light'. The project is to take four years, and calls for the considerable outlay of 19 million Sudanese pounds. High-level government support of WOALP seems to have been directly related to the development of a supportive infrastructure at local and intermediate administrative levels. A national literacy staff—much larger than foreseen in the Plan of Operation—was built up. This staff proved receptive to the training imparted in the project, and the indications are that the unit remains viable even without international assistance.

Participants

The project was localized in two areas. One was the irrigation area of Khashm al-Girba, where a settlement scheme has been initiated by the government. The other was Khartoum North, where the main industries are located. These two areas were selected as targets because they represented key sectors in the national economy and models for land reclamation and industrial development. A large home economics project for women was implemented in both the agricultural and industrial areas. Enrolments in the home economics subproject constitute almost 50 per cent (about 3,600) of the total project enrolment. The remaining 3,800 (all male) enrollees were distributed among seven other subprojects, the largest (2,000) being the agricultural subprojects in Khashm al-Girba. Of the total of 7,400 enrollees, only 2,800 completed the first stage of training. Dropout rates were high, ranging from 23 to 95 per cent, but the attendance of the remainder was good, ranging from 77 to 88 per cent.

Administration and organization

The executing agency for the project was Unesco, while the overall planning, direction, and co-ordination was the responsibility of the Ministry of Education. The work was the direct responsibility of the national director appointed to this ministry, who was assisted by a team of international experts headed by the chief technical adviser. Other United Nations agencies, while not signatories of the Plan of Operation, were close collaborators in the project. These included FAO, ILO and Unicef.

In addition to the national director, his deputy, and the supervisor of the agricultural subproject, the national staff were distributed among eight units: evaluation, methodology and training, production and audio-visual aids, agricultural extension, vocational training, home economics, field-work, administration and services. In actual practice, most of the work was accomplished by interdisciplinary teams, rather than by units working independently of one another.

A National Advisory Committee, provided for in the Plan of Operation, was established in order to ensure the participation of the government in the project. In 1972, the functions of this committee were transferred to the National Council of Literacy and Functional Adult Education. Its membership increased greatly to include the UNDP resident representative, the national project director, the chief technical adviser, and representatives from WHO, WEP, FAO and ILO, as well as representatives from numerous ministries and other bodies.

It appears that, relative to such massive operations as the Indian, Ethiopian and Iranian functional literacy projects, the organizational infrastructure of the Sudanese WOALP was small enough to be centrally directed, and did not require administrative cadres at intermediate levels such as the state or district. Such unified, tightly knit organization, was predictably more responsive and helpful than, for example, the complex, multi-administrative-level structure which existed in India. This would appear to have been, a major factor in the relative success of the Sudanese experience.

Teachers and other personnel

The build-up of national staff at all levels was impressive. Four courses were offered for supervisory personnel, three of these at the new (1971) National Institute of Functional Adult Education. These courses adopted the principle that students learn best by doing. Supervisor-trainees at the institute thus participated in the actual planning of a functional literacy subproject. The training of supervisors at the institute represented a break with the training scheme outlined in the Plan of Operation, which called for training to be conducted at the University of Khartoum. The establishment of the institute and the shift of training venue is another indication of the deep government commitment to functional literacy.

A total of sixteen courses were offered for literacy instructors, six each for the agricultural and industrial subprojects, and four for prospective home economics instructors.

Literacy instruction and agricultural/vocational instruction were carried out by same teacher, contrary to the practice in several other EWLP projects. Where the instructors did not have the requisite vocational skills, they had an opportunity to be 'apprenticed' to the trade they would teach, thus gaining first-hand practical experience in addition to formal training.

Instructors were drawn from the supervisory staff of the factories (foremen, technicians, etc.), from the ranks of school-teachers, civil servants, and other educated persons (graduates of intermediate or secondary schools). Most instructors were hired on a part-time basis, while many supervisors were full-time employees of the project. Supervisors included technicians, school principals, and university graduates.

The general impression one receives is that staff training and literacy instruction in the Sudanese WOALP was of higher quality than in many other EWLP projects. Indeed, a number of documents attest to this. However, it should be noted that larger numbers of instructors in this project were of a higher level of education as compared to other projects and were attracted, in part, by the payment offered. Those instructors with higher levels of education appeared, as a rule, to produce above-average results among participants in terms of traditional literacy skills, but were not necessarily those instructors who identified most closely with the 'functional' problems of the illiterates, nor were they those who appeared most committed to the programme.

Curriculum, methods and materials

Each of the eight subprojects progressed from inception through to completion and final evaluation via a logically consistent, nineteen-step implementation procedure, which included the integration of subproject objectives into locally and nationally defined development priorities. Additionally, provision was made for the gathering of baseline data in each case, and for periodic interim, terminal and long-term follow-up of the operation and the effect on participants of each subproject.

Project curricula, while generally tailored to individual subprojects, employed a problem-centred approach, wherein students were encouraged to participate actively in each lesson. The full syllabus was divided into three stages. In four of the subprojects, a primer was prepared for the first stage, together with technical notes, an instructor's guide, reading cards, posters and filmstrips. The objective of the primer was to help the participant reach an elementary level of reading and writing and to provide him with an overall view of the role of the specific trade or productive activity in the national economy, the major problems in the production operation and the relevant topics in elementary science, arithmetic, and socio-economic training.

The problem-centred approach, involving group discussion, appears to have been less than successful in motivating participants, if one can judge by the high dropout rates,[1] both in the Khartoum industrial subproject and in the agricultural project of Khashm al-Girba. Many industrial and agricultural problems are social in nature, and the programmes stressed technical problems. For instance, according to project survey data, farmers resist co-operatives and nomads resist integration, despite technical rationales favouring such developments in these areas.

The primer covered the Arabic alphabet and introduced an average of 250 words, mostly related to specific trades. The lessons usually included a pictorial illustration with a caption, a text centred around the problem and its solution, consisting of a number of sentences increasing gradually from two or three to ten.

Lessons started with a presentation of the problem either orally or through a filmstrip, visit or demonstration, and participants were encouraged to pool their experiences and to reach a group decision on the best method of changing attitudes toward the specific problem under consideration. The text was read first by the instructor and new words were presented by use of reading cards. Exercises were administered to ascertain understanding of the subject matter on the part of participants, their ability to read and write, and the level of language abilities acquired by them. Arithmetic and drawing were taught in relation to the subject matter.

In a second, more advanced stage, the participants were asked to read silently the text of the lesson, and after working with the new words, they engaged in group discussion linking the text with the ongoing professional upgrading or practical home economics. The text for this stage was longer and richer than the primer in technical vocabulary, and it emphasized

---

1. The apparently important role of motivation should not obscure the possibility that other factors—notably organizational—contributed to the high dropout rates.

understanding of the problems, the right way to do the job or to operate the machine, and objective thinking in a group setting.

In the third stage, follow-up booklets of both technico-vocational and socio-economic content constituted the main media of learning and professional upgrading. The objective of this stage was to reinforce newly acquired skills and attitudes. Participants were asked to read the booklet or bulletin in their leisure time, and to prepare for presentation and discussion. Unfortunately, a monthly bulletin, planned as additional follow-up reinforcement, was never actually prepared.

All the educational materials used in the three stages were produced in close collaboration with factory technicians, agricultural extension specialists, home economists, etc., who provided technico-vocational information in addition to examining the texts and the instructor's and trainer's guides.

The primer and advanced books were revised in most programmes after a trial period. A major modification was the preparation of 'introductory lessons' for the primer, with the objective of introducing the illiterate in a limited number of lessons to the Arabic alphabet and some of its mechanics. These introductory lessons were constructed within the functional framework. A recent experiment indicated that the lessons help to reduce difficulties encountered by the new learner in using the primer.

Significant emphasis was placed on the use of practical audiovisual aids such as demonstration farms, model poultry houses, production equipment and field visits. Posters, filmstrips and cassettes were also employed.

Because of the small scale of the project, sufficient materials were produced to meet the needs of participants at all stages of literacy. Indications are that the material produced was of reasonable quality.

Costs

In general, both the government and UNDP honoured their financial commitment as laid out in the Plan of Operation. The Unesco Literacy Division, EWLP Evaluation Unit, has provided the following summary cost figures:

| | Funding source | | Total |
	UNDP	Government	
Actual expenditure (U.S.$)	674,700	636,700	1,311,400
Planned expenditure[1] (U.S.$)	519;000	674,200	1,193,200
Percentage of planned expenditure actually utilized	130	94	110

1. Plan of Operation, January 1969.

The same source indicates that there was a wide discrepancy in overall costs per participant compared to costs per 'final participant' the figures being $86.90 and $271.62 respectively. The discrepancy reflects relatively high dropout rates, producing low cost-efficiency. The *per capita* and per 'final participant' costs are high relative to most other EWLP projects. Finally, Unesco estimates that about two-thirds of the *per capita* cost figures were related to research and evaluation activities. This relatively high ratio can be partially explained by the relatively low enrolment in the project, making it necessary to charge the cost of research and development activities to only a small number of participants.

Evaluation and research

The Sudanese WOALP resulted in mostly positive changes in levels of knowledge and skill acquisition, attitudes, consumption patterns and behaviour on the part of participants completing the course. Differences tended to be found in these areas both in comparison to participants' pre-literacy performance and in comparison to matched groups of non-participants (control).

WOALP, however, was a small experimental programme, closely integrated with very localized, economic enterprises. The terminal assessment of the UNDP resident representative points out that the groups selected were not totally representative of the Sudanese population. Illiteracy in most of the country is related to rural life based upon the simplest forms of agriculture—or nomadic. Additionally, industry employs only a tiny fraction of the Sudanese population—perhaps a few thousand at most.

The functional literacy courses for the eight subprojects were meticulously prepared. It is difficult to conceive of the same carefully detailed programming being applied to the development of functional literacy courses for the myriad of localized subgroups which make up the entire population.

Thus, the apparent success which WOALP realized can be generalized only with considerable caution. It may be wondered whether the government, which has wholly embraced the functional literacy concept and is attempting to employ it universally, has fully considered the cost and the logistical problems inherent in such a venture.

Generally, evaluation of the Sudanese project may be considered both multifaceted and competently performed. The evaluation and research activities of the project can be schematically divided into four types: (a) activities relating to the identification of programmes; (b) activities relating to the definition of content and organization of programmes; (c) longitudinal and cross-sectional studies relating to the measurement of results; and (d) several isolated studies relating chiefly to the experimental nature of the project (for example, a study which attempted to ascertain the effectiveness of recorded lessons).

Evaluation studies were carried out principally by the evaluation unit, and appear to have been planned well in advance of their execution. This is in marked contrast to several other EWLP projects.

Summary

The Sudanese WOALP appears to have been one of the more successful of EWLP projects in developing an organizational infrastructure for functional literacy instruction which could be carried on after the experimental project's termination. What limited success the project realized in this and other areas can perhaps be attributed to the government's commitment to the project (and to functional literacy in general), to the 'custom-tailored' nature of the various subprojects, to the smallness of the administrative bureaucracy, which enabled it to act and react quickly to project demands, and to the small size of the learner population itself, which enabled more thorough training of literacy instructors and preparation of literacy materials than was the case in most other EWLP projects. However, the project was relatively unsuccessful in terms of other areas, notably its high dropout rates and costs. The wide range of dropout rates seemed to correspond to basic differences in the rural and urban populations at which the project was aimed. While the urban-industrial-based learners constituted a relatively 'captive' audience, the rural participants were subject to inconvenient farm work schedules, long distances between home and class, and to given cultural rites at certain times of the year and during periods of family difficulty. The rural dropout rate decreased with the implementation of supportive group discussions and 'demonstrations', both of which solidified the participants' understanding of the importance of literacy.

A major paradox results from the government's strong support of functional literacy as 'the' method to be employed in its national campaign. While, in general, government support seems to be an essential component of project success, functional literacy programmes, by definition, must be tailored to the economic and literacy needs of specific groups. In an economically and culturally diverse country such as Sudan, it is questionable whether the financial, administrative and technical problems of mounting a national functional literacy campaign, following the pattern of the experimental project, can be overcome.

Syrian Arab Republic

Time perspective

A UNDP/FAO project in agricultural development began in the Syrian Arab Republic in 1965, and a functional literacy component was added in the second phase of the project on 18 November 1968. By a letter dated 19 June 1969, FAO formalized a subcontract with Unesco for the development of the functional literacy component. Field activities were prematurely terminated in August 1972, although the overall project was not completely closed until 1974.

Policy and objectives

The overall objectives of the Plan of Operation were to assist the government in the implementation of an agricultural development programme in the Ghab region by contributing to the training of personnel and the establishment of the necessary institutions as well as the settlement of farmers on an irrigated area of about 5,000 hectares. The Plan of Operation foresaw that special attention should be accorded to the training of national specialists such as engineers, technicians, rural economists, supervisors and agricultural and co-operative extension workers. The plan calls for the implementation of functional literacy among the farmers in order to facilitate the participation of themselves and their families in the process of agricultural development and to prepare them for responsibilities as landowners and co-operative members.

The target population was about 15,000 illiterates spread over 180 villages in the province of Hama.

The literacy operations were conceived as a component of a development project which implied that the goal was to train a number of farmers for the use of new or improved agricultural techniques, new crops, and new irrigation systems. This training was conceived in relation to overall economic objectives (for example, the introduction of sugar-beet as a new crop; the application of proper fertilizers and tested agricultural techniques; the use of irrigation and drainage, and transportation to the newly constructed sugar factories). Functional literacy was conceived as the means and the end in a continuing process of agricultural training.

While this concept has not varied, it has been enlarged with the introduction of co-operatives which, in turn, required the introduction of management notions necessary for this form of joint venture.

Participants

Over the three years of operations, the total number of participants were distributed as follows:
1969/70: eight centres (all for men), 280 participants.
1970/71: twenty-five centres (twenty-three for men, two for women), 500 participants.
1971/72: fifty-two centres (forty-three for men, nine for women), 1,169 participants.
An extension of 100 centres was foreseen for November 1972. Women were all involved in agricultural production since many of them received 2.5 hectares of land under certain conditions. Those who were married participated fully in agricultural activities. The age distribution ranges from 18 to 45 for men and from 16 to 30 for women. The entire population is involved in agriculture.

All participants were involved in the development activities of the Ghab region and, as such, the great majority cultivated land which was put at their disposal by the State as the result of an agrarian reform. Some participants were former fishermen who had not yet benefited from the agrarian reform and worked as paid agricultural workers. All participants were totally illiterate. Participation was completely voluntary as demonstrated by the refusal of one village in the experimental zone to open a literacy centre during the entire operation of the project.

Dropout rates during 1970/71 ran at no more than 5 per cent a month. FAO concludes that over the course of two training cycles, illiterate farmers can become literate at no more than 65 Syrian pounds per person (U.S.$17.80).

Administration and organization

The project was conducted under the authority of the Ministry of Agriculture and Agrarian Reform. A committee of co-ordination was established in May 1969 and presided over by the Minister of Agriculture or his representative; participants included representatives of: the Ministry of Culture and National Orientation, the Ministry of Education, the Ministry of Social Affairs, the Planning Ministry, the administration of major projects, the adviser representatives of UNDP, FAO and Unesco.

The secretariat of this committee was under the executing organ for the entire agricultural development project, which was the General Administration for the Development of the Ghab Region, a semi-autonomous body headed by a director-general. Under the director-general were directorates for land distribution, co-operatives, agricultural affairs, statistics and planning, training and extension, rural engineering and state farms. No agricultural extension programme existed in the true sense of the work, however, despite the unit under the director-general's authority, and this lack of an infrastructure on which to build the functional literacy project limited the potential of the activities undertaken.

Starting in 1970 the Ministry of Agriculture was more and more the sole executing ministry and there was a gradual withdrawal of the representatives of other ministries which had been attached to the project. In the summer of 1971, with the exception of one junior representative of the Ministry of Culture, the entire counterpart personnel consisted of civil servants of the Ministry of Agriculture.

Functional literacy was closely tied to overall agricultural development work. This explains why the first eight villages in which functional literacy centres were opened in 1969/70 were the key villages of the pilot zone. The development of functional literacy activities followed the requirements of the agricultural development scheme as decided upon by the national authorities, UNDP and FAO in the Ghab region. The selection of functional literacy centres, the calendar of the programmes and the content of the programmes were always established in close consultation with the national authorities and FAO. In keeping with the requirements of an experimental project, the literacy activities were first centred on a specific subject (sugar-beet). They were then diversified to take account of the agricultural calendar. Ultimately they also included the notions of management mentioned above. The target area was sufficiently homogeneous to permit the implementation of one programme only. The first cycles of the programme were structured over seven months, consisting of 280 hours, to be followed by four months of 'practical review' utilizing practical sessions and visual aids. It was foreseen that a second stage structured along the same lines would constitute the necessary follow-up but the premature closing of activities at the end of August 1972 prevented this.

Teachers and other personnel

During the first seven months of the first stage, instructors worked part time only, but for the four months' practical work, they were working full time with the participants in the field.

In 1969/70, the instructors were farmers or sons of farmers. In 1971, they were chosen entirely from among cadres or assistants to the local agricultural services, supervised by agricultural engineers in charge of sections. In 1971/72, a diversification took place but the majority (80 per cent) were farmers while a small number were assistants to the local agricultural services. Only one primary-school teacher was available and results were excellent.

Supplementary payments were granted to the agricultural assistants for their work as instructors. These payments totalled 25 per cent of the salaries, and when they ceased after the first two seasons, the training classes closed down.

A certain lack of commitment to the programme on the part of the instructors was noted. They took frequent absences on leave, and further felt that they were entitled to be absent during the vacation period of the formal school system. Thus, during long periods when participants in the training classes could have progressed, no instructor was available. Obviously, the instructors did not feel that the training programmes were one of their prime responsibilities nor that they should shape their schedules to the convenience of the participants in the training classes.

The number of years of formal education possessed by the instructors was as follows:

1969/70, from seven to eleven years.
1970/71, from four to seven years (except for two supervisors from seven to eleven years).
1971/72, forty-six from four to seven years, six from seven to eleven years.

Teacher training was conducted as follows:

1969/70, long initial training (two months full-time).
1970/71, short initial training (two weeks).
1971/72, short initial training (two weeks) with a recycling of two days every month and a review session each week for one morning.

Training of supervisory and administrative staff and materials production specialists was limited by the lack of counterpart staff for much of the early period of the project. The national director left for another assignment early in the programme and, until 1970, only two full-time and one part-time counterparts were available to work with the international team.

Curriculum and methods

The integration of literacy and professional training was carried out as follows:

1. By fully adapting the training schedule in the light of participants' preference and in relation to the agricultural time-table.
2. By presenting literacy in its most practical aspect and not as an intellectual exercise.
3. By avoiding any breakdown within a teaching session between training and literacy (a special daily guide was provided to permit full flexibility).
4. By producing unique material covering training and literacy both at the participant and instructor levels.

The global method was chosen as a logical requirement of this integration and was associated with visual preparation which was usually quickly understood by the participants. The first cycle permitted the learning of 600 words, including all Arabic signs. During this period of seven months, several categories of visual aids were utilized, to be followed in the second stage by specially prepared films. Generally, the curriculum was rather narrow in scope and objectives, in spite of baseline survey results (which were not available to project staff until functional literacy classes had actually begun) that indicated a high level of competence in the target population.

Teaching materials

A two-volume manual covering programme content on agricultural training, reading, writing, arithmetic, co-operatives and credit was produced for each cycle. In the first application, a special monograph on sugar-beet was prepared according to an integrated concept.

Instructors received for each daily session an integrated guide covering technical content and (schematically) the pedagogic progression of the session.

Problem-oriented posters were distributed to the groups and individualized posters were also distributed during the sessions. Additional posters and two projectors for sound films were available. Little in the way of follow-up materials was provided, and the FAO/Unesco final report recommends a programme in this area in the future.

Costs

According to the Unesco Literacy Division's Evaluation Unit, the UNDP contribution to the literacy component of the project totalled $251,400 while local government contributions totalled $44,700. FAO/Unesco estimated the *per capita* cost of a two-cycle literacy programme at approximately 65 Syrian pounds ($17.80). They further estimated, in the project's final report, that the problem of illiteracy among the active male population in the Ghab could be solved in two years at a cost of 160,000 Syrian pounds ($43,835). In addition, FAO/Unesco felt that there would have to be a substantial programme for the preparation and distribution of follow-up materials for the programme to have any long-term success. Otherwise, the new literates would have nothing to read.

A large part of the estimated cost of the programme was for the supplementary payments for teachers. As noted in the section on teachers above, the later, more successful phase of the project primarily used agricultural assistants as instructors and they were paid a supplement of 25 per cent of their salaries. When these payments were halted after the first two seasons, the training classes closed down.

It must be assumed that the FAO/Unesco cost estimates were based on use of existing agricultural staff with modest supplementary payments plus cost of preparation of teaching materials. The FAO/Unesco calculation that the problem can be solved in two years must also be based on the assumption that primary-school education covers all children in the region, thus precluding the need for functional literacy training for new batches of adult illiterates who miss such schooling.

Evaluation and research

No permanent evaluation was foreseen in this project, although two short-term consultant missions took place. The first, in late 1969 and early 1970, was devoted to the preparation of a baseline survey in the target area of the project at the community and individual level. This survey was published and served to help the planning of literacy activities in the villages reached. A second mission, involving two specialists, visited the project in spring 1971. It produced a report on the effectiveness of the work done and suggested a number of steps to ensure the longitudinal measurement of changes concerning all pertinent indicators selected by a panel on evaluation. Full instrumentation was developed for these indicators and contacts with local research institutes were established to ensure continuity in this work. The premature closing of the project prevented the implementation of this evaluation plan.

The second evaluation mission identified certain sociological and institutional problems which it felt would affect the success of the project. These included:

1. Tensions which were noted among the farmers and which appeared to be due to the nature of certain peasant institutions imposed upon them and not perceived as useful by the farmers.
2. Apparent lack of comprehension by the technical authorities in charge of the project of the cultural needs of the farmers.
3. Improbability of effective educational action through institutional structures which were not as yet functioning well.
4. Lack of effective administrative structure for the functional literacy component of the agricultural development project.

In the final report (1974), it is recommended that there should be an increasing involvement of the Ministry of Agriculture and Agrarian Reform in adult education in the agrarian sector, under the general co-ordination and control of the Ministry of Culture and National Guidance, which is charged with adult education on a national scale. It appears that the government is moving in this direction.

Summary

The overall impression derived from this project is that it functioned during its short life-span in a relatively efficient and effective fashion. 'Function-ality' was assured since the project was begun in response to a need on the part of agricultural technicians involved in an agricultural development project and the materials and methods fully integrated literacy with technical training from the very beginning. Since the project was a component of a larger agricultural project, there was never any question of a separate functional literacy infrastructure, parallel to the agricultural efforts.

Training was undertaken by agricultural assistants or literate farmers under the direction of agricultural specialists. This appeared to work well as long as there were modest payments for the instruction. One problem was noted: instructors, on the whole, did not give high priority to this part-time job, and absenteeism ran high.

Contrary to what was observed in several other projects, the classes and training programmes were well integrated with the agricultural cycle, rather than following the school cycle (which is geared to the needs of children and not to the needs of working adults). Thus, practical demonstration and integration of the training with meaningful field work were possible.

Interministerial co-operation existed in theory, but in fact was never functional. Furthermore, there was no real agricultural extension or education infrastructure in the Ministry of Agriculture which would have facilitated the work. The recommendations in the final FAO/Unesco report seem realistic, namely that the Ministry of Agriculture and Agrarian Reform should develop a programme and infrastructure to handle agriculture extension and education, under the co-ordination of the Ministry of Culture and National Guidance.

FAO/Unesco cost estimates would seem to indicate that functional literacy can be effectively undertaken as a part of other development schemes for a fraction of the *per capita* cost experienced on other projects where elaborate functional literacy schemes are set up parallel to other development efforts.

United Republic
of Tanzania

Time perspective

Following two Unesco missions in 1965, the Tanzanian Government
decided to adopt a selective and intensive approach to literacy, employing
the concept of functional literacy in so far as it was more directly linked to
production than other methods. An initial Plan of Operation was signed in
September 1967, with Unesco designated as the executing agency and the
Ministry of Local Government and Rural Development as the co-operating
agency (the responsibilities of the co-operating agency were transferred in
1970 to the Ministry of Education).

The duration of the project was to be five years. The chief technical
adviser and the team of international experts arrived in 1967, and the project
began operations in January 1968.

The first phase (preparatory) covered a planning period of about one
year. The second phase began with functional literacy classes in Swahili in
late 1968. The third phase (expansion), was delayed one year, began in 1971
and was completed in 1973. At that time, the national campaign took over
full responsibility for literacy activities, which continue to receive UNDP
assistance. The following summary relates only to the experimental phase of
the project, which ended in 1973.

Policy and objectives

The Tanzanian WOALP was implemented against a background of extreme
ideological consciousness. Beginning about 1967 (in the middle of the
1964-69 Five-year Development Plan for Economic and Social Development), President J. K. Nyerere published a series of treatises outlining his
desired course for Tanzanian development. After broad national discussion
these essays became the backbone of government development policy at the
most general level. They stressed a strategy of gradual development toward
self-sufficiency in skilled manpower and food which was to be

accomplished chiefly through the upgrading of rural productivity. This was to be achieved through the creation of agricultural co-operatives, and the adoption of non-traditional, but none the less labour-intensive, farming techniques. The plans were infused with a uniquely Tanzanian socialist ideology (the spirit of *Ujamaa*) which called for—among other measures—major expansion in primary and adult basic education. The goal was to provide each citizen with the tools of literacy and numeracy, as these were considered essential to political consciousness and participation, and to increased productivity.

The goals of the project therefore reflected national political/ideological concerns to a greater extent than did most other EWLP projects. These concerns were in addition to the narrower goal which linked literacy with increased productivity through attitudinal and behavioural change. Functional literacy was ultimately aimed at the development of the total citizen, not simply the citizen as producer.

The project's specific objectives included:

1. Teaching illiterate men and women basic reading and writing, and solving simple problems of arithmetic, using as basic vocabularies the words employed in current agricultural and industrial practice.
2. Helping them apply the new knowledge and skills to solve their basic economic and social problems.
3. Preparing them for more efficient participation in the development of their village, region and country.
4. Integrating the adult literacy and adult education programmes with the general agricultural and industrial development of the country.
5. Providing the necessary reading materials, imparting the knowledge of community and personal hygiene, nutrition, child care, home economics, which would help improve family and community life, providing opportunity for a continuing education and avoiding relapse into illiteracy.

Clearly, the concept of functional literacy fitted comfortably into the government's own development priorities, which were in turn shaped within a unique socialist ideological framework. The political climate was thus actively supportive of the project.

Another element of the United Republic of Tanzania's development policy was to encourage local 'self-reliance'—i.e. to develop the conviction at village level that local problems can be solved through local initiative and co-operative effort. The organization and implementation structure of WOALP was supportive of this 'self-reliance' concept. Particular efforts were made to ensure that literacy education was not viewed as an imposition—as a service rendered by a remote ministry through civil servants arriving from distant locations. Thus, the system of literacy class organization employed by the project was based on the policy stated in the National Five-year Development Plan whereby literacy would be implemented in response to local popular demand as people became aware of its functional importance.

Participants

WOALP was originally implemented on a pilot scale in one division of each of four regions which border the southern shores of Lake Victoria. These regions together contain about 2 million inhabitants, and they formed a high priority zone in the first and second Five-year Development Plans. The regions also play an essential role in the production and processing of the country's most important cash crops. In addition to their economic importance, the areas were selected because they had developed a strong institutional infrastructure, including numerous schools and co-operatives. It was believed that these would be supportive of the literacy effort.

A rough estimate of the illiteracy rate in the pilot areas (1970) was 60 per cent for adult males and 90 per cent for adult females. The original Plan of Operation called for the reduction of illiteracy in the adult population aged 15-45 in the pilot zones to 25 per cent. Two hundred thousand new literates were to be created. The operational phase of the programme began one year behind schedule, however, and these goals soon proved to be overly ambitious. The target figure was subsequently reduced to a more modest 75,000.

In 1971 the programme entered an expansion phase and spread to a total of twenty-three divisions in the four regions. According to the experimental terminal report of the resident representative, by 1973 when the project was terminated, an estimated 200,000 new literates had, indeed, been produced;[1] however, this figure was reached only by drastically reducing the standard for literacy (from standard 4 to standard 2 levels). When the experimental project ended, a total of 11,170 classes were operating, with an enrolment of 303,000. During the duration of the programme, an estimated 500,000 participants underwent some functional literacy training (466,010, according to Unesco's EWLP Evaluation Unit and some 550,000 according to final project reports). Current information (1975) indicates that more than 2.5 million adults are enrolled in the functional literacy classes of the national campaign, which began at the conclusion of the project in 1973.

A substantial majority of the participants were women. Most of the participants of both sexes were from rural households, and were engaged in cotton farming, rice cultivation, banana growing, fishing, cattle raising and home-making.

Administration and organization

Organization was characterized by extremely co-operative relationships between the international experts and the Government at the national level. When the programme commenced operations, the government body

1. This figure may include people made literate outside the experimental project, which would explain why it is more than double the figure made available by Unesco's Evaluation Unit and used later (page 174).

responsible for its implementation was the Ministry of Regional Administration and Rural Development (MORARD), assisted by two advisory commitees, an Interministerial National Coordinating Committee, and a National Advisory Committee on Adult Education, the latter with counterpart committees at the regional, district and local levels.

In June 1968, the government announced that the programme's locus of responsibility would be shifted from MORARD to the Directorate of Adult Education of the Ministry of Education. This shift, however, was not carried out immediately, being accomplished only in January 1970. The intervening $1\frac{1}{2}$-year period appears to have been characterized by a kind of administrative malaise. It was a period of indecision in which the programme suffered a number of quantitative and qualitative setbacks. When the ministry took over, almost all key national programme personnel were changed at virtually every administrative level, causing considerable confusion and placing added strain on the international experts in their efforts to preserve the programme's life and sense of continuity. These negative trends, however, were ultimately reversed. The ministry through the State school network, had a ready-made organizational infrastructure, and sufficient personnel to overcome the logistical problems which the massive expansion of the programme in 1970 created. MORARD would not have been capable of rendering this support.

Once the transfer of authority had been accomplished, daily responsibility for programme operation fell chiefly on full-time district education officers in charge of adult education, and on local primary-school headteachers, who served as programme supervisors at the operational level. The programme's actual teaching staff consisted largely of elementary-school teachers who, while supposedly contributing on a 'volunteer' basis, were none the less paid a small monthly honorarium, and were told that they would not be eligible for further formal training (leading to better jobs) if they did not participate in the functional literacy programme for two years.

Co-ordination between the ministries, while outstanding at the national level, was insufficient at the local level for much of the programme's duration, though it improved toward the end. The vocational-training component of the programme was never a strong point, chiefly because of the dearth of agricultural specialists at the field level. The literacy instructors eventually had to be trained in the skills required to provide adequate demonstrations and agricultural-technical knowledge. However, they were clearly not experts in these areas, and the practical/vocational component of the programme remained weak.

Teachers and other personnel

The international experts and high-level national counterparts assigned to the programme were generally of excellent quality, and committed to the programme's success. Throughout the programme's duration, however, the quality of the field staff (supervisors and teachers) was mixed.

Under MORARD, as noted above, national staff were too few in number. Most participated on a part-time basis, or as volunteers. The attrition rate for volunteer literacy teachers was high, adding to already strained training facilities. Training under MORARD was centralized, and conducted in four-week sessions by a national training team. Teaching quality and supervision during this period were generally poor to fair. When the Ministry of Education assumed programme responsibility, and the programme entered its expansion phase, some problems were alleviated, but others were created. Although thousands of primary-school teachers were 'made available' for service in the literacy programme, voluntary literacy instructors from outside the school system continued to be used, and continued to be less reliable than the instructors drawn from the primary schools. Instructor training, which had been a financial burden from the beginning, was decentralized, and developed a character unique among EWLP projects. The 3,000 literacy instructors required for expansion to take place necessitated the establishment in each division of a trainers' team composed of two primary-school headteachers, a rural development assistant and an agricultural assistant field officer. To cover the twenty-three divisions, 100 trainers were necessary. Their training took place in November 1970, and in January 1971, in two-week seminar sessions. Once assembled, the teams set about determining demands for classes, screening volunteer teachers and candidates, and arranging training sessions for both volunteer and primary-school teachers.

The project sponsored several kinds of training sessions: training for volunteer teachers (reduced from a four-week to a more concentrated three-week course); training for primary-school teachers (a one-week intensive course); and one-week refresher courses for experienced volunteer teachers, in which the latter received new training, discussed problems connected with teaching, and were urged to help learners finishing the two-year literacy course to develop their new skills.

The decentralized system of training was closely monitored to determine how it affected teacher quality, class attendance and other elements. It was subjected to constant improvement so that it could serve as a tool for extending the literacy programme to a larger area and eventually to the whole country.

At the request of the authorities concerned, all adult education tutors from all the national colleges of education were given special training by the project team, both in functional literacy and in preparing functional literacy teaching materials. Since 1970 all these institutions have been involved in preparing primers, teacher's guides and follow-up materials geared to the agricultural priorities in different zones of the country. Trainers' teams, composed along the lines of those organized for the pilot zone, were eventually formed in every region of the United Republic of Tanzania and given special training by the project staff on how to train functional literacy instructors.

While the quality of literacy instruction generally improved after 1970, the training of literacy instructors in agricultural and other vocational skills remained poor, and this was, in turn, reflected in their teaching.

Curriculum, methods and materials

The curriculum and methods were designed to be task-oriented, as opposed to the problem-orientation of several other projects. A considerable portion of the co-operative efforts of the international experts and their national counterparts was devoted to the production of instructional materials. Teaching materials were developed around six learning programmes offered by the project: cotton, banana and rice growing, cattle raising, fishing, and home economics. These primers were produced by unique 'writers' workshops'[1] composed of eight persons: two book production specialists, a rural institutions expert from FAO and his Tanzanian counterpart, the project's specialist on rural libraries, one specialist on fisheries, one on Swahili usage and one on *Ujamaa* villages. Two reading primers were produced for each programme (first and second year), together with a lesson-by-lesson manual for teachers and a booklet explaining how to conduct associated workshops. Together with the institute of Adult Education, the writers' workshops also produced a teaching programme on political structures in the United Republic of Tanzania. Some of these materials were found to be of general interest to the national literacy campaign, and were printed in large quantities for use throughout the country.

Supplementary materials included posters in the form of picture stories with little texts on civic and social subjects. For each, teacher's guides were produced, as well as follow-up materials to encourage new literates to apply their new skills.

Materials on arithmetic were developed in three ways: for the cotton and banana programmes, separate textbooks were written for each year of the teaching programmes, introducing problems based on farmers' everyday experiences—buying, selling and measuring; for the fishing, rice, and cattle programmes, the approach was based on experimental 'new mathematics' methods which had earlier been tested for primary-school use; in the home economics programme, arithmetic exercises based on everyday activities appear in the primers. Due largely to the high level of government support, large numbers of materials were produced by various institutions, only some of them directly related to the programme. In spite of this large volume, however, there were complaints throughout the project that too few follow-up materials were available, and that printing facilities were inadequate to deal with the demand.

In 1969, a monthly rural newspaper was initiated for each of the four pilot areas. These were written by teachers and rural development officers

---

1. According to an October 1971 survey, the first primer for the cotton programme was written not by the writers' workshops, but by the director alone.

and concentrated on local news and included a back page in extra-large print for new learners.

In 1972, a radio support project began as a means to counter communication problems, to promote interest and participation in the literacy programme and to produce programmes for active teachers. This project was intended to serve the national campaign starting in 1973; it provided a continous link between the project and the field, and by means of feedback recordings from the field as well as visits and reports, a communication channel from the field to the project headquarters was maintained. Radio programmes prepared by the project were also intended to be broadcast over the national broadcasting system. A radio production studio was established at Mwanza to work closely with the project headquarters, especially in respect of the training aspects, writers' workshops, book development, rural library, and rural press units.

Costs

The following cost figures, provided by the Unesco Literacy Division's EWLP Evaluation Unit, compare planned and actual expenditures for the project:

| | Funding source | | Total |
	UNDP	Government	
Actual expenditure (U.S.$)	1,327,300	2,870,000	4,197,300
Planned expenditure[1] (U.S.$)	1,181,900	5,326,400	6,508,000
Percentage of planned expenditure actually used	112	54	65

1. Plan of Operation, November 1966.

The figures indicate that the government failed to meet its financial commitment to the project, contributing only 54 per cent of the funds called for in the Plan of Operation. The inter-agency mission report of 1970 corroborates this, noting that government expenditures to 1971, while sufficient to allow the project to operate on an austerity budget, had fallen behind original expectations even though, rapidly increasing at that time.

The only major financial problem throughout the project related to the training of literacy instructors. The burden appeared to be particularly great prior to the decentralization of training in 1970, when the widespread use of volunteer instructors and the consequent high attrition rate, rendered training procedures highly cost-inefficient.

The Unesco/EWLP Evaluation Unit has developed estimates of *per capita* project expenses: $6.62 per participant, and $10.46 per final participant. About 25 per cent of these costs were for research and evaluation activities. While the figures compare favourably with *per capita* cost figures for other EWLP projects, meaningful external comparisons are difficult to make, since there was considerable variation between country projects on—among several variables—the level of literacy required for successful completion of a project. In the United Republic of Tanzania, this level was comparatively low, and a relatively large number of participants were thus capable of reaching it (see 'Participants'). In spite of the low *per capita* costs, however, it took 58 per cent more money to produce a final participant than to accommodate an enrollee, indicating considerable 'wastage' of participants.

Evaluation and research

The weakest area of the programme throughout its duration was the evaluation unit. A number of factors contributed to the less than satisfactory performance of this unit, including a very late start (resulting in a lack of baseline data), three UNDP/Unesco evaluation specialists all with different approaches, problems with transportation and unreliable interviewers, and the experimental nature of functional literacy evaluation itself. Because of the weakness of the evaluation unit, a number of precise measurements concerning the impact of functional literacy on various aspects of Tanzanian social and economic development were not obtained. A few systematic sample studies were conducted in 1971-72. These seemed to indicate that the programme was succeeding in terms of such criteria as the generation of wider consumption habits among participants, increased technical knowledge and application of such knowledge, and adoption of modern hygiene and nutritional practices. One study demonstrated the need for higher literacy instruction standards. A large number of graduates were found to have reached 'an insufficient level'.

In spite of these studies, much of the data demonstrating the programme's 'success' seems to have been based on impressions, gathered in the absence of controls and accumulated by a number of programme units in addition to the evaluation unit. Limited before-and-after studies of three groups (cotton, 1970; cotton, 1971; and home economics) seemed to show that the functional literacy classes had a direct influence on participants' behaviour *vis-à-vis* their participation in formal organizations, their knowledge of modern technology, their adoption of modern methods, their knowledge and adoption of improved health and nutritional practices, and their level of socio-economic aspirations.

Summary

This project again demonstrates the extreme difficulty of utilizing volunteers, or low-paid part-time workers, as literacy instructors. In this category of literacy instructors, attrition was high and reliability low, placing great financial and logistical strain on training schemes and recruiting efforts.

Project operations were improved when the administrative locus was shifted from the Ministry of Regional Administration and Rural Development to the Ministry of Education. The principal factor which appears to have facilitated this successful shift was the fact that the Ministry of Education maintained a 'ready-made', highly formalized organizational infrastructure, which operated at the local, regional and national levels and which therefore was capable of 'gearing up' to accept administrative responsibility for the project and to handle that responsibility well.

This shifting of administrative responsibility, while having several obvious advantages, none the less appears to have contributed to the weakness of the vocational technical education component of the project. The conduct of the day-to-day activities of the project under the Ministry of Education tended to follow well-defined and understood intraministerial communications channels, particularly at the local level. This may have discouraged the development of interministerial co-operation, resulting in the pattern—commonly observed in other EWLP projects as well—of literacy and vocational instruction being conducted as 'parallel' activities which were only loosely integrated.

The administrative shift could not have been accomplished without high-level government support for the project; the fact that the project was capable of responding effectively to the administrative problem, and to a number of other problems which developed during its duration, demonstrates the importance of high-level government commitment for success.

A fundamental question may be asked regarding the advisability or meaningfulness of utilizing formal primary-school literacy standards to assess literacy levels reached by adults in programmes such as EWLP. The educational objectives of functional literacy are obviously different from those of primary schooling, and cognitive processes between adults and young children also differ. The use of school standards in functional literacy programmes would tend, if nothing else, to distort the assessment of how well participants absorbed and utilized the vocational-technical skills they had been taught in the course of the programme.

Part   II
An analysis

In Part I of this report, an attempt has been made to provide a description of each of the eleven EWLP national projects, and in particular to draw the unique lessons offered by each. Keeping in mind the unique quality of each project, however, what major lessons does the programme offer as a whole? This is the question explored in Part II.

Because of the varying nature of information available on common problems encountered by projects, this exploration is necessarily qualitative. Some of the issues raised only affected a few projects; others were more widespread. The intensity of difficulties also varied, both from project to project and, within projects, from area to area. Obstacles were also perceived in different ways depending on the point in the development of the relevant project and the programme as a whole at which they arose. Perception was also affected by the ideas and concerns of the individuals involved. This report was drafted at one or more removes from the actual process of observation and recording. It is, therefore, unavoidably subjective on certain issues.

Despite these difficulties, it is felt that what follows does identify with fair accuracy some of the major bottlenecks encountered and dealt with, as well as some of the problems raised but not (fully) solved by EWLP. Thus, it constitutes a basic compendium of the programme's lessons.

Why EWLP?
The intentions

The Experimental World Literacy Programme was an unprecedented international effort to come to grips with a pressing educational problem. As such, it grew from a unique combination of intentions. In this chapter, intentions underlying EWLP are clarified in order to pave the way for decisions concerning the goals of future international action. Intention-related issues arising from the world programme may be placed in three groups: motivations for EWLP (what moved the 'actors' to act?), the idea of functionality (what was the intended conceptual novelty of the action?), and EWLP strategy (how was the new concept to be put into practice?).

Motivations

Why did the Experimental World Literacy Programme take place? Beginning with an important group, what were the major motivations of those who—nationally and internationally and in whatever capacity—took part in providing literacy through EWLP?

The altruistic rejection of the absolute growth of illiteracy[1] in the world was doubtless a fundamental motivation. This ethical response to a serious *Ethics . . .* problem was rooted in the will to make effective the right to education—the right of all to education—considered as an integral part of human rights as a whole. The motivation, determinant in certain cases, was then to offer illiterates the minimal instruction without which full personal development is difficult or impossible in the modern world, that is to enable them to throw off one of the strongest chains binding them to second-class citizenship. From the point of view of both the national beneficiary governments and international agencies involved, therefore, the experimental world literacy campaign constituted a crucial opportunity to merge in a

---

1. cf. figures in the Introduction to this report.

single joint venture the occasionally separate operational and ethical functions of multilateral international co-operation.

The strength of the initial ethical motivation to 'do something' about adult illiteracy was reflected in the fact that eighty-eight governments saw fit to send delegates (including no less than thirty-seven ministers, eleven vice-ministers and eight under-secretaries of state) to the World Conference of Ministers of Education on the Eradication of Illiteracy, held in Tehran in 1965.

Concern was not the prerogative of officialdom: nineteen international non-governmental organizations enjoying consultative status with Unesco sent observers to this conference. These included eleven who travelled to Iran from abroad for the express purpose of participating. A major conclusion was that:

Adult education (and literacy in particular) should not be confined to elementary reading, writing and arithmetic, but should also include both general cultural subjects and a vocational preparation in which account is taken of the opportunities for employment and the better use of local natural resources and which would lead to a higher standard of living [45].

Since the Tehran Conference, and as a result of EWLP, there has been a noticeable intensification of public concern about illiteracy. Sometimes of almost torrential proportions, a flow of speeches and writings have denounced illiteracy and demanded (or promised) with increasing force greater effort and expenditure for literacy work. Thanks in large part to the interest aroused by the programme, the publicly expressed motivation to overcome illiteracy has probably never been so strong as in the past decade, even in circles not previously notable for their interest in education and literacy. For example, bankers, financiers and industrialists expressed strong commitment to literacy at Unesco-sponsored round tables in 1969 and 1970.

. . . and the status quo
In the view of some analysts, however, the strength of the desire to make people literate (which led to EWLP) did not always and necessarily imply its purity. In this view (which is far from universally accepted), the motivation was not to 'do something', but to appear to do something, i.e. to hide a deep determination to maintain the *status quo* behind a mask of superficial change. The evidence of the past indicates that literacy receives only a small percentage of national education budgets which in turn entails a relatively minor commitment of resources by international funding agencies. If the illiteracy problem is to be overcome, then both national and international authorities will have to devote larger resources to non-formal education and literacy in the future.

Another, equally severe interpretation holds that in certain EWLP countries, it was precisely the conservatism of such groups—their survival instinct—that led them to believe that literacy action would help overcome sharpening dysfunctionalities in their societies, thereby enabling them to maintain power.[1] The 1974 Unesco Regional Meeting of Latin American Youth Experts (Tuman, Peru), affirmed that:

When the operation of the productive system begins to diverge from what is required of it, reforms are introduced to remedy this situation, both by improving the quality of education and by integrating sections of society hitherto excluded from it. . . . The so-called 'democratization of education' is therefore not an act of philanthropy on the part of the ruling classes but rather a dire necessity [35].

Referring to literacy as designed in the world programme, N. Salamé says:

It is no coincidence that financial and business circles are showing more and more interest in literacy work. . . . It might provide the dying man with bread—but so as to ensure that others get cake [40].

However they are interpreted, the motivations for literacy seem to have at least one common element. Individuals, governments, non-governmental bodies and international agencies may have undertaken EWLP out of ethical altruism or self-interest—or some combination of the two. But implicit in many EWLP-related motivations seems to be the notion of stewardship. National administrators and international aid often tended to do something to and—perhaps at best—for illiterates. International co-operation in EWLP was—according to the Tehran Conference—to be 'a reflection of world solidarity based on common interest' [45]. But the illiterates' interests were defined and interpreted by the literates.   *Steward-ship*

Often underlying the stewardship motivation is the view that illiterates are marginals. In a 1965 Unesco report on *Literacy as a Factor in Development*, their marginality appears as a collective phenomenon: *From margin-ality*

Illiteracy among adults implies the non-participation of entire sections of the population in the life of the national community . . . illiteracy is simply the manifestation at the educational level of a complex series of . . . factors which has prevented entire groups of human beings from participating in the process of development going on around them [24].

Illiterates also tend to be perceived as marginal in their individual attributes. Studies in Ecuador[2] underlined illiterates' lack of motivation for education, their absence of technical knowledge and community spirit, and their superstitious nature. Malgasy peasants have been described, in a similar survey,[2] as particularly backward with regard to health and technology.

Since (according to the views examined here) illiterates are marginal partly because of their illiteracy[3] it follows logically that literacy should

1. The assumption in such cases tends to be (as stated in public, at least) that there is communality of interests between upper and lower socio-economic strata. In other cases the contrary was so. The express aim of literacy was to help overturn what governments viewed as an unjust power relationship.
2. Reported in *Alphabétisation Fonctionnelle et Apprentissage: Rendement Interne*, Paris, Unesco, 1974.
3. As though all illiterates were completely cut off from the literate world; an assumption that is unfounded, given various (e.g. religious) intermediaries.

. . . to
integration

enable their integration to take place. Integration into the existing society does indeed seem to be a widespread major aim and motivation of those offering literacy. There was an early and continuing expectation in EWLP that literacy would enable adults to enter today's technical and economic world. A preparatory document for the 1965 Tehran Conference declares that literacy work

Enables the individual to fit into his occupational and social environment and . . . increases his value as a person. . . . It is inextricably linked with . . . needs inherent in the construction of the national community [24].

The implication is that the illiterate's life has somehow less human value than that of the literate. A particularly widespread aspect of the integrative motivation concerns language. A characteristic of certain EWLP countries was the more or less explicit aim to use EWLP educative action to implant more firmly the national, predominant or administrative language.

Depending on how it is brought about, linguistic and national integration can contribute fundamentally to nation-building. But regarding EWLP, a question that does not seem to have been asked with sufficient force (or, at least, answered with sufficient insight) is: integration from what marginal state into what society?

It would appear that, in certain instances, the 'marginal' view has tended, within EWLP, to reduce the illiterate to a caricature. He or she becomes a maimed human being for whom marginality even takes the shape of infantilization. In admittedly extreme cases, adult illiterates were said to have some skill with mental calculations, but were described as not understanding the mechanism of such calculations.

It would be facile to judge such assessments—which some might deem ethnocentric or paternalistic—with retrospective harshness. Surely the important thing is that in the future greater efforts must be made to understand illiterates on their own terms. Most often, they are caught between two worlds, 'torn', according to an Algerian survey (quoted in *Le Concept de l'Alphabétisation Fonctionnelle*), 'between old allegiances [to family and village] and new ones to which they submit against their will [factory and town]' [6].

This more relativistic standpoint adds an indispensable dimension of reality to evaluations of illiterates' mental abilities. After her 1965-67 research in the United Republic of Tanzania, an anthropologist with just such an approach (C. M. Varkevisser) warned that:

Rather than leaping to any conclusion that 'African' thinking takes place on a plane of abstraction different from (i.e. lower than) our own [European], we should consider the dampening effects of the almost mechanical imposition of a foreign system of education, neglecting indigenous aptitude . . . [44].

In short, illiterates often display quite sophisticated behaviour in their own contexts.[1] This is not to romanticize pre-industrial society, or to imply that illiteracy is not a major world problem. It is. But not just any kind of literate society is acceptable. For example, does the simple fact of being literate endow the European city dweller with community spirit, reduce his or her superstition,[2] or increase his or her human value? (It was implied by reports referred to above that these would be three attributes of a literate society).

The need for more modesty on the part of those planning literacy work *The need* is an important lesson of EWLP. Study of the programme led A. Meister to *for* 'denounce the tendency to confuse book knowledge with human *modesty* intelligence, man's understanding of his relationship to the world and other people'. (In 1581, the Spanish poet Gongora wrote—in a largely illiterate Europe—that: 'It may well be that the more aphorisms he knows, the more impressive the doctor.') Meister found that 'programmes had often underestimated [the illiterate's] intellectual possibilities. But attempts were made to deal with the assessment of adult perceptions and one is able to conclude that 'through the process of trial and error engaged in' during EWLP 'the image of the adult illiterate has emerged enriched' [28].

In countries where 80 to 90 per cent of the population is rural, illiterate, often propertyless and without access to basic social services, while 10 to 20 per cent is urban, educated in largely alien schools, owns or manages the means of production and consumes according to a Western-inspired standard—who is marginal? According to what criteria? Concerning motivation for literacy, who should be integrated into what society? On what terms?

EWLP has underlined both the difficulty and the necessity of answering these questions. They should not and cannot be eluded. Here, too, it would seem advisable to proceed with more care than in the past when determining (and judging) why illiterates think and act the way they do with regard to literacy.

Contrary to possibly over-optimistic hopes at its outset, EWLP did not spark in all its projects an immediate upsurge of interest in literacy among illiterates. Generally high dropout rates suggest (among many other things) that where initial motivation was high, it did not always stand the test of time. Why? The problem of 'change resistance' among illiterate individuals *'Change* and groups, has been seen by some as an important barrier to further *resist-* expansion of literacy work. *ance?'*

But was (and is) indifference or scepticism regarding literacy an expression of unreasoning fear of progress? Or do illiterates have their own logic, learned through prolonged contact with capricious nature, and not always generous humanity? According to such logic, is not innovation a

---

1. Have not illiterates survived for centuries in milieux (such as the Andean *altiplano* and the African Sahel) which would have proved lethally hostile for precisely those urban literates who judge illiterates insufficiently 'integrated into their milieu'?

2. cf. the current vogue of astrology in certain highly industrialized—and 'educated'—countries. In one such Member State, about $0.60 are spent *per capita* each year on rabbits feet and other good luck charms.

risk? And does not risk often mean catastrophe?[1] Common-sense lore around the world (often of peasant origin) is replete with the idea that 'A bird in the hand is worth two in the bush'. Meister points out that:

Poverty itself and often insecurity militate in favour of resistance to change in ways of living and working . . . in such circumstances that rejection of innovation was not only quite understandable but fully justified [28].

To some extent, the problem arises from a possible misunderstanding on the part of planners and administrators of illiterates' motivations. Exactly what would be revealed by a clearer perception of what does and does not motivate illiterates? The answer is closely linked with assumptions made about the functionality of the literacy provided.

Functionality

The notion of development-linked functionality lay at the heart of the experimental world programme. In a variety of settings, the stress on functionality offered the opportunity to put practical meat on the still-skeletal (if increasingly popular) call for relevance of education to its surroundings.

Briefly, the idea was to combine literacy and numeracy with a programme of education in basic vocational skills directly linked to the occupational needs of participants. Some humanist rigorists criticize this functional approach for narrowing the focus of education to what they deem a single and basely utilitarian role. Other, more radical critics (including certain partisans of P. Freire's psycho-social literacy method) maintain that it 'functionalizes' only certain aspects of literacy and skills training work, and that it particularly ignores illiterates' need for greater political awareness.

In striving to link literacy to development both theoretically and practically, EWLP has raised (if not always solved) a number of crucial issues. Discussion of these offers guidelines, or at least parameters, for planners of future literacy action.

First is the all-important question: to what aspect(s) of development should literacy be harnessed? The answer depends on where the bottlenecks of underdevelopment are thought to be situated. In 1962, A. Curle proclaimed that:

Countries are underdeveloped because most of their people are underdeveloped, having had no opportunity of expanding their potential capital in the services of society [7].

---

1. In Iran, changes in agricultural practices were accepted when they involved little additional investment of time or resources, and when the perceived benefits were relatively immediate. Otherwise, change was resisted (see 'Profile' in Part I).

This affirmation expresses the 'marginality' approach to illiterates in developmental terms. It also reflects the view prevalent in United Nations and Western academic circles at the beginning of the First Development Decade, that development was first and foremost a question of economic growth, stressing capital-intensive development and high-level technical skills.[1] From this point of view, education in general and literacy in particular were considered as means of 'developing' the 'underdeveloped' people in terms of giving them the knowledge and skills necessary to expend their 'potential capital in the services of society'. *Development as economic growth*

This concept unfortunately ignored two plain truths. First, a human being cannot be 'underdeveloped'. Secondly, the relative underdevelopment of certain economies is a partial result of the iniquities of the prevailing world economic system. Nevertheless, the concept clearly dominated thinking at the Tehran Conference in 1965. One commission summed up the concept as 'literacy combined with vocational training and leading to a quick rise in individual productivity' [15].

Already in the late 1960s and early 1970s, however, the narrow productivity-oriented focus of EWLP's developmentally functional approach to literacy was being called into question. Salamé, for one, concluded that:

There is a risk that functional literacy will supply the economy with individuals tailor-made to fit specific job requirements instead of enabling each individual to understand, control and dominate progress [40].

At the 1972 third International Conference on Adult Education (Tokyo), the Director-General of Unesco drew a balanced lesson from EWLP and placed the notion of functionality in a broad perspective. He said in his concluding remarks:

We do think that the idea of functional purpose ought to be kept in education since education is not an end in itself, and by insisting on its functional purpose we emphasize the relationship which exists between education and society's needs and between education and the motivations and aspirations of the individual which, as you know, have been too long disregarded.

He sounded a note of warning, however, on the economic focus of functionality:

There should be no misunderstanding on this point, even if other organizations sometimes use the idea of the functional nature of education in general, and of literacy work in particular, in a much too narrow, strictly economic sense which Unesco itself rejects [43].

---

1. This notion is gradually being replaced by the development and employment concept stressing intermediate technology of benefit to traditional—mostly rural—sectors. Such policies may make programmes of adult functional literacy more directly relevant to these new development goals.

The point, however, is not to discredit economically functional literacy in general, but to question narrowly productivity-centred functionality. Broadly economic literacy—stressing critical awareness of the producer-learner's problems and roles in society—would support rather than contradict the humanism implicit in the Director-General's remarks.

If development is mainly economic growth, as was widely accepted at the time EWLP was launched, then rather narrowly work-oriented literacy is its functional partner. This relationship assumes in turn that underdevelopment is a mainly quantitative problem (insufficient GNP) requiring a mainly quantitative solution (economic growth). Intimately linked with this quantitative approach was—and still is, in many quarters—the assumption that insufficient GNP was due basically to a lack of technology and that economic growth would be achieved primarily through dissemination of technology. The following short-cut syllogism therefore underlay the First Development Decade: development is economic growth; economic growth is a technical process; therefore development is technical.

echnical olu- ions . . .

This technical bias permeated sectoral as well as global development issues, including literacy. In the seminal thinking of a decade ago, when EWLP was being formulated, recent literacy action was deemed to have failed, primarily because of inadequate know-how. The problem being technical, it seemed logical that the solution should also be technical: the creation of a new literacy approach.

Already at the beginning of the First Development Decade, however, the 'growth' analysis of development was being called into doubt. U Thant himself stressed in his *Proposals for Action* for the decade (emphasis in the original) that:

> The problem of underdeveloped countries is not just growth, but development. Development is growth *plus* change; change, in turn, is social and cultural as well as economic; and qualitative as well as quantitive [42].

. . to non- echnical roblems

A crucial lesson of EWLP seems, then, to be the need to avoid viewing or designing literacy as an overwhelmingly technical solution to problems that are only partly technical. A broad, multidimensional approach to both development and literacy is required. Indeed, it would seem that literacy programmes can only be fully functional—and development contexts can only be fully conducive to literacy—if they accord importance to social, cultural and political change as well as economic growth. Not all EWLP countries realized this. A few did. Algeria, Guinea and the United Republic of Tanzania included in their aims the dissemination of literacy as a means of enhancing popular participation in social and political life.[1] Several other countries' approaches were focused more on literacy as an investment intended to result in higher worker productivity and hence in economic growth.

---

1. This intention was not followed in all cases in the preparation of materials, curricula or pedagogy.

It would seem that the theory of development from which the concept of literacy as a quasi-physical investment derives, seldom questions existing institutions although these may be obstacles to development. On the contrary such a theory tends to identify the illiterates as brakes on development. It assumes that illiterates do not produce more, not because they have no objective interest in being more productive, but because they are not educated. It further assumes that illiterates do not seek education, not because they have no objective interest in becoming educated, but because they are foolish or mischievous. From a comprehensive standpoint (development = growth + change), at least part of the objective interest that will motivate illiterates to become literate arises from their perception of the potential for appropriate change in their environment.

Thanks to EWLP, concepts have evolved. The programme has shown that the problem is no longer to determine whether literacy is a profitable capital investment. The question to be answered now is, rather, whether established institutions can accept the actual exercise of newly acquired skills, it being evident that their exercise presupposes far-reaching social, cultural and political change as well as economic growth.

The 'strategy'

A strategic approach to literacy was considered fundamental to the Experimental World Literacy Programme. In the past, Unesco major projects had focused international action on specified areas (e.g. arid zones, primary education in Latin America, Orient-Occident mutual appreciation) for periods running well beyond the Organization's usual two-year programmes. EWLP involved elements of this long-term focus. But its adoption of a strategy was intended to provide three additional advantages. First, considerably more money per literacy project was to be spent. Secondly, in order to attract such considerable funds, external sources (chiefly UNDP) would have to be convinced of the organizational efficiency of the programme. Finally, by concentrating its considerable and dynamically administered resources on eleven countries (selected from fifty-two national candidacies), EWLP intended to show tangible results.

This multifaceted strategy has generally been described as intensive, selective and experimental. Before discussing these three distinctive characteristics, however, it is perhaps helpful to dwell for a moment on the very notion of 'strategy'. The launching of the First Development Decade in 1960 seemed to usher in a new era of commitment and rationality. It appeared that during the 1960s the international community was going to prove itself capable of joining forces to achieve an aim of overriding importance. At that time 'development' and 'aid' still had the bright lustre of newly minted ideals.

Focus
Among other sectoral efforts, EWLP was meant to focus concern and resources on a single (albeit complex) development problem. Thanks to a rational strategy—the intentional mobilization of ideas, funds, men and women around a single goal—continuing attention has been irrevocably drawn to illiteracy.

Ironically, the necessarily focused orientation of the strategy has led some to question the usefulness of placing emphasis on sectoral problems. A succession of days, years, programmes and campaigns, sponsored by the United Nations system and delicated to issues as diverse as hunger, population, women and literacy, has tended to bewilder as much as enlighten. Drawing attention to sectoral problems may be a useful step but is only a preliminary one. Close-ups of isolated trees do not suffice to point to a way out of the woods. Referring specifically to literacy action, Unesco's 1974 Regional Meeting on Youth and African Cultural Values laid particular stress

on the fact that Unesco, in carrying out its programme, should try to avoid piecemeal or sporadic action and should make it possible to rediscover an overall approach linking together all its activities [47].

Another, equally paradoxical lesson of EWLP is the need to resist the spell of—or at least to examine more carefully—the apparent rationality of notions like 'strategy'. In the last ten years, 'strategy' has come to enjoy widespread favour in international development jargon. But what does it imply for an activity like EWLP? With its military overtones, it conjures up the image of a high command marshalling troops and attending to logistics—in effect, planning, mounting and (presumably) winning a war of some sort. For three reasons, this can be a misleading representation of what literacy action probably should be.

First, although war is seldom simple, literacy is infinitely complex. 'Strategy' may be convenient short-hand for a much more complicated (and problematic) idea. Has it not sometimes tended to replace the idea, thus over-simplifying the way the task at hand was viewed?[1]

Winning a war?
Secondly, 'strategy' suggests the goal of winning a war. Yet it was clear at EWLP's outset that winning the 'war'—the total eradication of illiteracy—was far beyond the programme's grasp. The intensity of certain current criticisms of the programme can probably be imputed in part to the exaggerated (or at least unrealistic) optimism it allowed itself to generate a decade ago.[2]

Thirdly, the military connotations of 'strategy' imply the existence of

1. Possible over-simplification also relates to the international insistence on a project approach, which attempted to provide aid in neat packages so as to enhance accountability to donors. This approach was to some extent at odds with such notions as 'co-operation' and 'partnership'.
2. In fairness, it may be recalled that Unesco and UNDP have steadfastly rejected the notion of the programme as a 'world campaign'. But the fact that EWLP is often referred to as such cannot be imputed solely to the confusion (or perversity) of public opinion.

an enemy. As long as the 'enemy' remains illiteracy, well and good. Unfortunately the sights of the 'high command' tended to slip somewhat from abstract illiteracy to a more tangible target. At the international level where the concept of functional literacy was elaborated, attention sometimes shifted from the ultimate goal of literacy to the intermediate necessity of convincing national authorities of the functional concept's utility. The persistence in descriptions of the programme of another set of metaphors—mercantile rather than military[1]—suggests that this was more than occasionally the case.

Referring to the design considered optimal by international agencies for national EWLP projects, Meister says:

It really is a question of production, all projects being designed to lead ... to enhanced intellectual production with their productivity norms, their costs, their inputs and their outputs [28].

Regarding the internationally conceived concept of functional literacy, many chief technical advisers had to devote considerable amounts of time to 'selling' the functional literacy 'packages' to host governments who did not always understand—let alone accept—the notion. *Marketing a product?*

In sum, it appears to have been thought at the international level that if largely illiterate nations were not making better progress with literacy, it was because singly they were incapable of doing so. Individual national incompetence had to be compensated for (in this view) by joint international competence under the intellectual leadership of Unesco. This assumption made possible, even necessary, the design of a single 'product' up to international specifications, whose 'marketing' was to be achieved through EWLP strategy.

This unfortunate logic ignored the wishes of at least certain of what the programme itself called 'clients'. Certain countries wanted national literacy campaigns and seem to have 'bought' the EWLP 'product' in part because they were not aware of all its implications, and in part because they saw no prospect of obtaining international aid in any other way. Predictably, national and international EWLP staffs of these countries' projects tended to work at cross-purposes—one cause of the severe problems encountered there. To a degree EWLP may even be said to have delayed progress toward mass literacy in these cases.[2]

Turning to the first major component generally attributed to EWLP strategy, what was meant by 'intensive'? Several things, although the links *Intensity*

1. The penchant of international aid administrators for military and/or commercial terminology possibly expresses (a) an assumption that the armed forces and profit-making enterprises are more efficient than intergovernmental administrations, and (b) a frustration with being—in terms of geography and substance—at one remove from the locus of action.
2. Thus EWLP's 'product' was too standardized, a kind of lowest common denominator pegged to the level of the least ambitious participating authorities (national and international) and insufficiently differentiated to take into account the orientation and potential of more ambitious aid. Could more varied sources of aid, with a broader mandate than that of UNDP in the 1960s, have better satisfied these diverse needs?

between them seem not to have been made explicit with great clarity. A 1964 Unesco statement quoted in *Le Concept de l'Alphabétisation Fonctionnelle* [6] defines EWLP intensity as follows:

These projects will be intensive in as far as they will tend to provide something more than basic elements of reading, writing and arithmetic.

Here intensity pertains to the process of what is to be done, and requires the broadening of the notion of literacy to include minimal technical skills. This interpretation of intensity corresponds to the medical meaning of 'intensive'. In a sense, illiterates reached by EWLP were placed under intensive care.

The intensification of the process undergone by illiterates, however, presupposes an increase in resources mobilized per illiterate. Intensity has thus been understood to involve the shortening of the overall time required for the acquisition of literacy. In most cases, this is tantamount to increasing the amount of resources focused on a given illiterate at a given time, or to what might be called the telescoping of resources. The approach was fully consistent with the literacy-investment concept examined above in the section on 'Functionality'. But there is nothing inherent in the notion of intensity to prevent its being applied on a broad, even mass basis.

In the context of EWLP, intensive was intentionally opposed to extensive, selective opposed to massive. Activities were to be intensive in that, covering limited zones and selected groups, with high potential multiplier effect, the number of participants would be rather small. In *Selectivity* EWLP, intensity became inextricably intertwined with selectivity— unnecessarily so, since Guinea, Madagascar, Sudan and possibly the United Republic of Tanzania were already prepared to move ahead on a broader scale. Once again, the programme offered a technical solution— intensification of the process of literacy—to a non-technical problem.

Like the notion of functionality, selectivity was the international agencies' alternative to the supposedly probable failure of mass literacy. In retrospect, it seems unfortunate that, in their comprehensible haste to act, EWLP's framers did not assess (or assess with more care) earlier successful mass literacy campaigns.[1] Had the Cuban[2] and similar experiences been taken more fully into account, the world programme might well have avoided certain pitfalls. It would possibly have been more flexible in its

1. Indeed, it may be asked to what extent pre-EWLP literacy and (adult education generally) was examined before being replaced by the programme's concept and strategy. Could the programme not have taken more direct account of problems met by fundamental education work in the 1950s and *animation rurale* of the early 1960s, in attempting to combine literacy and the provision of practical, social and productive skills in line with the wishes of the communities concerned?
2. In one year (1961) the adult illiteracy rates in Cuba was reduced from 23 to 4 per cent according to official figures, thanks to such bold steps as the temporary closing down of schools to enable pupils to swell the ranks of volunteer instructors (Somalia has recently adopted a similar measure in its literacy campaign). The Cuban effort was intensive but certainly not selective or experimental. Naturally, such campaigns have tended to be part of sweeping and radical socio-economic change. Cuba also began with a much lower percentage of illiteracy than most EWLP countries and in certain other respects its experience may not be fully applicable in all cases.

definition of functionality—thus achieving from the outset a result only reached at the 1972 third International Conference on Adult Education.[1] It might also have offered participating governments who so wished, critical—if financially limited—aid to undertake mass campaigns (Guinea, for one, consistently objected to EWLP's selectivity, which it would gladly have replaced with a national adult education and literacy campaign). This possibility only received renewed emphasis in Unesco's Programme and Budget for 1975-76, after more than a decade in disfavour.

The problem, then, was not primarily technical. Although doubtless in need of refinement, the methods for achieving mass literacy existed under certain conditions—the Cuban case being an indication. Globally, if not always nationally, means and men were also available. What was lacking? In the words of the then Director-General of Unesco, quoted in *Youth and Literacy* [14]: 'The resources, both human and material, exist; and where there is a will, there is a way.'

It is customary, in documents such as the present report, to skirt questions of national policy priorities, or to treat them in terms so diplomatic as sometimes to confuse rather than illuminate. To gain perspective on both past and future strategies, however, it must be understood that, at the beginning of EWLP, most countries knew how to approach (and in some cases achieve) much more massive literacy as part of broader socio-economic change, if they wanted to. In some cases, they appear not to have wanted to. It is often a question of political (and resource) priority rather than technical capability, not 'we don't know how to', but 'we don't really want to'. That the non-technical reasons for literacy are gaining increased recognition was reflected at the eighteenth session of Unesco's General Conference in 1974 which (in Resolution 1.25) called on Member States 'to identify the structural causes of illiteracy . . .'.

Confusion between the two terms of this proposition engendered further ambiguity regarding the third and final component of EWLP strategy, the programme's experimental nature. The still-debated question is: what kind of experiment was EWLP meant to be? Interpretations vary— and it is regrettable that there is still so much room for interpretation of such a fundamental issue—but on the whole there seem to have been two main and in practice divergent answers. *Experimentation*

On the one hand was what might be termed the technico-scientific approach, and on the other the activist-pragmatic approach. The first posited that considerable technical improvement in literacy approaches must be achieved through controlled scientific experimentation before massive expansion of literacy could take place. According to the Director-General's oral report on the subject to Unesco's General Conference at the thirteenth session (quoted in *Le Concept de l'Alphabétisation Fonctionelle*): *Technico-scientific approach*

The programme is basically designed as a significant experiment and hence of a kind which might, at a later stage, be far more widely extended. This experiment is

1. cf. the speech of the Director-General of Unesco quoted above in the discussion on 'Functionality'.

intended to confirm the fundamental hypothesis of a positive correlation between literacy and development [6].

Naturally, the technico-scientific approach did not consciously seek to offer reluctant national (and international) policy-makers a technical rationalization for eluding or postponing crucial literacy-related decisions. Quite the contrary, the intention was to offer sufficiently scientific evidence of functional literacy's economic value, under given conditions, to convince policy-makers that it was a good investment. Regrettably, EWLP's success in attaining this objective seems to have been rather limited, partly because the objective may have been unrealistic.

One reason was a reluctance of virtually all the governments concerned to support an experiment entailing systematic evaluation. Another drawback has been the widespread misunderstanding of the precise nature of the hypothesis that EWLP was testing.[1] The hypothesis just quoted (a posivite correlation between literacy and development) was quite clear, but soon after it was formulated (1964), i.e. when EWLP was becoming operational, a certain confusion seems to have set in. First, there were barely perceptible changes in tone. In 1964, the Director-General had said that EWLP was to 'verify' its hypothesis. Once under way, however, the programme was described as 'taking care to demonstrate its hypothesis'. But was EWLP endeavouring to verify/demonstrate the hypothesized relationship between literacy and development? Or was it trying to prove the assumed superiority of a given (functional) literacy approach? The answer was by no means always and everywhere clear. In some instances, the approach rather than the relationship was seen and treated not only as a hypothesis to be proved, but also as an already proven thesis.

In probably extreme situations, the thesis even took on an air of dogma. The tone of a 1969 Unesco working paper comes close to treating certain EWLP projects as heretical. It speaks of a 'mistaken view' of functional literacy,

an equally oversimplified approach . . . interpretations which are partial in both senses of the word . . . compromises between traditional literacy work and functional literacy work (by adopting the methods previously used) [27].

These reproaches are the more difficult to understand in that, at the time of their publication (1969), there was precious little for 'deviants' to deviate from in terms of methodology. Although functionality had emerged as EWLP's aim from the Tehran Conference in 1965, it did not begin to take *Towards* shape as a transmissible body of methodology until 1970.
conceptual Already in 1969 the imperative need for conceptual flexibility was
flexibility emerging as a major lesson of the programme. Previously, the programme

---

1. In several profiles (see Part I), it will be noted that evaluation specialists devoted themselves primarily to research and development efforts designed to evolve a doctrine and methodology that could in fact be evaluated.

could flatter itself on having made a sincere effort to adapt its activities to various socio-cultural and economic settings. Now the call for adaptability was addressed to the concept itself. A top-level meeting of national directors, chief technical advisers, a number of evaluators and independent specialists, and representatives of the United Nations, UNDP, Unesco and other Specialized Agencies involved in EWLP not only refrained from adopting a definition of functional literacy, but stated that 'a rigid definition of functional literacy was not desirable . . .' [26].

Misunderstandings also arose from confusion between the first (technico-scientific) approach to experimentation, and the second approach, the activist-pragmatic. The latter was activist in that it stressed forward *Activist-* motion rather than experimentation. In Unesco's 1967 instructions for *pragmatic* preparing EWLP projects, it was emphasized that the purpose of the world programme was not to carry out micro-experiments. Rather, according to the *Guide for the Preparation of Pilot Experimental Work-Oriented Literacy Projects* [15] distributed in that year, the aim was to demonstrate what could be achieved to strike a blow against illiteracy in certain countries. These were to be pilot projects rather than scientific experiments. The orientation towards—and commitment to—action was expressed even more strongly in Unesco's Programme and Budget for 1967-68. This document stated that EWLP projects would serve to prime the pump of national literacy programmes.

That confusion was rife was indicated by the very title of the above-mentioned *Guide* which referred simultaneously to 'pilot' and 'experimental' projects. The ambiguity was noted by UNDP which, at that point, stood squarely behind the technico-scientific approach to experimentation. UNDP (quoted in *Le Concept de l'Alphabétisation Fonctionnelle*) declared that:

'experimental' means that what the future holds is uncertain, while 'pilot' implies more to come. The use of the word 'pilot' in project documents has this unwarranted implication, which is also unfortunate in that it has diluted the emphasis on experimentation and promoted an attitude of 'get on with it', whether a scientific and tested basis for functional literacy existed or not [6].

To the extent that the second approach did concern itself with experimentation, it was pragmatic rather than scientific. It looked on EWLP as experimental in terms of a process of progressive enrichment. It thus opted for the accumulation through trial and error of new insights into the problems and methodologies of literacy work. In sum, it viewed EWLP as a *Runway* v. plane full of passengers rather than a prototype flown by a test pilot. *wind-*
Ambiguity arose around this distinction, too. For example, the same *tunnel* 1969 Unesco working paper that castigated certain projects as though they were deviants from a clearly defined concept (which did not exist), refers to

The novelty of the concept of functional literacy work and the need to define it in and through its practical application . . . [27].

On the whole, indeed, it seems to have been assumed from the outset that the technico-scientific and activist-pragmatic approaches had to co-exist within the experimentation component of EWLP 'strategy'. There appears to have been a degree of incompatibility between them in the programme. As in many bad marriages, their forced cohabitation has been rather fruitless, and marred by quarrels that, on occasion, pushed the major responsible international agencies near divorce.

What of the future? Certain lessons have been suggested above regarding the notion of strategy and the internal problems of its individual components. Here, a word may be said about the relationship between those components. Largely as a result of EWLP, there is now a fairly widespread impression that intensity, selectivity and experimentation are integral parts of an organically whole approach to literacy. That is, it tends to be assumed that none of the three can be viable in at least the medium-term future without the other two.

A mystique? In some instances, there even seems to be a certain mystique, whereby the three elements take on the aura of an indivisible trinity. In the mouths of some of its partisans, 'functional literacy' refers to a favourably judged process that is necessarily intensive and selective, and which (for financial and technical reasons) retains a strong element of experimentation, or at least research. Opponents also tend to link the three elements inseparably; in rejecting any one they are inclined to refuse all three. More discernment is doubtless required.

The wherewithal: resources, institutions and instruments

Internationally and in most participating countries, the Experimental World Literacy Programme succeeded in attracting to literacy unusual amounts—and sometimes resolutely new kinds—of resources. EWLP offers, then, a wealth of lessons to those who seek the quantitative quickening, and qualitative renewal, of the means necessary for literacy action. In this chapter, the means for literacy are examined in terms of EWLP's experience with: human resources (men and women with different levels of responsibility); material resources (buildings, books and other teaching tools); the institutional framework (how the international programme and national projects were organized); and evaluation (a crucial instrument, given the programme's experimental character).

Human resources

During EWLP, thousands of people around the world were recruited, briefed or trained, and employed in a wide variety of capacities to plan, supervise, staff and monitor functional literacy activities. The mobilization of so much and so many different kinds of man- and woman-power sometimes achieved remarkable results. It also occasionally created insurmountable problems. The results and problems offer guidance for future literacy efforts.

At the national level, and beginning at the pinnacle of the human resource pyramid, what may be said of policy-makers associated with EWLP? The newness of functional literacy (as defined by EWLP), and the programme's organizational complexity, made it desirable for continuity of top-level national, political and administrative figures. Such continuity seems to have been maintained in certain cases, e.g. Algeria and the United Republic of Tanzania. Elsewhere the lack of continuity was a serious hindrance. The change of president brought one country's project to a virtual standstill for almost a year. Another project suffered, in its first three years, from the fact that the Minister of Education changed no less than seven times.

National policy-makers

Equally important was the policy-makers' attitude towards educational innovation, a central feature of EWLP. In some cases, national policy-makers resisted the programme's innovative aspects; in others, however, there was an openness, even a commitment, to innovation. There, unfortunately, EWLP was perceived as unprepared, in at least a few of these instances, to be as innovative as national policy-makers. In such cases the programme was seen as designed to disseminate a pre-packaged, self-contained innovation with which national innovators were not expected to tamper.

Inter-national nourish-ment for national innovation

On the whole, the problem seems to have been that EWLP (a) designed what the international agencies saw as a single standard innovation at the international level (although ill-defined, as discussed earlier), and (b) expected national policy-makers to serve as relay stations in disseminating the innovation. In future, a more fruitful alternative would probably be to lay greater stress on aiding policy-makers so inclined to generate their own innovations in literacy (and other education areas). International experience could provide nourishment; but force-feeding should be avoided.

At the intermediate level of national staff, the programme's legacy consists of thousands of people who received training and/or experiences in areas (e.g. programming, curriculum design, evaluation, material production) of use in literacy education and other development fields. The lack of administrators, technicians, supervisors and field personnel, however, has been reported as a continuing major problem by Ethiopia, Iran, Mali and the United Republic of Tanzania. Iran's initial request for EWLP aid provided for 9,018 man/months of national professional services, which was reduced to 750 man/months in the plan of operations; the number of man/months actually provided was 1,322. Another country originally planned to place at the disposal of its EWLP project 150 agricultural agents, i.e. more than existed in the country at that time. Probably this was because the original planners did not consult all the ministries concerned, or go through a central planning body. In India, a high turnover rate and the fact that many staff members only worked part time on literacy compounded the problem of insufficient middle-level skills.

Lack of such personnel was not a problem everywhere, however. In one EWLP country, 40 full-time officials (not including supervisors) were responsible for a total of 7,000 learners. In another, the ratio at one point was 30 to 3,000. In these, and indeed all cases, productivity was largely dependent on the training and prevailing spirit of middle-level staff. All countries trained such staff at home and almost all abroad as well. Breaking with traditional formulae, some countries stressed practical training with apparently positive post-training results. In Tanzania, staff training included at times the actual preparation of literacy manuals. Sudan departed from its original plan to train supervisors at the University of Khartoum, and put trainees to work planning a functional literacy subproject.

It is hard to judge the spirit in which middle-level staff worked. In some cases (United Republic of Tanzania and Iran, for example) the prospect of making inroads into illiteracy and/or the opportunity to participate in an innovative educational venture does seem to have sparked at least initial enthusiasm. In several instances, however, morale was not as high as it might have been. The administrative mentality, often operating in a context of only minimal lateral support, sometimes proved incapable of generating the necessary dynamism and commitment. Field-work was often viewed as exile. The rut of administrative routine was too deep. According to Meister, 'in some cases literacy work was more formalized than functionalized' [28].[1] On the other hand, EWLP did produce national technicians who made important contributions at international meetings— or in some cases as international experts. *Enthu-siasm v. . . . . . . routine*

An important achievement of EWLP was to show that a wide variety of professional skills not usually allied closely with literacy must be, and could be, mobilized to enrich literacy work and post-literacy adult education. Specialists in various branches of development had to learn to express themselves in terms comprehensible to learners and new literates, without speaking down to them. Scriptwriters, journalists, radio producers and designers and producers of graphics have had to go through a similar metamorphosis.

The change did not, of course, begin (much less end) with EWLP. Considerable progress has yet to be achieved, both conceptually and technically (as will be apparent later in this chapter when material resources are examined). In Mali, the United Republic of Tanzania and other projects, however, the programme did stimulate media staffs to reorient their work toward broader needs than those of their traditional urban élite audience. The not always smooth changes in the labour market caused by recruitment and occupational modification of such staff were probably inevitable.

Regarding literacy teaching staff, an old issue sharply restated by EWLP was: to what extent can school-teachers be used as literacy instructors? At the outset of many projects, teachers (particularly in the rural areas) were looked on as a pre-existing cadre of literacy instructors. In India, most instructors were local school-teachers who worked part time in the project. Ethiopia and Iran also called on teachers (Mali did not). The assumption that school-teachers are naturally suited for such work seems to have been made in the United Republic of Tanzania, where pre-service literacy training was much shorter for teachers than for other categories of instructor. Sudan, too, exercised special care in training non-teacher instructors. *Profess-ional and . . .*

Because of the shortage of teachers, united with a desire for specialists to instruct vocational/technical aspects of the courses, all EWLP countries called on other kinds of instructors. Ethiopia, Mali, the United Republic of Tanzania and Iran drew instructors from one or more of the following categories: skilled workers, volunteers, students. The Syrian Arab Republic and occasionally Madagascar used farmers or farmers' sons; in Algeria fully *. . . non-profess-ional instructors*

1. Inter-ministerial secondments in Iran showed one way to achieve a more flexible and interdisciplinary approach.

one-third of instructors had not completed primary school. In fact, widespread and imaginative use of non-professional teachers may be the only way for countries with high illiteracy rates to become literate. The third International Conference on Adult Education (Tokyo, 1972) recommended that such nations should launch large-scale campaigns 'mobilizing for this purpose the whole literate section of the population . . .' [43].[1]

EWLP's call on instructors who were not professional teachers had causes other than the numerical lack of teachers. Emerging from EWLP, the task profile of the ideal literacy instructor includes teaching the three R's, classroom vocational teaching, practical training via demonstrations, animation and understanding of—and sensitivity to—adults of the least favoured socio-economic strata. By no means all school-teachers possess skills and attitudes commensurate with these tasks, and they sometimes look on literacy instruction as an imposition. Moreover, their background and training may make them quite unsuitable, while in terms of pedagogy, they represent school methods which are often inadequate or flagrantly alien; at the end of the research phase of the Iran project only 6 per cent of school-teacher literacy instructors used the group discussion method strongly urged in their training and manual. In terms of values and behaviour, they perhaps often aspire to enter the very white-collar urban social stratum that secretly scorns (or openly exploits) rural peasant illiterates.

Although often closer to illiterates socially and economically, non-professional instructors in EWLP (especially those drawn from the local community) were not always freer from alienated aspirations. In the United Republic of Tanzania, some jobless school-leaver instructors looked on their work as a path to more prestigious status in the village. In the Syrian Arab Republic, certain instructors felt they should be granted leave equivalent to

Attitudes, teaching skills and . . .

school-teachers' holidays. Realizing the importance of attitudes in addition to teaching skill, Guinea and some other projects used political as well as pedagogical criteria in recruiting instructors.

In functional literacy, as interpreted by EWLP, technical and vocational ability was also fundamental. In several EWLP projects, the trend was to use different instructors for literacy and vocational training—symbolizing the dichotomy between 'literacy' and 'functionality'. In India, agricultural counterparts were recruited to complement three-R instructors,

. . . technical ability

since these were mostly school-teachers with little or no knowledge of farming. The same was true of the Ethiopian project where, in addition, co-ordination between literacy and technical instruction seems to have been limited.

In terms of learner perception and grasp of the two areas, an integrated approach was considered preferable in theory and, at least occasionally, in practice. In Iran, Sudan and Mali, the same instructor was responsible for literacy and agricultural/vocational subjects. Training was crucial since

1. Such involvement can help to make technicians who are not professional teachers more sensitive to the human problems of development and change.

instructors without the requisite vocational skills were, so to speak, apprenticed in the trade they were to teach. In fact, one gets the impression that technicians who also taught the three R's achieved better overall results than school-teachers who instructed technical as well as three-R subjects. In the latter case, technical teaching often suffered.

More broadly, a consensus seems to have emerged from EWLP concerning the need to give great stress to in-service as well as pre-service training of instructors. Short initial training followed by periodic refresher sessions, on weekends for example, is thought to be more efficient (and probably no more expensive) than long initial training without follow-up. This preference arises both from the utility of repeated reinforcement of basic skills and from the opportunity provided for instructors to use class experience as a practical source for their own learning.

Even improved training, however, cannot overcome the fact that good literacy instruction will continue to be a hard, ill-paid and often thankless task whose reward is the sense of having taken part in a crucial venture of development. Many EWLP instructors did reap such a reward.

Turning to human resources at the international level, the perhaps overly influential role of permanent United Nations agency staffs in designing EWLP[1] meant that weaknesses among them would be multiplied many times over throughout the programme and projects. In Unesco, the *International* Literacy Division's situation was not unlike that obtaining elsewhere in *national* Unesco and the United Nations system. By and large, well-intentioned and *staffs* technically competent headquarters officers entrusted with EWLP tended to feel in regular danger of being professionally drawn and quartered by their numerous, urgent and sometimes contradictory responsibilities.

Headquarters officers' tasks included essentially the administration of projects. At least occasionally, however, they found themselves standing in for national authorities, as when Unesco staff defined the learning objectives of one national project. Caught between administration and action, officers found little time (and few built-in incentives) to improve their qualifications.[2] Periodic opportunities for self-assessment, such as the Director-General's annual report or the sexennial report on co-operation with non-governmental organizations, tended to be treated as irksome exercises whose results would probably (and in fact often did) go unread.

In addition, the rigid Unesco hierarchy precluded many of them from *Frus-* having a positive (or any) influence on the Organization's policies in the field *tration* v. of literacy. The resultant frustration of individual professionals probably had *esprit de* an adverse effect on the relevant unit's collective *esprit de corps*. The latter *corps*

1. cf. the discussion of this role on page 123 et seq., above.
2. While in-service training was mandatory for national staff in some projects, it was not even a real option for most international officials. Operational seminars organized toward the end of the programme could have offered an opportunity for upgrading, but they tended to serve as training courses for national personnel. Their most positive contribution—which could be used in the future—was to compress into a limited time most if not all steps in the literacy programming process: baseline study of needs, development of curricula and teaching aids, actual use of these, and evaluation. All these steps involved national and international staffs.

was certainly undermined, as elsewhere in Unesco, by the fact that non-professionals such as secretarial and clerical staff were seldom informed (much less consulted, despite their more than random interest and insight) about EWLP's progress.

In the future, the role of adviser to diverse national innovations (rather than designer and marketer of internationally standardized innovation) would imply changes in the situation of permanent international headquarters' staffs. Regular in-service professional improvement, carried out when appropriate in the framework of various kinds of literacy and adult education programmes (including those of various United Nations agencies), should become a requirement.[1] Acquisition of new knowledge and skills would necessitate modification of officers' tasks and organization. Tasks should encourage more 'think work' relative to amounts of paperwork. Also needed are the meaningful briefing and consultation of all staff—including non-professionnals—on the substance as well as the mechanics of the literacy work of concerned agencies. These reforms would doubtless have effects beyond units responsible for literacy. But far from being a reason for their postponement, this broader dimension should be viewed as an opportunity to apply certain lessons of EWLP to international development aid as a whole.

The same may be said of conclusions drawn from the world programme's experience with experts, of whom some 100 man- and woman-years of professional services in various areas of competence were supplied under EWLP. EWLP's stress on recruiting professionally *Experts:* competent experts was fully consistent both with the view of literacy as a *competence* technical problem and with its vocational interpretation of functionality. It *and . . .* does not, however, correspond to the above-urged need to view both literacy and functionality in a more flexible and broader socio-cultural perspective. Unesco's 1974 Regional Meeting of Latin American Youth pointed unanimously to the implications of this alternative view for recruitment and national approval mechanisms. It recommended that Unesco:

> revise the criteria on the basis of which experts are chosen. . . . They should take
> *. . . com-*   into account not only qualifications and experience but also social commitment. . . .
> *mitment*   Furthermore we believe that Unesco should carry out studies, and submit proposals
> to Member States, concerning machinery to ensure that some part in the selection of
> experts is played by bodies on which the people are represented [35].

This proposal may seem inapplicable in the near future in many Member States. But it might find takers elsewhere, at least on an experimental basis.

Such a broadened view of recruitment criteria, including what could be called human as well technical competence, is the more necessary in view of certain unsatisfactory experiences of EWLP. To be sure, there were very

---

1. If adequately implemented, the principle of time-study-entitlement adopted for an experimental period by Unesco's General Conference in 1974 would at least offer the option of such in-service training.

few instances of conflicts between experts and national staff as severe as in the case of at least one project that had to be prematurely closed on account of them. Nor, however, does harmonious co-operation seem to have been the norm, although problems were far from always attributable to foreign staff.[1] Still, it may be asked how long many experts' initial indignation at underdevelopment can avoid degenerating into indifference in the constant presence of extreme poverty. And how many persist in efforts to know and understand the cultures within which they work? (One EWLP expert told Meister of his relations with national counterparts: 'There is nothing in my contract to say I have to love them' [28].) EWLP has helped demonstrate that, as the present Director-General of Unesco wrote in 1974:

The time is long past when the 'expert' with assurance and good faith, could believe that he was the bearer of values, knowledge and know-how worthy of being transmitted and assimilated. Henceforth, the 'expert' is asked to avoid hasty adaptations and transfers. He is asked to make special efforts to resist the temptation of seeking to reproduce the context in which he was trained and the models peculiar to himself, in order to fit his actions into an original frame [25].

Usually limited to a pre-service visit to headquarters for lectures and appointments concerned mostly with administrative structures and procedures, experts' briefing requires thorough overhaul. Referring to briefing methods, A. Lestage points to

a built-in lack of coherence between the way in which the Secretatiats brief their experts and the [educational] methods which the latter are advised to use in the field [22].

To overcome this incoherence, a new pedagogy of briefing could be developed, replacing at least some lectures with more active (and stimulating) methods. Subject matter should be revised to achieve a better balance between administrative detail and substantive issues. Finally, more systematic use could be made of opportunities for briefing en route to, and on arrival at, duty stations, as well as during travel to and from leaves.

Briefing en route and on site

EWLP experience suggests that the overhaul of briefing and other adjustments to the expert system may not be sufficient to bring the provision of international manpower and womanpower in line with the needs of Third World countries. What may be required, to suit some needs at least, is the replacement of experts with a very different kind of external human resource.[2]

EWLP's lesson on this score may be stated as follows. The programme aimed to develop new practical approaches to literacy. It tended, however, to recruit experts from traditional academic disciplines with insufficient

1. Difficult communications, truly hard living conditions (i.e. not just lack of air conditioning and dry-cleaning) and uncommitted or non-existent national counterparts were not infrequent.
2. N.B. This is not a radical but an intermediate position between that of governments who wish (and should be enabled) to continue receiving traditional kinds of experts, on one hand, and those that have become or are becoming allergic to nearly all expatriate expertise, on the other.

practical experience in educational development in view of EWLP's ambitious goals. The dilemma appears even more clearly if one considers that most experts in EWLP (Third World) countries were from—or professionally trained in or according to the norms of—highly industrialized countries.

Asking questions

In other terms, it may be asked whether experts who are vehicles for the importation of skills and concepts are always and everywhere helpful to educational innovation in widely differing social, cultural, economic and political settings.[1]

What may be needed more in the future, in certain cases at least, is the international *animateur,* a partner who stimulates national personnel to think out literacy problems, and to seek innovative answers, on their own terms; who asks rather than answers questions.[2] He might also help them identify other individuals and groups whose experience would be compatible with national options and needs, as nationally interpreted. The facilitator approach, it must be noted, is not daringly new. It was used centuries ago by—among other non-'experts'—the Zen masters and Socrates.

Material resources

EWLP generated a vast quantity and broad diversity of material resources (e.g. over 100,000 separate sets of learning materials of two or more pages treating 7,120 different problems) which might not have existed had the programme not taken place. More important, it is the kinds of material resources produced—and the ways they were distributed—that offer guidance for future literacy action. Particularly rich in lessons was EWLP'S experience with the use of buildings and physical plant, printed materials, audio-visual and other teaching aids, and the logistics of resource distribution.

In many Third World countries, something of a myth has remained from colonial times about the minimal physical conditions in which proper basic education can take place. The rural primary school is often a village's most modern construction, perhaps the only one boasting a tin roof or built of reinforced concrete. Sometimes still viewed (even by villagers) as an outpost of civilization, such schools have the double drawback of being expensive and of cutting learners off, pyschologically and physically, from the reality around them.

1. Some observers are ready enough to admit the logic of this conclusion in as far as it concerns 'soft' skills such as pedagogy or teacher training. They maintain, however, that it does not hold true for 'hard' expertise, e.g. in technology, which they believe is universal ($E = Mc^2$, they argue, remains valid whether one is in Tehran, Timbuktu, Trondheim or Tomsk). Yet EWLP suggests this affirmation is subject to interpretation. The same slide-projector represents a qualitatively different kind of technology if one is in a country with $4.000 annual *per capita* GNP with spare parts available at the corner shop, rather than in a country with $40 GNP where spare parts have to travel for months (successively by boat, train, truck, bicycle and foot), and often arrive broken.
2. EWLP's experience with certain short-term consultants indicates the utility of this approach.

The world programme helped lay to rest the myth of the absolute need *The* for such buildings. It showed conclusively that adequate basic education can *building* perfectly well take place in a variety of settings. To be sure, school *myth* classrooms were used in Ecuador, Ethiopia, Iran and the United Republic of Tanzania and perhaps elsewhere, but the same countries also held literacy classes in community centres as well as factories and other work places. Varying combinations of churches, mosques, literacy centres and private houses were used in Mali (which did not hold classes in schools) and by Ethiopia, Iran and the United Republic of Tanzania. Where climate permitted, e.g. the United Republic of Tanzania, classes were also held in the open air.

The use of diversified settings for EWLP literacy classes contributed (if it did not lead) to the search for cheaper and pedagogically more appropriate educational plant. In Ethiopia, learners built their own class facilities. In the United Republic of Tanzania, a similar trend encouraged the government to apply a new policy under which rural communities are only aided to construct educational buildings if they themselves contribute labour and materials.[1]

Pedagogically, use of varied settings for literacy classes has helped link education with daily experience. Organized in factories, classes in Algeria, Ethiopia, Iran and Mali helped to focus teaching on the vocationally functional potential of literacy. The same may be said of agricultural demonstration plots in Iran, Ecuador, India and the United Republic of Tanzania, although these were sometimes difficult to find and had—at least occasionally—a rather tenuous and formalistic link with actual application. *Education* In one country, a demonstration plot was found to be barely larger than the *rooted* Unesco expert's office; so small, indeed, that the demonstration tractor *in reality* could hardly turn around on it. This situation was all the more absurd since the local co-operative could never hope to afford a tractor. Despite such problems, the teaching of literacy in real production settings encouraged (again, for example, in the United Republic of Tanzania) national policies for rooting basic education physically in the local context.

In some measure, EWLP fuelled a similar evolution in the field of educational printed materials. Developed from baseline surveys, Ethiopia's primers and other reading materials were related to key problems familiar to peasants in such areas as soil conservation and row planting. In Sudan, the advice of factory technicians, agricultural extension agents and home economists was taken into account during the preparation of printed matter in an effort to ensure greater relevance to technical needs as seen by these people. In certain other countries, a lower priority was given to such efforts. In one, there was no effective systematic consultation of technical services on the content of teaching materials. In another, a curious gap appeared between vocational materials, on one hand, and literacy primers, on the

---

1. The application of this policy during the United Republic of Tanzania's second Five-year Plan (1969-74) appears to have resulted in considerable savings of capital expenditure on formal and non-formal basic education.

other. In a third—exceptional—instance, it appears that functional literacy primers were simply a reprint of children's texts in which the word 'child' was replaced by 'adult'.

Follow-up reading: an auxiliary?

A problem in several EWLP countries has been the inadequate provision for follow-up reading materials. The very term 'follow-up' seems to have lulled several projects into assuming that such materials were of secondary or auxiliary importance only. Planning for the provision of appropriate popular reading materials is required concurrently with the organization of adult education services of whatever kind.

In certain cases appropriate materials have to be developed virtually from scratch. In the United Republic of Tanzania, for example, and despite earlier efforts in this field, many of the meagre stock of between 500 and 1,000 book titles existing in Swahili were not of a level or on subjects likely to interest new literates. Consequently, the government ran a national competition to obtain book manuscripts. There, and in Ethiopia, efforts have been made to place books at the disposal of new literates through mobile libraries. These efforts have encountered numerous obstacles, not least of which are poor production and distribution facilities. Creation of such facilities may be tantamount to setting up the material infrastructure of a literate society.

Possibly cheaper and more flexible than book production and dissemination is the use of newspapers for the circulation of ideas and information to and from new literates. In an apparently unique case, the United Republic of Tanzania devotes one page of a major national daily to news for new literates, printed with suitable vocabulary and typeface. More widespread has been the development of special newspapers for new (and other) literates, chiefly in rural areas. Judging from the experience of Mali (where the paper *Kibaru* is popular), the main advantages of such newspapers compared with books and/or the national press seem to be that they can: (a) treat several subjects simultaneously, and (b) give prominence to locally relevant and topical information.

An issue still outstanding in this area is the need to discover appropriate tone and style. Such papers tend to fail if they are overwhelmingly didactic, and correspondingly dull. Thus journalists must find ways of taking to (rather than at) new literates, and of presenting news as well as information. Here, the Tanzanian experience in using literacy organizers and instructors as on-the-spot reporters could usefully be studied.

Communication top-down . . .

. . . bottom-up . . .

Still more important is the question (topical in industrialized as well as Third World countries) of the direction of communication flow: who writes to whom? The easy and all-too-general answer is: top to bottom. That is, the power-holding stratum of society tends to send the messages it deems desirable or newsworthy to the powerless stratum of new literates in line with the integrative intention referred to earlier. Mali's experience suggests that there is no technical obstacle to a reverse flow, and that communication from the bottom to the top makes for stimulating reading. One newly literate reader recently wrote to thank *Kibaru* for enabling him to ask a public question of a government minister and to receive a public answer, all in the paper's columns.

The work of rural newspapers in the Tanzanian EWLP project suggests that in addition to flowing from the top down, and from the bottom up, communication via such media can move laterally among new literates. *. . . and* Indeed, unmanipulated horizontal communication among new literates *lateral* could be a vital fulfilment of literacy's promise. It could open the way for self-organization. This in turn is a precondition for a sharing or a shifting of power, from which the hitherto powerless may well benefit. For more than a few observers, the achievement of self-determination is literacy's ultimate functionality.

On the whole, then, the opening to new literates of rural newspapers and other media need not—must not—be treated as a transfer or adaptation of industrialized countries' models of mass communication to settings deemed to be 'underdeveloped' in communications (as in other areas).[1] Rather, efforts are needed to create alternative means of popular mass dialogue, in keeping with already existing communications traditions and with national needs and aspirations. This is one challenge that EWLP helped to define, if seldom to answer.

A similar challenge emerges from the programme's experience with audio-visual and other teaching aids. With few exceptions, the lack of equipment was seen by EWLP countries as a major factor hampering progress of their literacy projects, and was explicitly stated to be so by Ethiopia, Iran, Mali and United Republic of Tanzania. EWLP avoided recourse to the more expensive educational media, although these were coming into vogue at the time the programme was launched. Thus the United Republic of Tanzania explicitly rejected television. Simultaneously, several non-EWLP countries in a like income range were making heavy capital and upkeep outlays, and training a highly specialized cadre, to enable television to reach generally limited audiences of illiterates ; they considered they were obtaining justifiable returns for their investment, of course.

By and large, EWLP countries made fairly moderate use of (sometimes pre-existing) media to teach different groups concerned with their projects. In Iran, it was found that use of cassettes for limited periods in certain aspects of instructor in-service training gave roughly equivalent results to more classical kinds of technical upgrading. Films and/or slides were used in literacy classes—apparently without severe technical breakdowns—in Ethiopia, Mali, Syrian Arab Republic and United Republic of Tanzania. At least occasional supportive use of radio was made in the same countries, with the United Republic of Tanzania mounting special radio education campaigns for organized groups of new and other literates (one reached almost a quarter of the country's potential radio listenership) both during and after its EWLP project.

---

1. The traditional African *griot* and West Indian calypso singer were not less effective or more manipulative disseminators of news, in their contexts, than the mass-circulation European daily of our time. Hence the inverted commas around 'underdeveloped' here.

In general, then, there was apparently no major technical hitch in the sense of a technological unviability of the moderately sophisticated media employed. The main problem posed by EWLP's use of audio-visual aids seems to have been cultural rather than technical, and the more difficult to grasp (not to mention diagnose or correct) since it did not result from short-circuits or blown-out bulbs. Though probably affecting films, slides and similar aids, the breakdown seemed particularly evident in the most widespread and simplest media: posters, drawings and other graphics.

It did not perhaps require quite so complex a study as that carried out in Mali to determine that many aspects of the West's graphic code (arrows to stress certain ideas, a death's head meaning 'poison') are alien to the symbolic world of most Third World illiterates. Possibly more surprising is the fact that, despite the studies carried out in several EWLP countries, graphics designers tended to act as though illiterates had either no symbolic world of their own, or one so poor as to place them at the level of retardates.

Graphics for children?

The above-quoted study in Mali noted a general tendency for illiterates to be attracted by details of posters, and to neglect the central theme. An Iranian survey pointed to illiterates' difficulty in understanding the third dimension as presented in posters. With doubtless unintentional condescension, Unesco's *Practical Guide to Functional Literacy* analysed, in 1973, the 'errors' made by peasants in interpreting graphic representations and urged designers to avoid 'trying for aesthetic results'. The implied artistic poverty of the peasants was explained as follows:

As the peasants have very rarely seen graphic . . . representations, there is no cause for surprise at the sparsity of the list of details that they are able to 'see' [33].

Many anthropologists and earlier literacy and graphics specialists would have pointed out that all groups reached by EWLP have a well-developed aesthetic sense, and a rich (rather than poor) symbolic world, in which they are able not only to 'see' but also to create a wealth of often very fine graphic detail. If Europeans or urban-oriented élites have often been unable (or unwilling) to recognize the existence of such aesthetic richness among illiterates, it is hardly the illiterates' fault.

Different symbolic worlds

There are, thus, quantitatively[1] but also qualitatively different symbolic worlds. EWLP attempted to give illiterates access to literates' symbolic world through graphics designed by literates, but in doing so it underscored the need for those literates who organize literacy work (a) to recognize the internal validity of the illiterates' symbolic world, and (b) to attempt to enter and understand that world. What does the illiterate 'see' on his or her own terms? The aim of literacy organizers' attempts to answer this question should not be exclusively to improve the 'marketability' of their 'product' by making its 'label' more understandable to the 'clients'. An objective exploration of illiterates' symbolic world might, therefore, reveal original messages of perception, not to mention need and hope.

1. The Incas had neither alphabet nor ideographs; yet their *quipo* knot-writing was so sophisticated that it still baffles cryptographers today.

In summary, Western-style graphics are not necessarily appropriate for Third World illiterates, whose own aesthetic worlds should be taken into account in the preparation of graphics and other materials—the more so since those worlds may offer unique and original cultural contributions.

Assuming that adequate educational materials for literacy can be found, how can they be delivered to the right place at the right times? The logistics of resource distribution were a continuing headache in EWLP, and *Logistics* thus a source of guidance for future literacy action. The world programme had a two-tiered logistic structure. First, equipment and supplies were ordered—and shipped—from abroad. The flow was generally from industrialized countries to Third World (project) countries.

Administrative as much as geographical, delays were often inordinately long. In one case, more than a year elapsed between the purchase of books and their delivery. In another, no less than twenty-three months went by between the decision to buy a bibliobus and its arrival at the project. Production of printed material in Madagascar only began after a foreign-bought printing press arrived, toward the end of the project. In only a few countries was there a coherent effort to develop national publishing activities which would lead to self-supporting and continuous book production and distribution.

The second logistic tier was inside project countries. It almost always involved the distribution of goods (whether purchased abroad or nationally) from a major city—capital and/or port—to inland zones where the subprojects were located. Here again there were long delays. In several countries lack of transportation was a major problem hampering the promotion of adult literacy. Madagascar, where no EWLP zone was closer than 800 kilometres to project headquarters, had no infrastructure for distributing equipment and materials. Certain classes were several days' travel from even provincial capitals.

Viewed from a grass-roots standpoint, the two-tiered system of logistics made class members, instructors and supervisors—that is, the *Double* primary elements in learning and teaching—doubly dependent on external *dependency* factors over which they had little or no control. For much of their supplies and equipment, they depended on national project headquarters, which in turn depended on foreign sources, both for materials to be trans-shipped to classes and for equipment with which to produce materials for shipment to classes.

Curiously in a programme that publicly stressed its adaptability to diverse conditions, EWLP was not notable for stimulating the imaginative use of locally available materials and facilities, or the equally creative local generation of import substitutes when materials were not available. There were some interesting exceptions. In the United Republic of Tanzania, as a matter of policy, literacy instructors were trained to use sticks and pebbles to demonstrate certain arithmetic concepts, but, on the whole, EWLP did not actively encourage such inventiveness. It tended instead to prefer the routine kinds of classical technical assistance.

The institutional framework

Who decided what was to be done to whom, when it was to be done and how? Who implemented these decisions? Discussion of these basic issues of the EWLP institutional framework should help avoid certain pitfalls in the structuring of future literacy action. The issues appeared at the national level (internal organization of EWLP projects and their co-ordination with other development action), at the international level (internal organization of responsible agencies, and their co-operation with other concerned international bodies), and in the relationships between the international and national levels.

Autonomy   The desire to attain and retain autonomy of action influenced the
and . . .   institutional siting of almost all EWLP projects at the national level. The top-level international meeting on EWLP held in 1969 stressed that

> The projects must have administrative and financial structures capable of ensuring their effective and rapid functioning [and thus] retain the measure of autonomy which is necessary in experimental projects, in order to encourage innovation and research [26].

Several countries attempted to implement this principle at the outset by setting up separate project structures outside the institutional framework of other educational and developmental structures. This caused constant and unnecessary friction. In virtually all cases where the project phased into long-term activity, the structure was abolished and the programme was integrated into existing national structures.

Six countries originally placed their EWLP project under the control of the Ministry of Education, albeit generally in an *ad hoc* body. According to a document presented to the fifteenth session of Unesco's General Conference (1968), the autonomy of these bodies was

> often theoretical rather than practical, and in the majority of cases appears to be unable to meet the demands of projects the administration of which creates problems very different from those of institutions normally controlled by ministries of education [32].

In fact, five EWLP projects found themselves answerable to the same parent body as other forms of literacy work, which made for considerable sibling rivalry.[1]

The principle of administrative autonomy was also often undercut by governments' understandable desire to streamline proliferating bureaucracies. In addition, both autonomy and attachment to ministries of education

---

1. There was seldom peaceful co-existence. Where pre-existing literacy programmes prevailed, the innovative thrust of the EWLP project was sometimes blunted. Conversely, where the EWLP approach dominated, even successful non-EWLP literacy suffered; this seems to have happened with the *Periodista* campaign in Ecuador, where, to an extent, Peter may have been robbed to pay Paul.

were seen as contradicting EWLP projects' necessary link with development work.[1] Single-ministry monopoly of the national project was rejected by several countries in favour of integration into socio-economic planning or—at the very least—more or less strong co-ordination among ministries and between them and non-governmental bodies. The logic of the approach followed by EWLP required interministerial sponsorship which, in practice, was very difficult to achieve.   *... co-ordination*

Sometimes, efforts to integrate or co-ordinate do seem to have had a modicum of success. The Ethiopian project received interministerial attention as an integrated part of development work, particularly after an unwieldy National Advisory Committee was replaced by a smaller Executive Committee of bodies with direct operational responsibility. In Algeria, after a period of initial uncertainty, the EWLP project was brought in line with the national development plan. The two interdisciplinary consultative committees foreseen in the EWLP plan of operations did not play an important part in achieving this result, however, and interministerial co-operation in plan execution was never notably strong.

In general, EWLP countries' attempt to transcend vertical ministerial structures encountered stubborn adherence to sectoral approaches. One project's co-ordination committee met only twice in four years; another's, once in three years. In one country, agricultural extension workers theoretically attached to the project had no contact with literacy instructors, who were answerable to another ministry. In still another project, national, provincial and local co-ordination committees were simply ignored, and work was accomplished (or not accomplished) through traditional intraministerial channels. Finally, there seems to have been no satisfactory and replicable solution to the autonomy co-ordination dilemma. Of the various patterns tried, modified or discarded, none appears to correlate with success or failure.

The same conclusion probably holds true for another important issue, related in turn to the administrative traditions of the countries concerned, that of decentralization. Again, many attempts were made to find the most appropriate degree of concentration or devolution of responsibility. Iran moved from decentralization to centralization. The Algerian and Guinean projects evolved in the opposite direction. The overall EWLP trend was to settle on a compromise: a cup half-full or half-empty, depending on national history and preferences. But in no case can project success or failure be attributed to, or correlated with, the degree of (de)centralization that was finally settled on.   *National decentral-ization*

This is more regrettable since, in theory, EWLP required a degree of decentralization—and even learner self-government—hitherto rare even in adult education ventures. In 1973, the Unesco Secretariat (quoted in *Le Concept de l'Alphabétisation Fonctionnelle*) affirmed that

---

1. Is it not curious that in EWLP—and other—countries, ministries of education were not deemed to have a primarily developmental function?

functional literacy work cannot be designed from outside, in accordance with the mechanistic approaches of traditional pedagogy. It presupposes active participation on the part of those concerned at all stages of preparation and implementation.

Thus one of EWLP's basic tenets was 'the complete or partial assumption of responsibility for action by the socio-economic groups concerned' [6]. This implied the creation of specific machinery for planning and implementing literacy that would take learners" views, problems and hopes into account.[1] The almost universal absence of such machinery must be considered a failing of the programme.

Self-management

Alone with Guinea, and to some degree Algeria, the United Republic of Tanzania appears to have provided for a measure of learner participation in managing—if not planning—its project through class committees. The committees were composed of a chairman, secretary and treasurer elected by each class upon its formation, as well as the instructor. Class committee decisions covered enforcement of participant discipline, the spending of money made from demonstration plots, and the scheduling of classes. In practice, classes often modified their schedule and this sometimes required additional government expenditure for additional hours of teaching.

International agencies concerned with EWLP faced numerous thorny problems of internal organization. To a great extent, these were merely already existing difficulties which came to affect the programme. In this respect, the length and complexity of administrative procedures may be mentioned. So may the tendency of such procedures—and the political services of the organizations concerned—to control rather than support agency literacy activities. EWLP also raised a number of specific literacy-related problems. Uppermost among these seems to have been the continuing structural barrier between literacy and a host of other disciplines whose contributions could have been crucial to the programme. By focusing sharply on the economic functions of literacy, at least early in the programme, UNDP and Unesco tended to ignore its other important components and functions. At Unesco Headquarters, and more sharply at its regional adult education centres in the Arab States (ASFEC) and Latin America (CREFAL), the effect of EWLP was to restrict rather than broaden efforts in the field of adult education.

Noting the various sectoral barriers, Unesco's Director-General [43] told the third International Conference on Adult Education (1972) that

it will probably be necessary, if we are to do justice to the full richness and complexity of the concept of adult education, to recast the structure of the Secretariat accordingly. . . . In point of fact, adult education and literacy work are at present the responsibility of one sector of the Organization, cultural development of

1. Designed and controlled from outside and above, baseline surveys and other studies of learners' expectations and motivations cannot be considered satisfactory replacements for such institutions. Conversely, 'felt needs' should not be considered the only viable source of objectives. But a better overall balance could have been struck.

another and the use of mass media of a third . . . we shall, I think, have to try to achieve the reunification of these various elements.[1]

Some observers doubted that EWLP-related United Nations Agencies could reform themselves sufficiently. Following the pattern of certain bilateral aid programmes, they suggest major subcontracting with specialized and/or operational research bodies. In retrospect, it does seem that more use could have been made by EWLP of existing bodies, particularly in the project countries but elsewhere as well.

Inter-national decentral-ization and . . .

While not seeking to shift prime responsibility from its shoulders, Unesco (for one) did recognize its own limitations to a degree, and attempted to achieve a measure of institutional decentralization and diversification. Decentralization took the form of mobilizing already existing Unesco centres, e.g. ASFEC and CREFAL. It also led to the creation in 1968 of the International Institute for Adult Literacy Methods in Tehran. Host government support was unstinting and, after some initial hesitation, the institute embarked on a regular publication programme (although not the planned research and training programme). Nevertheless, this programme has often tended to be weighted towards authors from industrialized countries. It is now striving to become more fully multilateral, particularly stressing the horizontal exchange of ideas and information between Third World countries, in which it still does not have notably strong intellectual or political roots.

. . . diver-sification

Institutional diversification (on Unesco's part, at least) involved the organization of a number of experts' meetings and the creation of several advisory groups, including especially: the Literacy Sub-committee of the International Advisory Committee for Out-of-school Education, the International Consultative Liaison Committee for Literacy, the Panel for the Evaluation of Literacy Projects and the Expert Evaluation Group. Although most participants were highly competent and experienced, these gatherings and groups cannot be said to have had a sustained and positive effect on the formulation or implementation of EWLP. With the exception of the panel, the committees tended to be short-lived,[2] met irregularly, and had frustratingly imprecise and/or changing mandates. At least some of their members seem to have felt their function was to legitimize, rather than inform or enrich, Secretariat decisions and policies.

Inter-agency co-operation

To the surprise of certain EWLP critics, United Nations inter-agency co-operation with Unesco and UNDP worked well in certain programme countries. This appears to have taken place whether the other agencies had signed the Plan of Operation (FAO in the Syrian Arab Republic and India)

1. L. Edström points out that, according to current Scandinavian thinking, 'aid to education should increasingly comprise aid also to what might be called the societal and economic infrastructure of education'. He asks hopefully: 'Will we in the future have less of a sector-oriented, more of a problem-centred and integrated approach to educational aid?' [9].
2. Created before the programme, but not surviving to its end; or surviving to its end, but created only after it was under way.

or not (FAO, ILO and Unicef in Sudan). Unfortunately, it is impossible to detect a consistent pattern of structural reasons (as compared, for example, with personal compatibilities among experts of various agencies) for successful inter-agency collaboration.

Success was far from universal, whether in the field or conceptually. In a region of one EWLP country, a Unesco-UNDP subproject was undermined when another United Nations Agency paid higher wages and drew off staff to a project which was totally unco-ordinated with the literacy effort. Elsewhere, technical differences led to severe strain in inter-agency teams.

At the conceptual level, it may be regretted that there was not more exchange among various United Nation agencies concerned with innovative thinking and action in the field of non-formal education. Still more unfortunate was the fundamental disagreement at various times in the programme between Unesco and UNDP about the relative priority to be accorded to literacy programmes in the framework of economic development and scarce international resources.

It is important to note that the Unesco-UNDP rift tended to be viewed by several EWLP countries as irrelevant. Much of the imprecision of basic EWLP notions resulted from the fact that the Unesco-UNDP disagreement was never satisfactorily resolved. The resultant tensions could not but weaken the programme. The lesson is clear. Inter-agency differences of principle on issues as important as literacy should not be allowed to fester. Fought to a stalemate in the wings, they provide a far less instructive performance than if played out to their logical conclusion—an honest working compromise—in the centre of the stage.

NGOs   Regarding non-United Nations bodies, EWLP's relations with international non-governmental organizations (NGOs) offer particularly pertinent guidance for the future. Many Unesco-related NGOs were heavily or at least marginally active in literacy when the programme began. But the prospect of participating in a decisive joint effort elicited a groundswell of interest and commitment in the NGO community probably unprecedented in the history of Unesco-NGO co-operation. The NGOs were not satisfied with the usual and rather passive exchange of information among themselves and with Unesco. They decided to co-operate jointly and actively with the world programme, initially by organizing regional NGO seminars on literacy in the Third World. According to one observer, the first seminar (1966)

spun a living web of mutual knowledge and friendship among key individuals in national and international governmental and non-governmental literacy program-mes in East Africa. It powerfully stimulated governmental and non-governmental literacy forces to intensify and harmonize their activities [13].

A participant observed that: 'This seminar has made history—the first time the NGO Standing Committee and Unesco have co-operated in this way' [13].

Following the three seminars, however, the movement of joint and active international NGO participation in EWLP slowed, and then stopped. Some NGOs (particularly women's organizations and trade unions) have begun, or have continued, to co-operate individually with Unesco in the field of literacy. This co-operation has helped orient NGOs towards more practical projects, and towards more relevant kinds of literacy and adult education—both being positive results of EWLP. Joint action in the framework of EWLP, however, died a premature death, depriving the programme of an important consortium of partners. Why? NGO interest in the programme did not diminish; not immediately, in any event. Rather, it would seem that EWLP itself was insufficiently interested in (or capable of) surpassing routine NGO-Unesco relations and devising new structures dynamic and flexible enough to attract continuing and highly enthusiastic co-operation. *Structure and . . .*

One senses, however, that structural inadequacy was not the only—perhaps not even the most important—obstacle to co-operation. A more appropriate rigging probably could not, alone, have kept sufficient wind in NGO sails. What was lacking perhaps was not so much a structure, as something less tangible (but more powerful): a new spirit of co-operation. Unesco perhaps tended to view NGOs as willing to collaborate mainly when handed blank (and preferably large) cheques. Conversely, NGOs at least sometimes seemed to feel that EWLP-defined functionality might undermine the functionality in terms of which their own literacy work was being undertaken. Also, while Unesco urged NGOs to be more methodologically rigorous in their literacy work, NGOs tended to look on these urgings as having too complicated and too costly implications. On the whole, it seems in retrospect that a less orthodox and more flexible spirit of co-operation might possibly have catalysed continuing and enthusiastic NGO participation. An appropriate structure would probably have emerged. *. . . spirit*

This conclusion may also be valid for EWLP's national and international institutional framework. That is, the correction of structural inadequacies probably depends less on the search for a perfect organigram than on the spirit that breathes life into the organigram. Nowhere was the importance of this qualitative factor more crucial than in the relationship between UNDP/Unesco and national structures.

The Experimental World Literacy Programme was an attempt to mount an avowedly innovative (and adaptive) entreprise through the structures of traditional multilateral aid. Not infrequently, the reality of aid reduces notions like 'partnership' to euphemistic rhetoric. To a degree this may have happened in EWLP.

That EWLP projects received more external aid for literacy than would have been the case without the programme is probably incontrovertible, but it is the spirit in which the aid was given that requires examination. It appears that, in EWLP, the spirit of partnership was not seldom replaced by a kind of doctor-patient relationship. Meister points out that the international agencies concerned tended to view the illiterate 'as a patient needing to be cured of an illness'. Thus, in the framework of EWLP, aid to literacy may have become 'a sort of graft on to a culture which may or may not "take" and the consequences of which cannot be foreseen' [28].

Grafts, transplants and . . .

In general, grafts and transplants are a chancy treatment to be used only in the last resort. According to a French text on *Immunologie Générale et Immunologie Médicale,* genetic incompatibilities may lead to 'a serious and possibly fatal syndrome' [19]. This seems to have happened on one or two EWLP projects, which had to be terminated prematurely, apparently due in large part to fundamental conflicts between the ideas and resources made available by donors and the needs and aspirations of recipients.

. . . rejec-tion

Elsewhere, literacy projects survived after the programme although sometimes in a stunted, listless state, with little propect of attaining robust health in the near future. This is akin to a reaction among graft and transplant hosts known as runt disease. Whatever the symptoms, it does not seem an exaggeration to say that EWLP's attempt to graft or transplant literacy concepts and resources into nations deemed to be educationally 'ill' resulted in a degree of rejection, due to incompatibility. In this respect, for example, a number of EWLP countries strongly resented what they viewed as the imposition by UNDP and Unesco of built-in evaluation.

EWLP post-mortem analyses tended to debate the appropriateness of the treatment dispensed. Would medication have been more successful than surgery? Should cash have been given instead of equipment? Should more printing presses have been sent and fewer books? Should experts have been reduced and fellowships increased? These debates about the internal work-ings of aid have their use. Indeed the present evaluation has attempted to con-tribute of them, and so belongs to a growing body of literature in this vein.[1]

Nevertheless, the experience of the world programme calls into question not only certain kinds and structures of treatment, but also the very notion of aid as a treatment applied by the 'healthy' to the 'ill'. A more pluralistic policy is definitely necessary. Under such a policy, countries wishing to continue to receive aid for literacy in the traditional spirit could naturally do so, but where there is a desire for innovation and renewal, a different spirit must come to prevail. There, the traditional relationship of what *Le Concept de l'Alphabétisation Fonctionnelle* calls 'centre' and 'periphery' [6] should be questioned.[2]

Centre/ periphery

Common sense suggests that the views of the United Nations and its Agencies are not central—and those of Third World countries peripheral—to the problem of illiteracy. EWLP thus has opened the door to a radical

1. See, for example, the following: Unesco's journal *Prospects,* summer 1974 issue, which analysed aid to education; *The Future Role of UNDP in World Development,* New York, UNDP, D.P.-114, March 1975; and Seth Spaulding, 'Needed: New Forms of Technical Cooperation in the Development of Education', *Focus: Technical Cooperation,* 1974/1, p. 3-7, Washington, D.C., Society for International Development.
2. The notion is reflected in a letter from an EWLP literacy expert to the Unesco Staff Association's newspaper as 'those feelings of frustration and incomprehension which are often (but not always) the corollary of remoteness and isolation [18].

revision of the United Nations system's current operational approach. External aid that artificially maintains the life of externally generated projects should be replaced with true co-operation conducive to internally generated change.

This is a major lesson of the programme. Generally, the achievement of national literacy is comparable to a genetic mutation. As such, it cannot be grafted or transplanted from the outside, and probably happens when the organism itself adapts to evolving conditions. The point is not to halt international co-operation, of course. Quite the contrary; co-operation should be enhanced, so as to become true—not rhetorical—partnership. One-way dependency should give way to increased interdependence. Just such an approach is beginning to gain acceptance in current United Nations system thinking about the forms its aid should take in the years to come.

Evaluation

EWLP began at a time when concern for rigorous assessment of education and international aid was growing quickly. This topicality, coupled with the programme's intentionally experimental character, gave evaluation a central role. At a 1965 meeting of a Unesco literacy experts committee, research and evaluation were declared to be the *raison d'être* of EWLP. Evaluation in EWLP has doubtless stirred great interest in the assessment of innovative non-formal education in the Third World. It has also stimulated the development of applied methodological research in this field. This is in contrast to evaluation of many other kinds of externally aided educational evaluation work which Unesco's 1975 *Operational Evaluation: A Basic Guide for Teacher-Trainers* reports as having 'met with remarkably little success' [30].

Understandably, evaluation of EWLP has not been exempt from growing pains. First of all, each project underwent a long initial process while the general concepts of the functional approach were being spelled out in operational terms. To the extent that evaluation depends on clearly defined programme objectives, little useful evaluation foundation could be laid. Furthermore, difficulties may be traced in part to a degree of confusion concerning purpose and priority. This confusion was largely responsible for further problems concerning the design, structure and timing of evaluation of the programme, all of which affected its results.

All of this likewise stemmed in part from the already discussed conflict between the technico-scientific and activist-pragmatic approaches to experimentation in EWLP. The technico-scientific approach to experimentation engendered summative (final) evaluation. This was evaluation conceived of as serving the long-term improvement of literacy thanks to a global assessment of the national project, the results of which could only be known *post facto*.[1] The chief proponents of summative evaluation were the United Nations agencies involved in EWLP, and particularly UNDP, which

Summative evaluation

1. This is opposed to formative evaluation, which is ongoing and decision-serving.

was intent on determining functional literacy's viability. National authorities (and perhaps not a few foreign experts) tended to perceive summative evaluation as an external imposition of little practical use. They either resisted it (Guinea, Madagascar and Mali) or accorded it a relatively low priority (India).

Summative evaluation tended to predominate in several EWLP countries.[1] It was intended to elicit scientific and internationally comparable data in areas related to EWLP's basic hypothesis about literacy and development. Its design required considerable innovation and resulted in methodological progress, for example EWLP's internationally Standardized Data Reporting System (a system established for reporting project data) and a number of measurement indicators used in the technical reports being prepared by Unesco. The summative approach's ingenious footwork however does on occasion seem to have taken EWLP unnecessarily far from the most useful path of evaluation it could have followed.

The research requirements imposed by a design intended to differentiate between results attributable to the three R's and those caused by (or correlated with) vocational training or other aspects of project activities were not acceptable to some programme governments. In certain projects involving agriculture, there was increased use of fertilizer due to: (a) newly literate farmers' ability to read, write and do arithmetic; (b) their familiarity with the advantages of fertilizer; (c) their skill in fertilizer use; (d) the creation of a structure for free distribution of fertilizer, or (e) some other project-related (or other) factor? Summative evaluation could perhaps reasonably have been expected to provide answers to such fundamental queries.

The rather narrow vocational productivist focus of the predominant evaluation design meant that certain important effects (positive or negative) in other areas and at other stages of literacy work tended to be overlooked. What was learned about those organizational structures that were most effective? What effect on conceptions of teaching (and on the individuals concerned) was produced by the mobilization of numerous non-professional instructors? What impact did projects have on other forms of literacy? On other kinds of adult education? On schooling? On mass media? On book production? On national (and international) staffs? EWLP does not seem able to offer even beginnings of answers to these types of questions.

The option for a scientific and internationally comparable approach further limited results in two ways. First was a comprehensible but regrettable tendency to over-quantify at the cost of ignoring research procedures capable of generating pertinent—including qualitative—data. Single-minded preoccupation with ever more sophisticated quantification at least sometimes blinded EWLP evaluators to simple truths that were in plain view. On occasion, it thus led them into dead-end logic. In one country, possession of a fountain pen was used as one of sixteen items

*Quantity
v.
quality*

1. Although there is not necessarily a theoretical dichotomy between summative and formative evaluation, they were frequently treated as mutually exclusive concepts during EWLP.

indicating consumption of durable goods in pre- and post-teaching tests given to learners and to a control group of illiterates. Although it is not suggested that qualitative evaluation should predominate, in future a better balance between quantitative and qualitative evaluation of literacy action should be struck. EWLP evaluators' inability or unwillingness to develop simple instruments of systematic qualitative assessment was possibly one of its chief methodological drawbacks.

The second limit was imposed by EWLP's concern that evaluation results should be internationally comparable. There seems to have been increasing pressure to produce evidence that functional literacy was indeed worthwhile. This, in turn, led to the formulation of centrally imposed evaluation directives. The underlying assumption was that the programme's hypothesis was universally valid, whatever the local or national circumstances.

But the rigidity of EWLP approach to functionality led, at the conclusion of the projects, to the selection by the Evaluation Unit attached to Unesco's Literacy Division of very limited evaluation criteria to treat the varied data generated by the national projects. For example, under the general heading of transformation of the milieu, indicators were devised for testing changes in new literates' behaviour in the following categories: means of production, volume of production, monetary income, income in kind, consumption of durable goods.[1] These indicators say virtually nothing about vital behaviours concerning social, political or cultural 'transformation of the milieu',[2] even though pertinent data were available in certain project evaluation studies.

In addition, the criteria finally retained tended to reflect a given model of society whose values were rejected outright by more than one EWLP country and seriously questioned in several. Thus, the use of 'consumption of durable goods' as a criterion of 'transformation of the milieu' was, to say the least, a curious projection on to poor nations of a consumer-oriented system peculiar to certain highly industrialized societies. In one EWLP country where *per capita* annual GNP is less than $200, this 'consumption' criterion was broken down into indicators that included safety razors and wrist watches,[3] relatively luxurious articles of individual consumption. There was not a single criterion or indicator to ascertain whether newly literate communities[4] undertook joint efforts to 'transform the milieu' by

1. A similar critique may be made of the heavily value-laden orientation of the two other major categories of behaviour chosen for evaluation: 'insertion into the milieu' and 'mastery of the milieu'.
2. Certain efforts were made, however, to ascertain changes in socio-cultural attitudes (as distinct from behaviours).
3. A recent study made by War on Want (United Kingdon) showed that the 1 billion CFA francs repatriated annually by 100,000 emigrant workers from a rural region in one African country are spent primarily on consumer goods similar to these, as well as to purchase property in the capital city. This income has done nothing to 'transform the milieu' of the region in question (which happenened to be situated in the Sahel).
4. The only specifically social (as opposed to individual) behaviour measured by the EWLP evaluation was 'participation in formal organizations'. This was not treated under the category of 'transformation of the milieu' but under that of 'insertion into the milieu'.

the creation of a social infrastructure such as schools, clinics, pure-water wells, etc.[1]

Structure
Often perceived as an external intrusion, internationally favoured summative evaluation tended to be structurally side-tracked by certain national project authorities.[2] Independent as they were of projects which were already autonomous, even those evaluation units that could have contributed to ongoing decision-making, sometimes found themselves at two removes from power. The low priority most units enjoyed meant that they were chronically under-staffed—so much so in at least two cases that external experts had to undertake full executive responsibility, which only further estranged evaluation from national structures. In one of these a UNDP expert found the unit constantly 'on the defensive' and saddled with ill-qualified staff.

In this context, it may be emphasized, however, that the technical assistance concept in use treated the evaluation expert as an adviser and training resource person for national staff rather than a researcher who could take on the complex responsibilities demanded of a national evaluation unit. The resident foreign expert evaluator, furthermore, ran the risk of losing touch with the rapid developments in his field. He was also subject to many and conflicting pressures to support the project on the one hand, and to provide donors with objective and reliable data about its performance, on the other.

Part of the national staffing problem admittedly arose from the scientific aspirations of EWLP evaluation. These raised the threshold of minimal necessary competence above the ceiling of available man- and woman-power in most programme countries. A fruitful alternative (to be noted for the future) might well have been to adapt evaluation structures more thoroughly to existing national resources[3] of different kinds rather than insist on maintaining an international 'standard', which may anyway be ethnocentric or otherwise ill-suited. The experience of Mali's tomato production programme, in which learners undertook a continuing self-evaluation could usefully have been studied in this innovative context. (In Mali also, secondary-school pupils proved useful in collecting data.) Terminal self-testing might also be applied, in certain cases at least. E. Rogers and M. Herzog have shown a highly significant statistical correlation between Colombian farmer-learners' assessments of their levels of literacy attainment (positive and negative) and external measurement of those levels [38].

---

1. Baseline studies in Mali did take socio-economic infrastructure into account, but they were not followed up in post-teaching evaluation.
2. The substantive isolation of the Unesco Evaluation Unit from the Regular Programme officers of the Unesco Literacy Division (in which the unit was physcially located) reflected this situation at the international level.
3. In some cases this may require a merger of sorts beween evaluation and ongoing knowledge-testing used for other purposes (e.g. marking). It should not be forgotten that these two kinds of measurement serve overlapping but distinct purposes.

A major lesson of EWLP evaluation's timing is the need to schedule *Timing* more realistically at the national and international levels; this is valid for summative and formative (decision-serving) evaluation. In some instances, sufficient time does seem to have been allowed in EWLP. The Sudanese evaluation unit, for one, planned its studies well in advance of their execution. On the whole, however, evaluation exercises tended to be characterized by initial, growing and, on occasion, irreparable delays. The international preparation and national use of the baseline survey was an important case in point.

The baseline survey was meant both to provide information on the basis of which teaching objectives could be determined and to serve as a pre-literacy benchmark against which learner change could be measured. In this double role it was a major point of juncture between international and national concerns, i.e. between summative and formative evaluation. Not surprisingly, this mutal reinforcement of interests placed the baseline survey in a particularly advantageous position. It proved useful for both purposes in a number of cases, but as often as not it arrived too late for one or the other. By definition, a baseline survey is more useful if carried out before the intervention to be studied begins. EWLP's baseline instrument, however, was distributed by Unesco in July 1967, when the Algerian, Ecuadorian and Iranian projects were either in, or fast approaching, their operational phase. In Mali, baseline results only became available once teaching of the first batch of courses had begun.

There were a number of reasons for these delays. One of the most critical was the imprecision that reigned from the beginning of EWLP, about both the purpose of evaluation and the basic concepts and goals of the programme as a whole. According to R. Mager:[1] If we don't know where we're going, we can't know when we've arrived.' The world programme appears to have been in this dilemma. It embarked on a voyage with only a hazy idea of its destination.[2] Could it have been expected to measure with any precision its advance toward an imprecise goal? Colombus set out for India but was happy enough to land in America. Because of its attempt primarily to measure progress toward (imprecise) goals, EWLP summative evaluation collected little data to indicate where it actually fetched up. Did the programme discover a new world of literacy? It is perhaps too soon for definitve judgements, but for the present its evaluators seem to have little way of knowing.

Fortunately, stress was laid in some cases on formative (rather than summative) evaluation early enough to offer national decision-makers useful information. For instance, Bazany (evaluator for the Iran project), stated that

---

1. Quoted in *Operational Evaluation,* op.cit. [30].
2. So hazy, indeed, that it was only possible to formulate precise hypotheses once the programme was over.

functional literacy considered as an instructional theory was little more than a loose agglomeration of assumptions and inferences supported by unsystematic findings and a considerable element of faith.

He then pointed out, in essence, that summative evaluation of a classical nature was impossible. Instead, a new variant of the formative evaluation approach ('evaluation-research' in his terms) was found more appropriate in that project.

This approach consisted of field studies designed to indentify appropriate objectives and modifiable and unmodifiable factors that might influence the achievement of these objectives. Then, various organizational and pedagogical approaches were tried, field-tested (assessed) and modified, on the basis of field experience. As Bazany observed, this formative evaluation approach assumed that

the problem is primarily one of evolving rather than evaluating an instructional technology. The evaluator is an active participant in programme development, not solely the judge of its outcome [4].

Indeed, through such formative evaluation (closely akin to research and development) various useful lessons were learned, a number of them described elsewhere in this report. Unfortunately, only the Iran team (and then very late in the project) gave primary emphasis to this approach, although some other projects included elements of this kind of formative evaluation.

Confusion as to the purpose of evaluation, a narrowly-focused and quantity-oriented evaluation design laden with a not always appropriate set of values, structures that tended to side-track rather than expedite evaluation, chronic delays due in part to attempts to evaluate progress toward EWLP's imprecise goals—these and other problems weakened the EWLP's self-assessment effort. In the end, rather a lot was spent on an evaluation that produced generally disappointing results.

In common with much evaluation of more traditional kinds of education (e.g. schooling), but with the difficulties compounded by its innovative nature, the EWLP assessment was unable to collect sufficiently systematic, comparable or comprehensive information. Although perfection would have been impossible, a great part of the data provided to the Unesco Evaluation Unit proved unreliable and/or invalid. Moreover, both the design of evaluation and the interpretation of its results are largely conditioned by the values of the designers and interpreters.

In the final analysis, it may be wondered in retrospect if international summative evaluation of EWLP did not assume an importance somewhat out of proportion to the results yielded. Indeed, future evaluators of such efforts—not only in literacy but in education and still broader development fields—might do well to heed the Malaysian proverb and 'Beware, lest the leash cost more than the monkey.' This being said, it does seem that, if kept

Monkey or leash?

simple, conceived clearly, designed flexibly and imaginatively, and scheduled realistically, evaluation has an undeniably valuable potential role in literacy work. Its value may be greatest at the national level in helping decision-makers; on condition, of course, that decision-makers (a) do not place blind faith in evaluation, and (b) sincerely want evaluation to inform—rather than merely legitimize—their decisions.

Doing the job: implementation

The combination of motivations (see page 115 et seq.) and resources (see page 131 et seq.) resulted in the implementation of the Experimental World Literacy Programme's projects. The basic question is: what happened? The answers and their related guidelines for future action fall into the following categories: curriculum (what was taught?); learners (who was taught?); methods (how was teaching done?); language (what were linguistic achievements and problems?); and timing (how were the programme and projects scheduled?).

Curriculum

Integration A major feature of EWLP was the principle of integration, which was to guide the identification and organization of subject matter in curricula.[1] As the curricular expression of functionality, it was expected to be one of the programme's most practical innovations, at least in comparison to such unintegrated forms of education extant in certain EWLP countries as foreign-inspired primary schooling.

The application of the principle of integration to the selection of subject matter was meant to ensure the practical relevance of the curriculum to learners' daily lives. In a very general way (and as common sense might well have predicted), learners seem to have appreciated this attempt to achieve relevance. Activities in the Mali groundnut programme, for example, were the more popular for their linkages with student concerns, among other reasons. In Ethiopia, curricula were focused (and vocabulary chosen) in function of learner 'centres of interest'.

Obstacles were encountered by integrative identification of subject matter, however. For one thing, the very principle was sometimes misunderstood (or not accepted) at the outset. It was not until two years

---

1. Interested readers will find numerous examples of contents and articulations of the curricula actually used in EWLP in the *Practical Guide to Functional Literacy* [33].

after its project began, for instance, that India opted for curricula based on learners' problems. Another issue was: how were problems to be identified? The methods applied by EWLP became increasingly sophisticated, at least in certain projects, as the know-how about the functional-literacy approach accumulated. In all projects, some type of problem survey was carried out at the individual and/or group level. In some projects, surveys were carried out among supervisory personnel and development agents; in others, the potential participants were interviewed. In some, both types of studies were undertaken, ensuring that both the technical expertise and felt needs of future learners could be taken into account. Some studies were not completed in time to be of use. Not all studies completed were useful for curriculum development. One reason was that they revealed problems that could not conceivably be solved by literacy.

Relevant portions of surveys were translated into curriculum materials in various ways, e.g. writing workshops, discussion groups with illiterates, operational seminars, and field testing followed by revision. In some instances, progressively improved versions of curricula on the same subject matter were prepared.

Who determined what was a 'problem' and what was not? There was *What is a* undoubtedly a need to harmonize learners' perceptions with those of other *'problem'?* parties involved (entreprises, educational authorities, development bodies, etc.), but too often perhaps this need was used to legitimize the setting of instructional objectives that did not sufficiently take learner aspirations into account. In almost all projects, moreover, objectives were set in an un-balanced way. In two countries, only the economic development authorities identified the problems. In three others, the decision was taken by the literacy projects, which were unable to obtain the participation of development authorities. In still another, expatriate experts decided virtually alone.

Despite these obstacles, EWLP does offer evidence supporting the link between a problem-oriented curriculum, on the one hand, and results judged to be favourable, on the other. Analysis of all programmes that produced statistically significant socio-economic effects deemed to be positive led the Evaluation Unit attached to Unesco's Literacy Division to formulate the following hypothesis:

The more closely content focuses on problems actually encountered by workers in the course of their productive activity, the more effective the functional literacy programme [2].

Data selected from two projects (India and the United Republic of Tanzania) tend generally to confirm this hypothesis.

What degree of specificity of problem focus in curricula is most *How* advantageous? The logic of work-related functionality suggests that *specific?* functional literacy's efficiency ought to increase with the degree of curricular specificity. For example, subject matter related to a single product should yield better results than teaching about several products within the same professional branch, which in turn should be more successful than curricula covering several branches each of which includes several products. Study of the Iranian sugar-beet programme, which was highly specific, seemed to bear out this assumption. However, enrolment data indicate that many participants in the sugar-beet programme were not sugar-beet growers, perhaps suggesting that problem orientations need not be occupationally specific to the learners. Furthermore, analysis of the more general Iranian agricultural programmes revealed (statistically significant) socio-economic changes judged by EWLP to be positive. It may therefore be concluded that very high curricular specificity is not necessarily a sufficient precondition for the success of a programme. This would appear to place in serious doubt one of the basic tenets of functionality as defined by EWLP.

In fact, research on all EWLP programmes that produced statistically significant socio-economic effects deemed favourable showed that, rather than high vocational specificity,

the more the content of the course takes into account the workers' cultural environment, the more effective the functional literacy programme [2].

A dynamic environment seems to be more conducive to success than a static one. The above-mentioned research concluded that functional literacy

brings about a change for the better on condition that it is associated with a process of genuine innovation (of a political, social or technical nature) in which the participants are themselves involved [2].

By and large, then: (a) relevant problem-based curricula seem to have produced results judged to be positive[1] by EWLP when (b) subject matter was not necessarily narrowly, rigidly or mechanically specific in terms of learners' jobs, but when (c) it took into account a broader environment that was (d) characterized by true innovations that personally concerned the participants.

In EWLP the principle of integration was meant to be applied to the organization and presentation (as well as the preparation) of literacy curricula. How did this work out in practice? Efforts were intended to bring about two kinds of integration in particular: between the three R's on the one hand and additional (especially vocational) subject matter, on the other; and between theoretical and practical aspects of subject matter.

The systematic extension of literacy curricula to include, in addition to the three R's, other (vocational) subject matter was a major innovation of EWLP. In this regard, the balance between the two subject areas varied widely from project to project.

---

1. EWLP value judgements on the effects of literacy were discussed briefly during the examination of evaluation in the previous chapter and will be analysed more fully in the next chapter when the programme's socio-economic effects are considered.

In Sudan, only three or four new words were introduced in each class session because stress was placed on transmitting technical knowledge. At the other extreme were Algeria and Mali, where the three R's occupied 80 per cent of class time. Other countries fell somewhere between these poles, nevertheless favouring the three R's. The overall average for the eight countries for which data are available was two-thirds of the time devoted to the three R's and one-third to other material.

The achievement of a balance between the three R's and other subjects was not sufficient to ensure their integration. Different instructors and texts sometimes reinforced their not infrequent separation in curricula. This organization and presentation doubtless reflected the sharply categorized structure of formal primary schooling, but it seems to have been alien to many adult learners. It may consequantly have made learning more arduous than it would have been were the subjects integrated rather than juxtaposed. *Three R's v 'functional' subjects?*

In this area, EWLP's practice fell short of the programme's innovative principle. Integration was too often interpreted as merely requiring the addition of primarily vocational subjects to the three R's in literacy curricula. Even Unesco referred on occasion to these added subjects as the 'particularly functional' parts of the teaching programmes. The need to 'functionalize' the three R's as well was too often underestimated or ignored altogether. Iran and Madagascar were fortunate exceptions. There, reading, writing and arithmetic were used as a means for transmitting the technical content of subjects presented elsewhere in the literacy curriculum.

An overriding reason to integrate the three R's and vocational subjects was the need to ally theoretical and practical material. Unlike schooling, EWLP projects could not wait until the acquisition of hermetically divided areas of knowledge eventually facilitated better performance in farm or factory. Academic categorization had to give way to immediate and progressive syntheses of theoretical knowledge and practical know-how. *Theoretical and practical subjects*

The importance of integration in the organization and presentation of curricula has been underscored by attempts to evaluate EWLP scientifically. Projects were studied where statistically significant (and favourably judged) socio-economic effects were detected among new literates. The conclusion was that 'the integration of educational content increases the effectiveness of functional literacy work' [2].

Learners

Who enrolled in EWLP classes? What were actual participation rates? And, in broader terms, what was the quality of participation? The answers to these questions are perhaps of particular interest to the organizers of future literacy action.

As propounded by the EWLP, 'functionality' treated literacy as an economic investment destined to yield short-term results through the improvement of vocational skills. Projects designed in accord with this interpretation could not but project a certain ideal learner profile. To a degree, enrollees corresponded to that profile. In terms of age, for example, nearly three-quarters of all EWLP learners were in the 15 to 34 age range, i.e. in the group most likely to have an immediate (and possibly innovative) economic impact. The Unesco Secretariat prided itself on this result, which it called an important intellectual and vocational investment [1]. Vocationally oriented programmes (chiefly agriculture, but also including industry and artisanry) were organized for 91 per cent of EWLP enrollees, while only 9 per cent were involved in non-vocational (social and women's) programmes. Since vocational programmes were open to women, and since women play a very important agricultural role in many EWLP countries, the fact that females accounted for some 55 per cent of all programme enrollees may further enhance the economically functional profile of learners although in many cases they had no other choice of courses.

Equity v. . . .

The figure on female participation, however, also seems to bespeak strong equity, compared to other forms of education in EWLP countries (e.g. schooling) which generally feature much higher enrolments of males than females. Such equity was not deliberately sought by EWLP. In Iran, for example, project organizers seem to have had considerable difficulty in limiting enrolments in agricultural classes to farmers, so great was the social demand for literacy from an increasingly diverse population. In terms of future action, EWLP's more than occasional preference for the most favoured of the impoverished—a kind of 'élite'—seen as needing only a small educational push to move over the threshold of modernity, may well limit the replicability of its approach. What of the truly disinherited, often the majority of a nation's population, who find themselves very far from the

. . . the 'élite' of the impoverished

threshold? In Sudan, groups selected for EWLP literacy were unrepresentative of the often still nomadic population. Yet the Sudanese authorities intended to generalize literacy, albeit progressively, once the programme's experimental work was completed. Dilemmas like this seem inherent in EWLP's narrowly economic functionality.

On first sight, enrollees' participation rates in literacy classes organized under EWLP seem far from satisfactory. In Madagascar, married learners proved much less likely to drop out of courses than single men and women, but family responsibilities made absenteeism more frequent among them than among other non-dropouts. In Sudan, while absenteeism among those who stayed in classes was relatively low (ranging from 12 to 23 per cent) the dropout rate among initial enrollees took a heavy toll (23 per cent to 95 per cent). The Ethiopian project found that adults hoped to attain results more quickly than the classes could produce them. Slow progress seems to have been an important cause of a high dropout rate. Of every eight people enrolling in the project's first stage, only one reached the last stage. Algeria did better, but fully one-half of the enrollees in its project dropped out before completing both cycles. The implications are rather staggering. No matter how widely the EWLP approach was applied, it would be impossible to achieve universal literacy.

Lest these figures be judged too harshly, it is well to recall that, in most cases, they seem on a par with other literacy efforts and other forms of basic education. It might reasonably have been hoped that education relevant to learners' problems and aspirations would have attracted more persistent participation. Either EWLP literacy was not perceived as relevant enough in those terms or (when it was so perceived) even relevance was incapable of exercising exceptional magnetism. In any event, experience of EWLP does not appear to offer a clear set of practical measures which literacy organizers can take to ensure more satisfactory rates of learner participation. Perhaps, indeed, it is less a question of taking practical measures than of creating a favourable psychological (and hence political) climate. Further, it may be thought that the selective and experimental dimensions of the programme perhaps limited its potential for generating such a climate.

Issues of climate affect not only the rate but also the quality of learner *Quality* participation in literacy. Quality of participation pertains to the atmosphere *of partici-* and spirit of learner relationships both inside classes and in literacy-related *pation* class dealings with various local institutions.

Within classes, it may be wondered to what extent disparate individuals who probably only knew each other in non-educational settings (if at all) coalesced into learning groups. Such grouping may have been inhibited where stress was placed on individualistic and hence competitive motivations for literacy, such as personal upward mobility. On the other hand, where groups did form themselves as small communities around literacy activities, they could fulfil a number of useful functions.

In industrialized as well as Third World countries, there is often something of a stigma attached to adults who take part in education, which is normally thought to be reserved for children. The creation of a group identity that positively values adult learning can help offset doubts in the minds of adult learners and of their neighbours. The actual process of learning can also be facilitated through group interaction. On this subject, Guinea attempted to achieve learning objectives through the creation of a group spirit in its literacy classes, but there is little evidence that many EWLP projects recognized—much less took systematic and explicit advantage of—the potential for peer teaching among class members. This *Peer* possibility might fruitfully be explored in the future, the more so since *teaching* various forms of peer teaching are still a lively tradition in at least some highly illiterate societies.

The development of strong group identity and autonomy in literacy classes has also been seen as a means of reducing the anxiety that new literates may have felt under certain circumstances in connexion with their explicity intended role as innovators. Social sanctions may be less severe if whole groups change behaviour with the support of external authorities. Isolated innovators may be treated as renegades or outcasts. Cohesive groups of innovators, although sometimes suspect at first, may come to be considered as pioneers.

Part of this problem relates to the question of who is innovating and who is judging. Let us take the case of a coalition of chemical manufacturers, local money-lenders, profit-motivated landlords and government officials who conceive of development as economic growth. This coalition is likely to view attempts to encourage the innovative use of artificial fertilizer rather differently from the penniless and landless peasant who is expected to become the innovator.[1] In other words, group cohesion *per se,* when sought as a means of favouring innovation, is not always a sufficient indicator of who will benefit most by the innovation in question.

In favourable contexts, nevertheless, group identity and cohesion can be a useful goal in literacy classes. How it can be brought about depends partly on teaching methods (discussed in the next section) and partly on other factors. Uppermost among these are class size and instructor attitudes.

Instructor to learner ratios

Probably the lower the instructor to learner ratio the better; in the Cuban campaign it was of the order of 1 : 7. But EWLP generally contended with severe man- and woman-power constraints. Iran's original project request planned a 1 : 11 instructor to pupil ratio. The figure dropped to 1 : 6 in the Plan of Operation, which proved optimistic since, in reality, the ratio was 1 : 34. This was very close to the Tanzanian average of about 1 : 35, and of the same order of magnitude as the average figure in India, 1 : 30.

These statistics do not give an exact idea of real class sizes since actual attendance rates were not up to initial enrolment rates. Also one instructor may have taught two or more classes or, conversely, a single instructor may only have been responsible for teaching part of a class's schedule. National project-wide class sizes ranged from an average of twenty-two in the Syrian Arab Republic to an average of forty-six in the United Republic of Tanzania, with the programme-wide average of national averages being thirty-seven.

Instructor attitudes towards class participation, however, may on occasion have been more influential than even class size in determining learner participation. Authoritarian attitudes of the more schooled towards the less schooled may exist (or at least be expected by the less schooled) and reflect existing power relationships in formal education or the community at large. As a result, even where instructors attempt to encourage participatory behaviour on the part of learners, their intentions may be misunderstood (by the learners, among others) and be followed by little effect. Alternatively, they may be all too clearly understood (by landlords, officials, etc.) and perhaps even judged subversive.

Community/class relations

There is, then, a vital link between the quality of participation within literacy classes and the quality of their relationships with the surrounding community. Most projects did considerable pre-class spadework at the village level. In the United Republic of Tanzania, for example, centre committees were created preceding the already-described class committees, which were elected only once classes were formed. They involved community leaders, local administrative officials and political cadres in planning and launching the classes, and thus gave them an investment in

1. This *scénario* is very close to the actual situation in at least one EWLP country.

class success. In the Ethiopian textile subproject, the co-operative attitude of Bahr Dar mill management seems to have been a key factor in the good results obtained. Conversely, in another EWLP country, the 'negative attitude' of farm officials was the most frequent reason given by new literates (32 per cent of those surveyed) for dissatisfaction with their programme.

It may be pointed out that good co-operation with the surrounding *milieu*—in whatever kind of education—is not positive *per se*. Some observers would maintain that if the village or factory power structure exploits illiterates, then good co-operation may (a) dissuade them from becoming literate, or (b) teach them that by becoming literate they can abandon the ranks of the exploited, possibly to join those of the exploiters.

A final point on the quality of class/community relations concerns the kinds of institutions with which literacy instructors and students co-operate. General EWLP practice, where co-operation was actively sought, seems to have been to prefer structures identified as 'dynamic', 'modern' or 'development-related': co-operatives, factories, plantations and the like. An important opportunity may have been ignored to enlist traditional popular institutions (often of pre-colonial origin) in the execution of tasks compatible both with the functions of such institutions and with the needs of literacy.

In Ecuador, *mingas* (communal labour) has been revived in connexion *Non-* with various local development efforts. Could it not have played a role in *Western* the country's EWLP project, for example in building or refurbishing *institutions* facilities for classes, or in offering a socio-economic framework for practical demonstration activities?[1] The *kisumba* (village-level young adults peer group) traditional in Sukumaland, where the Tanzanian project was focused, could perhaps have made similar contributions. Given its cultural and educational—in addition to productive—functions, the *kisumba* might also have been appropriate for enhancing a literacy-conducive atmosphere, or even organizing literacy classes. The same may be said of the Malian *ton* and the informal mutual-aid and savings 'societies' found in Ethiopian towns and cities, generally comprising from six to a dozen young men who have emigrated from the countryside.

Naturally, one must proceed carefully and take into account the full complexity of the situations obtaining in the countries mentioned.[2] The cases quoted are, therefore, only symbolic of the networks of traditional popular institutions that still exist in many Third World countries. The point is not to bring about their artificial reanimation, but to be aware of non-Western modes of communication, affiliation, learning and power. This awareness might be viewed as a possibly important step towards ensuring that literacy is spread in ways consistent with the desire of growing numbers

1. In Iran, the Koran was studied with a view to identifying texts compatible with motivating illiterates.
2. Nevertheless, the underlying concern does seem to correspond to (for example) Tanzania's declared aim of building a society rooted in the values of *ujamaa*—traditional African 'familyhood' or 'communityhood'.

of Third World countries to resist external cultural penetration in line with the Declaration of the Intergovernmental Conference on Cultural Policies in Asia (Yogyakarta, 1973) that 'collective self-realization and the authentic liberation of peoples is the quintessence of the humane society' [20].

In summary, it has been suggested that although EWLP learner attendance rates were on a par with those of other forms of basic training, still better rates can probably be attained where there is psychological (and political) mobilization. The importance of group spirit in classes has been pointed to, as has the potential of peer teaching and the need to maintain a reasonable instructor to learner ratio. The quality of relations between the class and surrounding institutions—including traditional non-Western institutions—has also been stressed.

Methods

According to Unesco's 1967 *Guide* for the preparation of EWLP projects, a broad objective of the programme was to develop a new method of literacy adapted to adults' needs [15]. As in the field of curriculum, however, innovative work does not seem to have had a notable impact on literacy in the narrow sense of apprenticeship in the three R's.[1] Teaching of arithmetic was modified on occasion but, in general, projects seem to have used a mixture of methods ranging from school teaching to literacy teaching designed prior to—or outside—the programme.

On the whole, efforts to build a new adult-oriented pedagogy (sometimes called andragogy) were focused on the vocational and other non-three-R subjects. In this area an at least occasional failing was the tendency to transfer school pedagogy with little or no adaptation, much less original innovation. This contradiction reached extreme proportions in Algeria where the curriculum laid great stress on techniques of popular participation in the governance of self-managing farms but where teaching methods were school-like, that is, highly directive. The form of learning directly undermined its content.

Despite such hindrances, three basic elements of adult-oriented pedagogy were used on a fairly widespread basis in the programme, and seem to have shown their worth. The first was a strongly inductive approach to learners' acquisition of knowledge. In the school class, knowledge is transfered almost exclusively from the teacher to the taught. In *Adults'* contrast, several EWLP projects gave explicit recognition to adults' *experience* experience and insights as a valid starting point for learning.

and The sequence of the Guinean teaching contained no less than eight *insights* steps but began with group discussions. In Madagascar, the educational

---

1. There was (and perhaps still is) confusion about the innovative intentions of EWLP regarding methodology. Was 'the functional literacy method', so often referred to, an attempt to link literacy and development? Or was it also to be a new way of teaching the three R's? (concrete examples of methods used in EWLP projects may be found in the *Practical Guide to Functional Literacy* already referred to).

process also started with group discussion, during which participants analysed their technical problems and reviewed solutions. Only afterwards were these possible solutions grouped into key sentences as a support to literacy instruction. Lessons in Sudan began with the presentation of a problem in one of several ways (oral, filmstrip, etc.) after which learners were encouraged to pool their experiences and reach a group decision on the best solution. Observation and analysis of inductive learning[1] in the framework of EWLP led Meister to conclude that

overall, the teacher's view of the adult pupil has been enriched by the realization that the illiterate adult knows and understands many things; their approach has therefore become more and more andragogic [28].

Secondly, EWLP succeeded on occasion in showing the value of practical demonstrations, curriculum-related work and other forms of experiential learning (learning by doing). The locale of teaching and learning *Learning* frequently shifted from classroom to demonstration plots, fields for actual *by doing* production and workshops of various kinds. In Sudan, substantial use was made of field visits, demonstration farms, poultry houses and production equipment. Guinea, too, stressed practical demonstrations in factories and fields. Ecuador attached demonstration plots to its project, as did the United Republic of Tanzania where each agricultural class had a *shamba* (field) on which demonstrations took place and learners carried out productive work, which at least sometimes yielded a financial profit.

A study was carried out of the effect of demonstration fields on the adoption of new crops and techniques by farmer-learners in six Iranian communities. Results showed that the behaviour change varied as a function of learners' real prospects of post-class application of new knowledge and skills. Thus effects deemed positive were not found among illiterates below the age of 25 who did not own or have access to land. The reverse was true of older and autonomous farmers.

The study attempted to determine differences in the rate of adoption of new crops and techniques between older autonomous farmers in classes with demonstration plots, and two kinds of control groups: (a) classes without demonstration plots, and (b) farmers not attending literacy classes. Statistically significant differences were found between the first (experimental) group and both control groups. The evaluators concluded that

the use of a demonstration plot in the village in conjunction with a functional literacy course contributes significantly towards the adoption of new crops and new farming methods by older and independent farmers [2].

A final pedagogical lesson of EWLP would seem to be that it is advisable to use a variety of methods and techniques. This was not an explicit hypothesis *Variety* at the start (or finish) of EWLP nor was systematic research done on the

---

1. Group discussion is not necessarily inductive learning. Leaders with 'hidden agendas' and subtle managerial techniques can rigidly structure discussion that seems superficially non-directive.

subject, but the adult status of learners, the orientation toward practical relevance, and the diversity and complexity of subjects covered seem to have led to the empirical use of several teaching methods in almost any given EWLP class. A typical Sudanese class had recourse to: (a) oral exposition by the instructor; (b) oral exposition by visiting technical staff (e.g. extension workers); (c) joint class discussion (problem-focused and/or analytic and/or solution-oriented); (d) audio-visual aids (particularly film-strips); (e) individual and joint use of textbooks and reading cards; (f) field visits; (g) practical demonstrations.

EWLP's methodological variety, which was by no means limited to Sudan, may have helped maintain adult interest and attendance thanks to what is technically known as 'stimulus variation'. Equally important, it perhaps facilitated learning by bringing the teaching/learning process closer to the multi-sensoral world in which illiterates (like other people) live. In this connexion, more study would be necessary to determine the most favourable mixes and balances among various methods in relation to different kinds of subject matter. More research—and experimentation—would also help determine the utility of other suggestions made here, particularly regarding ways of taking advantage of adult learners' experience and insights, and more systematic efforts with experiential 'learning by doing'.

Language

Language was an area of both achievement and dilemma in EWLP. At a time when there was sometimes considerable hesitation over abandoning colonially-imposed languages as media of school instruction, the pro-gramme gave generally strong impetus to the rehabilitation of Third World tongues in education outside the school. In certain cases EWLP's influence was strong. Partly thanks to the programme, for example, a special team in Mali achieved a number of remarkable results. This team worked on the transcription in Latin characters of the national languages: Mande, Peul, Tamasheq and Songhai. It prepared a lexicon of Bambara (a variant of Mande), selected words expressing the notions of Bambara grammar and of arithmetic, and prepared a French-language *Grammaire de la Phrase Bambara*. In India, functional literacy training and materials had to be distributed in no less than nine languages, which seems to have required the development of number of 'new' words in certain instances. This raises a broader and longer-term issue of particular relevance to countries with a number of languages, some of which may be spoken by relatively few people. Although it is good conceptual sense for people to be made literate in their own language, the long-term implications of developing reading materials in these languages should be taken into account. Mali, for one, recognized the need for continuous attention to the problem through the establishment of a national linguistics centre.

But the multiplicity of languages used in EWLP also created a number of problems. Most of the Indian materials were translated from Hindi, and even careful testing and revision does not seem always to have attained the double aim of maintaining the original and precise meaning while making it thoroughly comprehensible to non-Hindi speakers. The translation problem was compounded—occasionally several times over—by the fact that original texts were sometimes written by foreign experts. In one country, for instance, technical flash cards were designed in English and translated into the national language. When independently translated back into English they departed markedly from the original text. In another case, materials were originally drafted in Russian, then translated into English for discussion by national and international staffs, and then translated yet again into the national language for distribution to learners who did not speak Russian or English—or the national language, for that matter.

Language is not only a tool for communication. It is also a vehicle that *A vehicle* expresses and transmits values. The drawback of the linguistic gymnastics *of values* just described was not, therefore, merely the difficulty of ensuring exact translation. Materials were not only written in foreign languages, they also tended to be conceived in terms that were doubly foreign since they generally reflected (a) an imported technical rationality (that did not take sufficiently into account the non-European technical rationality of most learners), and (b) inevitably alien value patterns.

Because of this tendency, an unintended effect of EWLP in certain instances may have been to bolster—rather than curtail—a lingering mentality of inferiority and/or dependency *vis-à-vis* former colonial cultures. This 'second-best' view of the national language seems to have filtered through in one EWLP country, despite its efforts to carry out literacy in that language. A new literate was asked (in the language of the former colonial power): 'What is science?' His answer (also in the former colonial language) enumerated in correct detail the various branches of exact and natural sciences, but when asked the same question in the national language, the new literate simply replied (also in the national language): 'Science is what will save humanity.'

Another crucial issue was the inverse relationship in certain projects between EWLP's role of disseminating a national language and its function of transmitting knowledge. In more than one country, the programme was used to spread (or impose) a dominant language among minorities who, in addition to being illiterate, did not speak that language. To some degree, it played a part similar to that of the European and North American primary school fifty or a hundred years ago in the construction of a centralized state through the assimilation of ethnic or cultural minorities.

This teaching of a language largely for its own sake, however, clearly undermined the transmission of new knowledge and skills. In one subproject, there was no statistically significant improvement in knowledge of the national language among minority illiterates between tests taken before and after the eighteen-month course. Since the national language was also the medium of instruction, this failure probably explains the great proportion of negative results revealed by tests in other (vocational) aspects of the subproject. Analysis of all EWLP projects whose socio-economic effects were judged statistically significant and positive led evaluators to the conclusion that

the closer the language used to present the content and materials of the course to the workers' everyday language, the more effective the literacy programme [2].

Timing

The Experimental World Literacy Programme saw the interplay—if not always the intermesh—of numerous, diverse and sometimes conflicting calendars. A review of the different kinds, levels and reciprocal relationships of calendars impinging on this major international literacy effort offers some useful lessons. Individual class sessions varied in length from forty-five minutes (Sudan) to two hours (Ecuador, Ethiopia, India, Iran, Mali, Syrian Arab Republic), with a programme-wide average of one and three-quarter hours. Although evidence on the question is not abundant, it does seem likely that a two-hour sitting may be rather long, keeping in mind the imperative need to maintain interest and avoid fatigue. Appropriate session length depends on a number of factors, of course. One is the extent to which classes are literally 'sittings': how active are they and how much variety of activity is there?

Another point is whether sessions take place in the evening, i.e. after the working day (with a consequent need to have artificial light and to take into account learners' personal and family responsibilities) or during work hours. In Ethiopia, Mali and the United Republic of Tanzania, classes were held both during and after working time, while Iran organized its courses after the work day. The United Republic of Tanzania—perhaps building on its experience with EWLP—has recently decided that all salaried persons may use the equivalent of one paid hour per day for educational purposes.

Length and scheduling of individual sessions are also related to the sequencing of lessons within the overall course time-table. Should classes take place every day? Two or three times a week? Once a week? The programme offers no hard-and-fast answers, but it seems advisable to space lessons sufficiently to enable assimilation of their content. Yet the overall learning process must also be sufficiently intense to enable learners to see *Interest* results—for the shorter the time needed to succeed, the greater learner *and* interest will be. All programmes were divided into two or more stages. In *results* this context, 'success' might mean finishing a given stage. Time allotted in principle to the first stage (for example) ranged from twenty-six to thirty-eight weeks. An exceptional subproject took nineteen months to complete stage one and was notable for a loss of learner interest and high dropout rate.

Staging cannot be arranged only in terms of maintaining student interest, however. In one country, EWLP class scheduling imitated the school year, which prevented the project from following the agricultural calendar. This may have suited educational administrators, but it was illogical in terms of learners' needs. Similarly, another country arranged classes throughout rice planting and harvesting seasons, with a consequent two-thirds absenteeism rate. It is, then, essential to link the literacy calendar with that of the development programmes in terms of which literacy is meant to be functional.

Development calendars v. . . .

Unfortunately, this requirement may on occasion contradict the needs of good teaching. This is because of the almost inevitable incompatibility between the sequencing and timing of production and learning respectively. India and the United Republic of Tanzania, for example, did subordinate the scheduling of literacy classes to the agricultural calendar but this led to a separation (rather than functional integration) of theory and practice. Ethiopia had a similar problem as the local agricultural cycle sometimes did not coincide with material being covered in the curriculum.

. . . good teaching

Moving from the class to the national level, difficulties were encountered in the timing of EWLP country projects. The 1964 session of Unesco's General Conference established three to five years as a suitable overall project length but the project preparation *Guide* published in 1967 indicated that one criterion for selection of countries to participate in the programme would be the extension of projects over a five- to ten-year period. Although disconcerting for governments involved, this was farsighted. Delays were experienced at almost every level of all projects, not to mention at the international level. In one country, no less than thirty months elapsed between the original request and the start of operations. While the original request allowed for an overall operational period of fifty-four months, the project took in reality seventy-three months to complete. Not surprisingly, a 1969 meeting on EWLP noted that 'the programme has fallen seriously behind schedule' [26]. The lesson for the future is to avoid over-ambitious scheduling.

Delays were perhaps due in part to the stage in national planning schedules at which EWLP appeared. In Algeria the project overlapped the 1967-70 and 1970-73 national plans. In Sudan, it began half-way through the 1961-71 development plan. Iran's project began once the 1962-67 plan was under way, but finished at about the same time as the 1967-71 plan. In the United Republic of Tanzania, work began half-way into the 1964-69 plan and ended during the 1969-74 plan. On the whole, there was something of a mis-match between international programming and national planning, with resultant strains of substantive readjustment and resource juggling.

The mis-match was inevitable, in view of the incompatibility between lengths and dates of the national plans of the various countries involved, but the resultant strains might have been reduced or avoided had the international programme been scheduled more flexibly, given the inherent difficulty of programming an innovation. More time for preparation (EWLP allowed itself a single year) and post-operational conclusion of evaluation could be sandwiched around a considerably longer time of actual work. A decade would seem a minimum for any world literacy programme[1] and even a decade might not prove flexible enough to suit already mutually incompatible national-plan schedules, not to mention overlapping (and sometimes contradictory) approaches to international agency programming.

No time limit ?

Perhaps it would be wiser—if international programming is to suit national needs (and not vice versa)—to impose no time limit on future world efforts in this field. EWLP's experience suggests that the tortoise may be more likely than the hare to cross the finishing-line first. At the international level, illiteracy may prove more vulnerable to persistent long-term action adapted to diverse national paces[2] than to occasional short sprints which all participants are expected to run at the same speed.

1. This corresponds to the trend towards longer international programming periods, e.g. the UNDP shift to five-year country programming and the increasing importance given by Unesco to six-year (medium-term) indicative planning.
2. Including intensive and massive projects at the national level.

The results—effects on participants; what did it cost?

In trying to the determine what the Experimental World Literacy Programme actually achieved and what changes resulted from it, it is well to be prudent. Perhaps because of its newness among international non-formal educational efforts, EWLP's evaluation encountered severe difficulties.[1] On the whole, it did not yield internationally comparable results, and even regarding national projects extreme care must be exercised in interpreting the data. Considerable precautions have, of course, been taken to collect reliable data and to base analyses on such data. Nevertheless, nearly every figure quoted in this chapter must be considered as at best an estimate of a given national reality, made under generally difficult circumstances. Moreover, it must be remembered that comparisons between doubtful representations of national realities makes it even more difficult to assess the viability of the functional literacy approach as applied in EWLP.

By and large, it is also impossible to state with much confidence what would have happened if EWLP had not taken place. World attention might be less aware of the growth of illiteracy today were it not for the programme. Such affirmations, however, can only be speculative, the more so since EWLP did not take place in an international void. It was part of a sharpening awareness of, and growing effort in, literacy. Certain of its apparent results may, then, be due to other factors or forces. Similarly, the programme may have had far-reaching impacts that cannot yet be positively attributed to it.[2]

With these provisos clearly in mind, what can be said about EWLP's results? The basic questions are: What was learned? What was done with what was learned? What were the costs and economic advantages of literacy as achieved in EWLP? And what were the programme's impacts on further educational action?

1. Problems affecting the EWLP evaluation were discussed above on page 151 et seq.
2. Perhaps summative (terminal) evaluation of such international aid efforts could usefully wait five or ten years, since this larger time span may be necessary to ascertain who learned what lessons with what result.

What was learned ?

What did the million-odd illiterates reached by the programme actually acquire in the way of skills and knowledge? There was wide country-to-country variation among pass standards and rates of learners who took examinations on completing different parts of their course. The following table gives success percentages for projects on which data are available. The figures refer to samples, of limited scope in some cases, of participants who finished a full literacy programme (usually two cycles). Thus, success percentages among initial enrollees were comparably smaller. The percentages given here range from the classes with lowest success rates to those with highest rates in each project. The wide variation is due, in some cases at least, to the fact that teaching materials and methods were employed during the project with the result that lower tests gave higher success percentages.

	Ecuador	Ethiopia	India (Jaipur)	India (Lucknow)	Iran	Sudan	United Republic of Tanzania
Writing	38-97	50-93	74	71-80	40-100	62-92	
Reading	73-100	58-97	96	89-94	10-89	70-97	
Arithmetic	2-89	55-91	76	75-80	3-91	40-93	7-17
Vocational training	6-95	50-92	85	88-93	—	41-96	

In rounded absolute figures[1] the number of people progressing from (a) initial enrolment through (b) sitting for final examinations to (c) success in those examinations were as follows (in projects for which data are available):

Country	Initial enrolment	Examinees	Pass
United Republic of Tanzania	466,000	293,600	96,900
Iran	97,400	46,900	13,900
Ethiopia	36,800	21,700	9,300
Ecuador	17,500	10,000	4,100
Sudan	7,400	2,400	600

The actual significance of these pass figures in terms of learning is hard to determine. Test levels and criteria varied widely from subject to subject, context to context, project to project and perhaps also within projects. Arithmetic considered 'basic' in an automobile repair course might be 'avanced' in a weaving programme. Automobile repairs (or weaving) also require very different amounts of learner effort depending on previous familiarity with cars (or looms). Similarly, 'written expression' means one thing for examinees writing in their mother tongue and something quite different and much more arduous for those who have had to master both writing and a new national or foreign language.

Another important factor affecting examination performance was the level of pre-course knowledge. It was generally assumed in EWLP that the

1. In all cases these figures are estimates of varying reliability.

beginning learners were fully illiterate. This was far from always the case. In Ecuador, at least a few participants were primary-school leavers anxious to acquire vocational skills. In Iran, a baseline survey found that many learners were already able to do arithmetic on enrolment. Indeed, ignorance of reading and writing is probably never automatically linked with inability to do mathematics since all societies have their own kinds of numeracy that do not require reading or writing.

Conditions and methods of measuring knowledge and skills also influenced results, both internally and with regard to national and international comparability. 'Yes/No' test questions were used in at least one case. They are, however, patently an irrelevant imposition in cultures where it is impolite to say 'no'. Measurement of individual achievement is alien to communities that prize group solidarity. In such settings it is perhaps also unreasonable to expect a farmer-instructor to exercise Western-style detachment when marking papers written by his neighbours and friends.

There was widespread frustration among EWLP organizers and evaluators over the obstacles to reliable testing. The examples just given suggest that these obstacles may sometimes have stemmed from the irrelevance (or threat) of 'modern' assessment methods to the 'traditional'[1] mores of illiterate communities. In future, a sensible and sensitive approach *Sensible* might be to attempt to devise tests more compatible with local customs, even *and* taking into account the extreme difficulty and expense of such an effort. *sensitive* Attempts in this direction could even enhance (rather than undermine) *testing* certain nationally favoured values. Why stress and test individual achievement if group solidarity is fundamental to a culture ? Could not joint examinations requiring co-operation rather than competition be devised?[2] The question is perhaps worth at least some experimentation.

A more flexible international approach to assessment of learner progress would have implications reaching far beyond the redesign of testing instruments. Also necessarily at stake would be curricula, teaching methods and personnel, and the very function of literacy in a given zone or country. More pluralism would doubtless make international comparability of result measurement even more difficult than it was in EWLP, but that is possibly not too great a price to pay for achieving the relevance that, in principle, lay at the heart of the idea of functionality. Giving priority to the needs of national—rather than international—decision-makers would also better reflect the idea (now generally accepted though not always practised) that aid should be partnership, rather than an unequal relationship between 'donors' and 'beneficiaries', with accountability solely owed by the latter to the former.

Seeking to place the levels of learning attained by new literates in a broader educational perspective, EWLP organizers and evaluators inevi-

1. Perhaps sometimes equated with 'backward'.
2. Some two decades ago, *animation rurale* educational programmes in Morocco relied heavily on group testing whose instruments were based on Moroccan folklore and mores.

tably drew comparisons with primary schooling. Naturally, schooling fulfils certain specific roles not played in functional literacy, and vice versa. Excluding these non-comparable functions, however, it does seem possible to make broad comparaisons about the area of overlap, i.e. the skills and knowledge comprising the fundamental training that both literacy and primary schooling seek to provide.

Analysed in these terms, it appears that the level of basic training acquired by new literates can be roughly likened to the amount of basic training acquired in a given length of primary schooling in the same country. The basic training acquired by a primary-school pupil over a period of two years was more or less achieved by new literates during courses lasting a total of 700 hours (Ethiopia), 600-700 hours (Mali), 560 hours (Syrian Arab Republic) and 270 hours (United Republic of Tanzania). In Algeria and Ecuador, it was four years, for respective totals of 426 hours (three cycles in Algeria) and 400 to 746 hours (two cycles in Ecuador). In Iran, a five-year equivalent was attained in two-cycle programmes varying from 208 to 554 hours. Conventional wisdom[1] has it that a minimum of roughly four years is necessary for primary schooling to become self-maintaining. In the light of the above figures, it would seem indispensable for EWLP countries to offer further education to new literates if these are not to relapse into illiteracy.

What was done with what was learned? EWLP's overriding goal was that functional literacy should change the new literates' relationship to their socio-economic milieu, and the milieu itself. The programme evaluation sought to detect these changes in three major respects: 'insertion into the milieu', 'mastery of the milieu' and 'transformation of the milieu'. About 160 observations and measures were made in various projects. In overall terms, the influence of functional literacy was judged to be plausible and favourable in about 42 per cent of the observations.

However, a relatively low percentage of new socio-economic behaviours sought through the various curricula were actually adopted (e.g. estimated at 30 per cent, in Iran); of these changes, a number were never the less considered significant.

Looking more closely at the results, one may begin with 'insertion into the milieu'. Here, indicators were devised to ascertain changes in areas such as interest in further education, management of personal finances, exposure to mass media, the seeking out of technical advice, use of the three R's, and participation in formal organizations. Eighty-six per cent of actual changes observed were judged satisfactory (56 per cent were statistically significant) as against 14 per cent declared unsatisfactory (6 per cent were statistically significant).

Insertion into what milieu?   These results, and particularly the values attached to them ('satisfactory' or not) raise a fundamental question: into what milieu is the illiterate to be 'inserted'? Point by point examination of certain 'insertions' attempted

1. cf. for example, D. Harman, *Community Fundamental Education* [17].

and observed in India and Iran—probably reflecting similar efforts in other EWLP countries—offer at least the beginnings of an answer.

The Jaipur and Lucknow subprojects in India gave rise, among their farmer-graduates, to significantly increased desire for technical information and to significantly intensified behaviour designed to satisfy that desire. That is, they were stimulated and enabled to seek out in the maze of possible sources of technical information those most likely to help them solve their daily and mainly farming problems, usually—although not always—posed in individual terms.[1] This seems to have been linked to the fact that the project stressed the economic gain that the individual could expect to reap by becoming literate.

On the other hand, the results regarding participation in formal organizations were less conclusive. There was only a tendency (not statistically significant) for new literates in the Jaipur and Lucknow subprojects to increase participation in bodies such as co-operatives, youth clubs, political parties and village councils. Certain observers explained this trend as expressing a lack of propensity for social affiliation in the two districts studied, and/or defective organizational structure (one might also wonder if, in fact, it is known how to teach these behaviours).

Participation in formal organizations

Perhaps, too, the organizations selected as indicators were not perceived by learners as useful means of attaining the individualistic and productivistic aims stressed by the subprojects. Additionally (or alternatively) such organizations may be perceived as part of a local power structures not particularly favourable to at least certain strata of new literates. Studying the role of *panchayats* (village councils) in the first decade of Indian independence, S. C. Dube[2] concluded that, despite the democratization function assigned to them by the central government, they tended to be dominated by land-holders. Consequently, the intentional concentration of power in the councils' hands by higher authorities

has been construed by some villagers as an effort of the government to maintain the status quo within village communities, and indirectly as a step to support the domination of landowning groups [8].

In Iran, an effort was made to evaluate literacy's impact on the use of writing and arithmetic in the maintenance of savings and bank accounts. A favourable trend (not statistically significant in the first case but significant in the second) was found, but in the second case it could not be determined whether the trend was attributable to literacy courses, or to the concurrent opening of a bank branch accessible to the new literates under study.

Also in Iran, functional literacy was determined to have had a favourable impact on family planning, i.e. was identified as a plausible cause of the trend toward reduction of the family size considered ideal by new

1. Some of these problems were considered 'collective', but only a minority actually demanded joint action for their solution. The 'collective' problems were 'collective' in that most were faced by many or most individuals in the community.

2. Observations by O. Lewis [23] and M. Opler [31] echo this report in vivid terms.

literates to two or three children. This effect was described as placing new literates before the respective advantages of large and small families, a choice between more children or the hope for a higher material living standard, with stress on the latter. It may be interpreted as having (among other things) enabled the people concerned to understand better the long-range implications of such choices and thus to choose more rationally, although subsequent behaviour has yet to be demonstrated.[1] In this interpretation, literacy is seen to be at the very least a vehicle for increasing the responsibility of new literates in selecting family size.

According to another view, underdevelopment does not result from large populations so that development does not follow automatically from birth control. In this interpretation (which is not of course shared by all observers), the poor family that assumes responsibility for limiting its size, simultaneously and tacitly accepts responsibility for its poverty—without obtaining any assurance of being able to improve its lot. In essence, it is probably unrealistic to assume that functional literacy with a population education component will in itself have significant impact on family size decisions unless the educational effort is in the context of other development activities which offer tangible incentives for small families.

More examples could be given of EWLP socio-economic effects regarding the insertion of new literates into the milieu. These suffice, however, to suggest the outlines of an answer to the question: insertion into what milieu? From the foregoing, one can begin to see the kinds of behaviours deemed important by the planners and evaluators of EWLP

A profile projects. The participant who was deemed 'successful' seemed to: (a) actively seek information likely to help solve mainly personal problems, generally posed in vocational terms; (b) prefer such activity to participation in formal community organizations; (c) take advantage of his or her new literacy and numeracy skills to maintain personal bank and savings accounts;[2] and (d) aspire to reduce the size of his or her family in exchange for the prospect of a higher material living standard.

This admittedly sketchy profile (which—it must be stressed—is by no means necessarily representative of all programme results) diverges slightly from the ideal 'inserted' new literate projected by the evaluation criteria. These criteria reflected 'functionality' as understood (or misunderstood) nationally and internationally in EWLP.

As regards these four behaviours, at least, the programme was most successful (in terms of its own evaluation criteria) when it reproduced the narrowly economic interpretation of functionality. This was notable in respect of knowledge and skills that could be put to work for primarily personal material benefit, whether immediate (wanting and seeking

1. This in an area where larger-term socio-economic effects of literacy (like other international aid programmes) cannot yet be measured.
2. Given the relatively favoured status of people liable to have bank or savings accounts in most Third World countries, this expected behaviour lends further substance to the 'élite of the impoverished' idea already discussed.

vocational information), intermediate (replacement of children with material goods) or longer-term (savings).[1] It was less successful when it expected new literates to participate in formal organizations, either because the new literates were not gregarious or possibly because such organizations did not enhance their prospect of primarily personal material benefit or did not favour them in the local power structure.

The milieu into which new literates are inserted—i.e. the behavioural profile into which functional literacy helps them to grow—would thus seem to be defined by the values of a society in the process of a certain kind of modernization. This modernization appears to correspond rather closely to a model of development embraced and propagated by industrial nations (perhaps particularly those of Western Europe and North America). An earlier discussion (see page 151 et seq.) concluded that just such a model was projected by at least certain of EWLP's evaluation criteria. It can now be hypothesised that, in the instances just examined, the programme was more successful than not in achieving the insertion of new literates into a milieu corresponding to this model. Before testing this hypothesis against other classes of socio-economic results—mastery of the milieu and transformation of the milieu—a word may be said about the process of insertion.

In the cases just described, EWLP's function was apparently to provide both a stimulus (the prospect—if not always the reality—of primarily personal material benefit) and the means (various information and skills) for giving a 'satisfactory' response to that stimulus. Was, then, the process akin to behaviourist conditioning? The very notion of 'insertion' suggests that something was done to illiterates by external agents, and that the something in question was determined by those external agents, who also decided whether responses to their stimuli were 'satisfactory'.

Without more complete data on the 'insertion' effect of functional literacy, the question can only be asked, not answered. But it must be asked, for it is fundamental. Did the Experimental World Literacy Programme tend to stress knowledge and know-how at the expense of know-why (critical awareness of one's role in society)? If so, it may have been successful in adapting the new literate to existing circumstance. But education should also help learners to know how to shape the environment.

Knowledge know-how and know-why

New literates' mastery of the milieu was the second broad class of intended socio-economic effects examined by EWLP evaluators. Here, indicators were prepared to measure changes in such areas as behaviour at work, knowledge of modern technical practices, adoption of such practices, and conservation and reproduction of the labour force. In this class, 93 per cent of changes recorded were judged satisfactory (51 per cent significantly so), while 7 per cent of changes were deemed unsatisfactory (2 per cent significantly so).

In India, the Jaipur and Lucknow subprojects were evaluated for their success in encouraging the effective use of certain new resources (improved

1. One EWLP primer exhorted learners to 'make money—don't waste time'.

seeds, fertilizer, pesticides, related tools) and in the case of Jaipur a certain number of associated practices (row planting, extensive cultivation, irrigation). On the whole, results were found to be positive, more clearly so in Lucknow than Jaipur, where only a positive trend was found—probably because of the disruption in farming caused by a concurrent period of drought.

There were, however, interesting variations within the generally positive results. In Lucknow, for instance, although new literates were found to be much better informed about sorghum than the control group of non-learners, they did not tend to apply their knowledge. This seems to be due to the declining profitability and popularity of sorghum compared to wheat. Regarding wheat, a widespread and marketable crop, the Lucknow subprojects achieved results assessed as extremely favourable. A trend in the same direction was found in the Jaipur subproject. There, the aim was to bring about adoption of new high-yield strains of wheat and millet, and learner response to this innovation was judged positive.

In both cases the socio-economic strata reached seem to have been largely made up of small peasants. Indeed EWLP's apparently greater success in contributing to adoption of at least some technical practices recommended in agricultural courses (a positive programme-wide average score of + 54 per cent) compared to industrial courses (a positive programme-wide average score of + 45 per cent) may perhaps be attributed to the fact that agricultural participants were frequently autonomous farmers or small landholders and thus better placed to apply immediately the new practices taught them than workers who were limited by the constraints of enterprise production.

Joining the green revolution

In India, and possibly elsewhere, it seems that thanks to the Experimental World Literacy Programme small peasants—members of what was earlier called the 'élite of the impoverished'—were enabled to join the green revolution. Thus the programme helped answer criticism (notably by Ladejinsky [21]) that India's green revolution was primarily benefiting already wealthy landowners, which most Lucknow and Jaipur learners plainly were not. By joining the green revolution in India and elsewhere, however, new literates exposed themselves to its servitudes, even if their personal incomes tended to rise. A brief discussion of the green revolution is therefore vital to understanding the milieu the new literate was to master, and the ways in which this mastery was to make itself felt.

The green revolution requires considerably increased investment, not only in the new strains of seeds but also in the additional resources and tools that, as EWLP taught, are necessary to achieve increased crop yields per land area. According to Rochin's report on West Pakistan, larger farmers may often be in a better position to purchase such accessories than small landholders [36]. Paradoxically, newly literate farmers who join the green revolution may find themselves in a double dilemma since if they are able to purchase new seeds and necessary accessories, how much of their new income has to be re-invested in this way?

Like EWLP, the green revolution tends to be more or less highly selective. In geographical terms, it is generally limited to areas most likely to yield short-term profit. According to Cleaver's study, the green revolution in India seems likely to be incapable of affecting meaningfully zones outside the 20 per cent of cultivated land that is irrigated (only half of it with sure water) [5].

Socially, the green revolution is also selective. It tends to favour the already favoured minority of the rural population, but its benefits do not generally reach the majority. According to Rudra *et al.* [39] and Ladejinsky [21], wealthy Indian farmers already seem to be extending their holdings, thus raising land prices. Cleaver [5] predicts a possible 'considerable rise in rural unemployment in those areas where mechanization proceeds rapidly'. Bardhan [3] points to a trend, in areas of India where the green revolution has been effective, for real wages of agricultural labourers to decline.

In the light of this discussion, what seems to be the provisional profile of a new literate as 'master of the milieu'? There is no doubt that, in the case discussed at least, he or she does exercise increased mastery of his or her milieu. But is it not mastery of a rather narrow technical and economic kind corresponding to the profile suggested earlier of the new literate 'inserted into the milieu'? In acquiring this kind of mastery of the milieu, to what extent has the new literate become dependent on which external socio-economic processes and forces? Has literacy enabled the new literate to know and understand these processes and forces? To come to grips with them? To have a voice in controlling them? What implications has the new literate's accession to mastery of the milieu for the fate of his or her less favoured neighbours and compatriots?

It is probable that these questions have no simple or single answer, either for any specific case examined or for EWLP as a whole. They are none the less probably legitimate and basic enough to require answers in future literacy (and other aid and development) efforts, particularly where the United Nations and its Specialized Agencies—with their special commitment to human rights—are involved. In seeking answers, President Nyerere of Tanzania has some provocative thoughts on education and human beings' relationship with their milieu. He makes

Creators or creatures?

a serious distinction between men and women who are skilful users of tools, and a system of education which turns men and women into tools. I want to make quite sure that our technical and practical education is an education for creators not for creatures . . . that our educational institutions are not going to end up as factories turning out marketable commodities. I want them to enlarge men and women, not convert men and women into efficient instruments for the production of modern gadgets [29].

The third and final broad class of EWLP's socio-economic effects examined by international evaluators was the participation of new literates in the transformation of the milieu. In this respect, indicators were devised to to detect changes in areas involving the means of production, the volume of production, cash income, income in kind and the consumption of durable goods. On the whole, 90 per cent of recorded changes (the absolute numbers of which were relatively small) were deemed to be satisfactory (41 per cent significantly so) and 10 per cent were judged unsatisfactory (7 per cent significantly so).

In the Lucknow subproject (India), a list was drawn up of sixteen material goods whose pre- and post-course possession was noted among EWLP learners and non-participants in the literacy programme. The list included items such as bicycles, sewing machines, pressure lamps and chairs. At the end of the course, new literates were found to possess markedly more of these goods than the non-participant control group. Evaluators concluded that increased consumption was a probable consequence of income growth due, in turn, to enhanced agricultural knowledge and skills and resultant innovative professional behaviour.[1]

Stimulus, response, reward

The results help to fill out still further the provisional profile of the new literate emerging from EWLP, in the case analysed at least. The new literate 'inserted into the milieu' has been stimulated by the prospect of personal material gain and equipped with the knowledge and know-how to supply appropriate response to that stimulus. As a 'master of the milieu', the new literate does seem effectively to supply the appropriate response. It is only logical then that, completing the circle, the new literate should be rewarded: he or she (and family) appears to gain access to increased personal consumption of material goods.

In summary, considerable caution must be exercised in interpreting the success criteria discussed above. Relatively few (probably less than a third) of all socio-economic changes advocated in the various programmes were, in fact, ever adopted by participants. And these changes, on the whole, were those which were perceived by participants as having some immediate personal benefit and requiring little expenditure of time and resources to achieve. Thus, notwithstanding the high percentages of such modest changes which were regarded as 'positive' by the Evaluation Unit attached to Unesco's Literacy Division, the fact is that these positive changes were very modest in nature and few in number.

If such modest changes in the three major classes of behaviour evaluated can be said to prove that EWLP was successful, and to the extent that this logic of project success served the development model chosen by participating countries, the programme was worth while. However, the question remains as to whether the narrowly economic and individualistic nature of EWLP's logic did not diverge from—or even contradict—the kind of development to which at least a few participating countries aspired.

Whatever the answer to this question, it is clear that evaluation

1. The validity of this study is open to question. Considering the high dropout rates, the successful participants were a highly self-selected group in the experimental (literacy class) population that cannot be appropriately compared to a random sample of the control (non-literacy class) population.

providing immediate information could only reveal the short-term and most mechanistic socio-economic effects of the world programme. This necessary focus may have biased at least some of the questions asked in this chapter. It certainly makes it difficult even to guess at some of the longer-term and possibly profounder effects wrought by EWLP. Such results doubtless already exist in latent form, and will make themselves felt in the future, if for no other reason than the liberating potential of literacy.

Possibly of necessity, evaluation took into account chiefly the intelligibility and utility of certain messages for learners who were viewed primarily as receivers. Nevertheless, the distinguishing feature of verbal and written symbolism is that it can have a wide variety of functions. It is endowed, in particular, with the ability to broadcast as well as receive, and to broadcast an almost infinite number of entirely new messages. Unlike computers, human beings cannot be programmed to respond only to certain stimuli, or to give only certain responses to those stimuli.

An already palpable effect of EWLP in certain Malian villages appears to have been at least the beginnings of a new social dynamic involving a redistribution of socio-political initiative. In the United Republic of Tanzania, Hall and Mhaiki report as follows on the results achieved by 1972 by adult education, including that country's EWLP project:

Other uses of literacy

> Stories are now being told of farmers learning to read and write and denouncing individuals who had cheated them by mis-weighing their crops when they brought them for sale [16].

Such are the inevitable uses of literacy where domination and exploitation persist, as Shakespeare well understood. In *The Tempest*, the powerful Duke Prospero uses magic (which might be likened to modern technology) to conquer a tropical island and enslave its one inhabitant, Caliban.[1] Having given Caliban enough instruction to understand orders, Prospero can hardly be surprised when his slave turns learning to other purposes:

> You taught me language, and my profit on't
> Is, I know how to curse. . . .

Costs and project economics

What did the Experimental World Literacy Programme cost? Who paid for what? What does it cost to produce a new literate? How could costs be reduced? Was basic training provided under the programme cheaper than basic training provided by alternative sources? Attempts to answer these

---

1. 'Caliban' is an anagram for 'cannibal', a word stemming in turn from 'Carib'. Fernandez Retamar views the Prospero/Caliban relationship as typifying that of colonizer to colonized [11]. A symbolic parallel is found in Mozart's *The Magic Flute* when the simple bird-catcher Papageno is punished for mocking the powers-that-be by being obliged to sing a whole aria with his mouth padlocked shut.

questions are perhaps particularly subject to the warnings expressed at the beginning of this chapter. Nevertheless, even attempts to find answers may be of interest. The total cost of EWLP during six years of operation was of the order of $32 million[1] with expenditures per national project ranging from $300,000 to $6 million. The governments concerned paid roughly two-thirds of global costs, although the proportion of national financing varied in function of the size and nature of projects. National financing accounted for 70 per cent of expenditure in projects that tended toward a massive approach, but as little as 25 per cent of spending in the more properly micro-experimental projects. This means that the smaller and more experimental a project, the larger was the financial responsibility of international financial resources. This correlation probably expressed the earlier overriding but now changing preference of the international agencies concerned for what was previously called the technico-scientific approach to experimentation, contrasting with the activist-pragmatic approach. The latter approach seems to have been more popular with national governments, particularly those who viewed their EWLP project as a prelude to broader literacy action.

Regarding international aid to national projects, some project country nationals may have expected that it would take the form of direct cash flows, capable of easing (no matter how little) sometimes disastrous economic stituations.[2] But EWLP followed the traditional pattern of technical assistance under which help was furnished primarily in the form of expert services, fellowships and equipment—but not cash. Disappointed nationals may, then, occasionally have seen the programme as something of a 'Now you see it, now you don't' conjuring trick.

How were budgets used? A study of one EWLP country pointed to the need to separate operational costs from research and development costs. Excluding spending on research and development, the cost per enrollee was $17, and per participant completing both parts of the literacy programme approximately $31. These costs rise to $26 and $50 respectively if spending on research and development is included (see the cases in Part I for figures on each project).

In more detailed terms, this study found the following breakdown into percentages of overall expenditure: remuneration of instructors, 30; preparatory and research studies, 23.5; administration expenses, 21; transport, 8; training of instructors, 6.5; teaching materials, 5; classroom equipment, 4.5; audio-visual material, 1.5.[3] Figures available on other

1. This figure does not include the cost of a certain amount of staff time, or of aspects of the international evaluation.
2. International aid's overall impact in this broader context was pointed to in 1970 by the Principal Secretary of the United Republic of Tanzania's Ministry of Finance when he observed (quoted by Rodney) that 'losses from sisal price declines [sisal is a chief Tanzanian export] have more than equalled total gross aid receipts over 1964-69' [37].
3. These figures do not seem to include capital expenditure, e.g. construction costs, since they refer to the expansion—rather than to the experimental phase—of the project in question. Nor do they appear to cover the cost of international experts. The item 'preparatory and research studies' seems to include baseline studies, curriculum development and evaluation.

projects suggest that this may not be an especially atypical budget, and that instructor remuneration was generally the most expensive single item of global spending, combining national and international outlays for operations and research and development. If salaries of all kinds were grouped, this category would make up over 80 per cent of all project costs, with remuneration of instructors making up less than half of all project salaries. Other salaries, of course, were for those involved in research studies, administration, preparation of materials, etc. Such high non-teaching personnel costs indicate a rather large and perhaps cumbersome infrastructure in most projects.

What did it cost to make a person literate? The following figures *Per* should not be compared at face value since they are unweighted. That is, *capita* they do not take into account sometimes wide country-to-country variations *costs* in testing levels or in the amount and quality of learning required to achieve what was defined as literacy.[1] Keeping these differences in mind, the rounded costs per participant taking the final examination in countries on which data are available were as follows.[2] These figures include national and international financing, take capital as well as running costs into account, and compare total expenditure (operations plus research and development) with operational costs alone (not including research and development):

	Total estimated cost per enrolled participant	Total estimated cost per final participant	Estimated cost per final participant excluding research and evaluation (operations only)	Estimated total cost per participant passing final examination
	U.S.$	U.S.$	U.S.$	U.S.$
Sudan	7.00	272.00	110.00	269.00
Madagascar	112.00	126.00	48.00	—
Ecuador	70.00	123.00	70.00	300.00
Iran	49.00	100.00	76.00	332.00
Algeria	71.00	99.00	83.00	—
Ethiopia	54.00	92.00	63.00	212.00
Mali	14.00	35.00	17.00	—
United Republic of Tanzania	7.00	10.00	9.00	32.00

One way of reducing costs might be to carry out more careful analyses of the administrative and organizational patterns in each project than was possible in the profiles of Part I of this report. It would certainly seem (as mentioned above) that many projects spent large percentages of their budgets on administrative and project support infrastructure. Others spent much less by assigning responsibility for various aspects of the programme to officials in charge of other technical or social services.

Secondly, the foregoing table shows that costs per successful

1. In the United Republic of Tanzania, for instance, reading, writing and computational skills roughly comparable to second year of primary school were accepted as criteria of literacy compared to fourth- or fifth-grade levels in several other countries.
2. In all cases, these figures are estimates of varying reliability.

participant were much higher than costs per enrolled participant because of the high dropout rate. Reasons for high dropout rates in many projects are not entirely clear, and relate to factors over which projects may have had some control as well as factors over which they had little influence. It is reasonable to conclude, however, that those projects which had lower dropout rates did something that was more effective in holding participants, and reduced wastage and effective cost per successful participant.

Thirdly, given the experimental nature of EWLP and the rather large amounts already spent on research and development, it may be that economies of scale (the bigger the project, the lower the cost per learner) could be achieved by extending literacy work to larger audiences. Since the methodological research and development have already been carried out, expansion, according to such reasoning, would essentially require the replication of operational spending.

The prospect of achieving economies of scale also seems substantiated by the fact that the lowest *per capita* costs appear to have been achieved in projects reaching the largest audiences. Iran, Algeria, Ethiopia, Mali and the United Republic of Tanzania, the countries with comparatively low total costs, respectively reported the following numbers of candidates for final tests: 46,239, 38,784, 21,722, 50,000 (approximate) and 293,586. Conversely, countries with relatively higher total *per capita* costs—Sudan, Madagascar and Ecuador—had a rather smaller number of final candidates—2,363, 3,826 and 9,988 respectively.

Economies *of* *scale*   Unfortunately, the possible economies to be reaped by extension of the scale of functional literacy do not seem likely to be as great as initial theory suggests. Research and development costs may decrease in cases where widespread application of programmes already devised during EWLP is possible. As earlier chapters of this report have suggested, however, curricula and pedagogy probably require considerable revision. Moreover, pre-existing programmes will have to be modified, or new programmes prepared, if extended literacy is to be functional in terms of the specific problems and aspirations of additional groups with geographical, professional and/or ethnic particularities. Technical assistance should keep these possibilities in mind when helping governments to develop national capacities. Equally compromising for the prospects of economies of scale are trends already detected by evaluators within EWLP regarding operational costs. Although these do seem to fall off with the expansion of literacy, there appears to be little hope for a radical reduction.

Finally, a mass campaign implies a commitment of the government to move towards a fully literate society requiring an infrastructure of reading materials, newspapers, libraries, reading rooms, extension materials, and all the other things necessary to support the intellectual interests of literate people. Thus, a long-term plan for a literate society must take into account expenditures that probably far exceed the cost of the original literacy programme in order to establish and maintain such an infrastructure.

Limiting ourselves for the moment, however, to the costs of literacy programmes, what can be done to reduce such costs? Basing themselves on available EWLP data, Unesco/UNDP analysts identified four 'sensitive' cost factors and attempted to project the magnitude of savings that might result from slight variations of each.[1]

Average class size was the first factor. It was assumed that class size would be increased by 1 per cent. A reduction in overall costs of between 0.4 and 3 per cent—depending on the project—was considered a probable result. This means that for each new group of 100,000 enrollees, savings ranging from $22,000 to $300,000 could be realized, depending on the average size of classes. Naturally, pedagogy as well as economics should inform any decision to increase class sizes. Although classes with a 1 : 8 instructor to learner ratio (e.g. Guinea) might not suffer irreparably from adding a few more pupils, the EWLP-wide ration of 1 : 30 or more should probably not be stretched much farther, assuming that there is any truth in conventional wisdom on class size and assuming the need for participation in discussion and in technical activities involving demonstrations and the like.

The second sensitive area covered the educational know-how required to construct programmes. Such know-how results from research and experimentation which, as already seen, can absorb a percentage of budgets that grows as projects become smaller and more experimental. Here, a 1 per cent reduction results in a saving of between 0.6 and 0.9 per cent of research costs per learner. In certain cases, this economy would not result from standardization of programmes, given the already-mentioned need to remain functional in terms of specific learner groups. It would, rather, arise from the improvement and normalization of programme design techniques. Once again, however, projections should be conservative rather than optimistic, since constant self-assessment would probably require continuing readjustment of even these techniques.[2]

Most projects, of course, assumed that a materials development and validation infrastructure was needed for the project, quite independent of anything else going on in the country. Many countries have (or are developing) various kinds of curriculum centres designed to prepare more effective teaching materials for the schools. In addition, many countries have agricultural, health and other extension services. With an increasing concern for lifelong education that does not compartmentalize educational opportunity as rigidly as in the past, it would seem reasonable to consider ecucational materials research and development centres which would not be limited to the preparation of literacy materials or school materials or extension materials. The process of definition of educational objectives, the design of instructional or educational materials to suit a particular organizational 'strategy' involving formal or non-formal education, and the validation and revision of such materials involve similar skills and

1. In each case, all other costs were supposed to remain unchanged.
2. Indeed, 'normalization' may be an illusion in a field like literacy, where innovation is permanent, and the only basic constant may be perpetual change.

resources. The need to have separate expensive centres for literacy materials would appear to be open to question. In fact, the creation of teaching materials and literature in the national languages, is compatible with this idea.

A third flexible cost factor is expenditure on teaching staff. Given the above-noted importance of such expenditure in virtually all EWLP projects, this is perhaps the most influential single item of operational budgets. A reduction of 1 per cent here leads to a saving of more than 0.5 per cent, i.e. an average possible economy of about $40,000 for each new group of 100,000 enrollees. Because of relatively high salaries, fringe benefits and other career perquisites, school-teachers and civil servants seconded to literacy work generally cost more than non- or para-professional instructors. It is therefore in this second category that imaginative efforts might reap considerable savings. The United Republic of Tanzania's experience suggests that it is cheaper (although perhaps not radically so) to use literate peasants as instructors rather than professionals. Other categories could also be tapped. Students at universities, teacher-training colleges and secondary schools, for instance, might be required to make a given number of people literate as a condition for graduation. In such cases, the teaching work could add an invaluable experience of reality to the education of student-instructors, who tend to come by definition from the more favoured socio-economic strata.

Finally, evaluators attempted to project savings that might accrue from reducing running costs. Unfortunately, this factor was found to be too dependent on other factors to be treated in isolation from them. It was nevertheless thought likely that savings could be achieved if literacy action were more integrated into the institutional framework (farms, factories, development agencies, etc.) of the localities where it takes place. Duplication of staff, plant and so on could be reduced, for example, if a given enterprise assumed prime responsibility for organizing courses.

Functional literacy v. primary schooling   Was functional literacy provided by EWLP cheaper than education furnished by atlternative sources? Data allowing a reliable and comprehensive comparison between EWLP projects and other kinds of literacy in programme countries are, regrettably, unavailable. This leaves only the possibility of comparing functional literacy with equivalent amounts and kinds of primary schooling. The difficulty of such comparisons has been referred to in the discussion of EWLP result measurement. Despite this difficulty—and keeping in mind the very vulnerable and provisional nature of the following figures—it does seem possible to make at least an educated guess about comparative costs. This guess is based on the comparison of equivalent amounts (lengths) of equivalent kinds of education (basic training), and explicitly excludes contents and functions of literacy and schooling respectively that do not refer directly to basic training.

It was possible to make the comparison for eight EWLP countries. In only one (Sudan) does basic training furnished by primary schools seem to have been cheaper than that provided by the EWLP project. In the seven others, literacy was cheaper by percentages that ranged (per candidate at the final test) from 55 per cent in Madagascar to 86 per cent in Algeria and 89 per cent in Mali, and (per successful new literate) from 2 per cent in Ethiopia and 28 per cent in Ecuador to 63 per cent in Iran and 85 per cent in the United Republic of Tanzania. In other words, it appears that for an identical expenditure EWLP was able in each case to provide basic training to a certain number of additional people. Keeping in mind the above criteria (cost per candidate at the final test in Algeria, Madagascar and Mali, and per successful new literate in Ecuador, Ethiopia and the United Republic of Tanzania), the additional numbers of learners trained by the programme compared to what schools could have done at the same cost, seem to have been roundly as follows: Ethiopia, 310; Ecuador, 2,010; Madagascar, 2,360; Iran, 16,600; Mali, 44,430; Algeria, 46,320; United Republic of Tanzania, 130,700.

In contrast, an identical expenditure on schooling and literacy in Sudan may be supposed to have enabled the school to provide basic training to 320 more pupils than the EWLP project.

It can certainly not be concluded from these figures that the Third World should immediately replace primary schooling with EWLP-type functional literacy, if only because of the possible margin of error affecting the collection and analysis of the figures themselves. On the other hand, this comparison does offer two conclusions that may be drawn with fair certainty. First, functional literacy as organized under EWLP does seem to have provided important aspects of fundamental education rather more cheaply than existing forms of primary schooling could have done. Secondly, cost-conscious educators could therefore usefully re-examine existing forms of primary schooling with a view to introducing certain elements of functional literacy. EWLP may not offer irrefutable evidence of the necessity to 'de-school' society, but it does strongly suggest the need (and a way) to 'de-school' the school.

To de-school or not to de-school

Impacts on further educational action

EWLP did not, single-handedly, 'de-school' the schools, but there are signs that, here and there (and mostly in programme countries), it at least influenced them. In one case, the school seems to have had greater influence on the EWLP project than vice versa. Elsewhere the reverse may be true. Organizers of one project noted with satisfaction that school-teachers who doubled as literacy instructors began to display less authoritarian attitudes toward children. In two countries, adult education methods have been introduced into the curricula of teacher-training colleges. Iran is studying the possibility of reforming all training of school-teachers to make it more responsive to local reality, i.e. more functional.

EWLP's influence has also been felt outside the framework of formal schooling. One project was requested to assist in training community development instructors. More to the point, several EWLP countries have continued and expanded literacy in a more or less functional spirit since the end of the programme. Mali is reported to have planned the opening of some 450 new literacy centres with bilateral help during 1974-76. Sudan, which built up a much larger national staff than provided for in its Unesco/ UNDP plan of operations, has persevered with literacy work. The United Republic of Tanzania has expanded its experimental pilot project into an ambitious mass campaign, and is the first country of sub-Saharan Africa that seems to have a serious chance of eliminating mass illiteracy.

In forty-one countries that did not take part in the programme, discussion, research, experimentation and/or pilot projects related in some way to one interpretation or another of the notion of functional literacy have been noted as having taken place or being under way. These range from experiments in the Napieoledougou region of the Ivory Coast and in Indonesian rice and rubber plantations to research or other preparatory activities in the Central African Republic and the Libyan Arab Republic.

On the whole, however, in both EWLP and non-EWLP countries, and whether United Nations related or not, functional literacy activities tend to be limited, fragmented and incidental. The 'eventual World Campaign for the Eradication of Mass Illiteracy' for which the Secretary-General of the United Nations hoped a decade ago, EWLP might 'prepare the way', is certainly no nearer than when the programme began. This state of affairs is possibly disappointing to some of the programme's more ardent well-wishers who may have expected it to unleash a massive world-wide assault on illiteracy. And that is the world programme's last, and most poignant lesson. Neither literacy nor development as a whole can be willed into existence by international agencies that are inter- (but not supra-) governmental. Such agencies probably go awry if they try to replace the muscle of national governments. At best they can prick the conscience of national governments. It is perhaps in this role that they can best respond to the hopes of those to whom they have ultimate ethical, if not yet legal, accountability: 'We the peoples of the United Nations . . .'.

Appendix
Recommendations of the Expert Team on Evaluation of Experimental Literacy Projects

3rd session, Paris, 15-18 July 1975

Literacy is necessary *both* as a national priority to raise the cultural level of the population, to break with a past of ignorance linked to domination and exploitation, and to build a democratic society, *and* as a duty of international solidarity in the perspective of a new world order aborning.

For these reasons the concept of functionality must be extended to include all its dimensions: political, economic, social and cultural. Just as development is not only economic growth, so literacy—and education more generally—must aim above all to arouse in the individual a critical awareness of social reality, and to enable him or her to understand, master and transform his or her destiny. Limiting literacy to narrowly economic aims implies the risk of diminishing considerably the importance of this task and of preventing the mobilization of hearts and minds without which no sustained development is possible.

I Policy, planning, organization

1. Literacy policy and planning must seek to integrate national necessities with the needs expressed by different social groups. No literacy process can be effective unless these groups realize that literacy serves their own interests as well as those of the nation.

   For this reason, literacy must often be linked to changes in other fields, such as:
   (a) economic and social reforms (it is useless to teach a farmer to increase productivity if the greater part of the fruit of this labour goes to a landlord);
   (b) scientific and technological research (to improve the instruments and methods of work and production);
   (c) a policy of labour-intensive rather than capital-intensive investments (taking into account the products and branches of activity), etc.
2. Literacy is but one element of a process of lifelong education. It should be allied with knowledge appropriate for improving the individual's condition, always taking into account his or her social environment (see above) and natural environment (savannah land or forest, dry or humid zone, etc.). Rudiments of citizens' rights and duties, of history and geography, hygiene and book-keeping are indispensable for all.

3. It is desirable to tackle the elimination of illiteracy in a long-term perspective. Within such a perspective and in liaison with economic, social and cultural planning, medium-term plans should show, for each period, precise aims and the means for achieving them, taking into account differences between regions, activity sectors, sexes, towns and rural zones, ethno-linguistic groups, etc.

4. Such planning should also be as decentralized as possible, in both preparation and execution, so as to reflect clearly the problems of each region and thus arouse the interest and participation of the population in all ways possible: individual initiatives, non-governmental organizations, voluntary associations, trade unions, youth clubs, etc., and in all forms: contributions in cash or kind, teaching volunteers, voluntary construction of facilities, etc.

5. The government should set forth the major orientations for action, sensitize the population particularly through the mass media, and furnish technical and financial aid to the least-favoured groups.

   It should set up the mechanisms for intersectoral co-operation at the national, regional and local levels, ensuring that a single body assume responsibility for the leadership of literacy work and that this body be part of a general structure of formal and non-formal education.

6. For literacy to be effective and lasting it must be sustained by an infrastructure that not only provides literates with abundant reading matter but also maintains their taste for learning and broadening their horizons: information media, stable and mobile libraries, means of producing and disseminating the written work, small museums, cultural clubs, not to mention the schooling of children (who ask questions of their parents).

7. Experimental projects can often be useful before launching literacy campaigns. In such instances, care must be taken to ensure that the human, material and financial resources used are of a kind allowing for later generalization.

II Methods, contents, materials

1. The experience of EWLP has demonstrated the utility of a centralized structure responsible for designing and preparing teaching materials which may be used not only by literacy agencies but also by all bodies and institutions dealing with animation, information and training.

2. Similarly EWLP brought to light the advantages of a methodology based on the definition of educational aims linked to general development aims and on the identification of problems that constitute blocks to the achievement of development aims.

3. The preparation of curricula and materials must be based on the use of baseline and context surveys carried out among the concerned populations and taking into account the needs expressed by them. The content of functional literacy curricula must be realistic and simplified, closely linked to the concrete problems of individuals and groups. It is often possible to prepare modules including specific notions common to several groups, thus facilitating the expansion of functional literacy.

4. Literacy work in mother tongues is in principle more effective and better reflects the reality of national cultures. It does, however, raise problems in certain countries (untranscribed languages, a gap between the written and spoken word, numerous ethno-linguistic groups, lack of instructors and books, costs, etc.), and such problems should be taken into account. Linguistic research is necessary to

improve the efficiency of literacy (dictionaries, vocabularies, grammars, literature for new literates).

5. Teaching methods must be in harmony with curriculum content: thus if the content of a curriculum relates to self-management, the teaching method cannot remain directive and teacher-centred.

6. The process of functional literacy must be designed so as to enhance the ability of individuals and groups to express themselves, orally, in writing, or in other ways (painting, sculpture, theatre, dance, mime, etc.). Illiterate adults must not be mere receivers of knowledge, but also creators of culture.

7. In the preparation of curricula and the definition of methods, account may suitably be taken of adult psychology, and of the adult's previous knowledge and motivations so that the process of education may encourage and spark off a dynamic of self-learning.

8. The improvement of methods and materials could be facilitated by the preparation and dissemination—in particular under Unesco's sponsorship—of manuals, practical guides, bibliographies and teaching documents. Similarly, the dissemination and exchange of experience and sample materials should be encouraged and organized systematically, in particular through the network of existing international pedagogical centres.

III Personnel

1. Literacy, and adult education more generally, should call on all existing human resources and not only professional teachers. Experience shows that more often than not instructors from the same ecological and vocational background as illiterates are more successful in carrying out literacy than school-teachers because they understand illiterates' problems better. In the same way, technical staff who teach reading, writing and arithmetic achieve better results than school-teachers who instruct both the three R's and technical subjects.

2. Whatever the personnel, including volunteers, they must be trained in pedagogical communication in the broadest sense of the term. Short initial training followed by continuing in-service training (through periodic sessions of evaluations and up-dating) is better than prolonged initial training without follow-up.

.3. Training concerns not only the instructional staff but all people who have a role in literacy: organizational training, training in the use of mass media, libraries, etc.

4. Since the administration of literacy programmes should be as decentralized, light-structured and diffuse as possible, it should be taken over by the very setting in which literacy work takes place, i.e. essentially by the instructors and learners (self-management). External staff should intervene as little as possible, and then primarily to ensure the design of programmes and the creation of a link between them and other development programmes.

5. Institutions of higher and secondary education should pay more attention to literacy. Universities could deal with problems of pedagogical research, innovation, evaluation and integration in general development, training of specialists, and scientific and technical popularization. Teacher-training institutions of different levels could deal with the concepts of adult psychology and pedagogy to be taught to student teachers to prepare them for educating adults as well as children. Certain principles and means are common to both types of

education: active methods, group dynamics, participation, responsibility, interest-centred themes related to the milieu, etc.

IV Evaluation

1. Evaluation should be both internal and external. In the first place, it must be self-evaluation undertaken by the participants themselves enabling them to realize what progress they are making, what problems crop up, and how to solve them step by step.

   Secondly, evaluation should be carried out periodically to ensure plan execution with a view to improve or revise the plan. This must be action-oriented evaluation and may be limited to a few simple but crucial indicators that are easy to apply: attendance rates and quality of results (knowledge, attitudes and behaviours) in relation to curriculum contents and teaching methods.

   To improve the efficiency of action is a more important function of evaluation than the international comparison of data collected.
2. Evaluation must take account of the cultural context of each experience and not transpose mechanically evaluation designs prepared for differing societies. This requires of the evaluator not only technical knowledge but also sensitivity to and respect for the culture within which he or she is working.
3. Evaluation must not be limited to opinion polls, but must also include refined anthropological studies to compare attitudes and behaviours, expected results and actual results.
4. Evaluation must include a cost-efficiency analysis, taken in the broadest sense (including social, economic and pedagogical factors) so that efforts to reduce costs do not lead to a lower output ratio.

   EWLP's experience shows that functional literacy is an economically advantageous proposition and that school pedagogy can benefit from its pedagogical approach.

V International co-operation

The group notes with satisfaction that the implementation of the Experimental World Literacy Programme and of its evaluation are an interesting example of co-operation between UNDP and Unesco. It hopes that this sort of co-operation will come to encompass other fields, and that it will discover still better procedures.

Generally, there should be integration rather than juxtaposition of national and international efforts, and co-ordination both between bilateral and multilateral assistance and within the United Nations system itself.

In the framework now offered by the opening of new dimensions of international co-operation,[1] the group makes the following suggestions:

1. Development can only be autonomous and sustained if the countries concerned rely first and foremost on themselves. External aid can only 'top up' national efforts, enabling those to achieve maximum efficiency.
2. Such co-operation must be tailor-made in response to needs expressed by the countries and taking into account means available, with priority given to the least-favoured nations for which special programmes might be foreseen.

   Within overall national responsibility for designing, implementing and

---

1. cf. the document 'General Review of Programmes and Policies of UNDP' (DP/114, 24 March 1975).

evaluating programmes, assistance could be given to non-governmental organizations which have shown themselves most useful in the struggle against illiteracy and for mass education.

3. International co-operation should aim to develop the production of national materials for literacy rather than favour the consumption of imported goods (for example encourage the creation of national education-related industries for making paper, teaching materials, etc., rather than import such articles). Special attention must be paid to the problem of paper so that its present scarcity does not inhibit educational efforts of poor countries.

   External aid must in no case compete with existing or potential national production (of equipment, for example).

4. Aid procedures must be speeded up so as not to delay certain literacy activities. Procedures should also be made flexible enough to suit the diverse needs of each country. For example, in most cases short-term qualified consultants are preferable to long-term experts. It should also become possible to use external aid to finance local fellowships and the salaries of national specialists, etc.

5. Co-operation among developing countries must be encouraged by international organizations, in particular through exchange of information, documentation and experience, the organization of meetings of specialists and officials (an extremely important form of aid to exchange), study tours, regional training courses, etc.

6. Encouragement should be given to research and evaluation programmes undertaken by national, regional and subregional agencies (e.g. universities and research institutes).

7. Literacy is a long-range effort; national and international financing bodies should make commitments for periods of several years so that literacy programmes may be carried to a successful conclusion.

Bibliography

1. *Alphabétisation fonctionnelle et apprentissage: l'efficacité interne de la méthode.* Paris, Unesco, 1974.
2. *Alphabétisation fonctionnalle: relations entre les effets économiques et sociaux et l'intervention pédagogique.* Paris, Unesco, 1975.
3. BARDHAN, P. The green revolution and agricultural labourers. *Economic and policical weekly* (Bombay), July 1970.
4. BAZANY, M. Evaluating an experimental functional literacy project: the Esfahan experience. *Planning out-of-school education for development.* Paris, International Institute for Educational Planning, 1973.
5. CLEAVER, H. The contradictions of the green revolution. *Monthly review* (New York, N.Y.), June 1972.
6. *Le concept de l'alphabétisation fonctionnelle: genèse, objectifs et hypothèses du Programme expérimental mondial d'alphabétisation.* Paris, Unesco, 1974.
7. CURLE, A. Educational strategy for developing societies: a study of educational and social factors in relation to economic growth. London, Tavistock, 1962.
8. DUBE, S. C. *India's changing villages.* Ithaca, N.Y., Cornell University, 1958.
9. EDSTROM, L. A Scandinavian perspective on aid to education. *Prospects,* Summer 1974.
10. FAURE, E. *et. al. Learning to be.* Paris/London, Unesco/Harrap, 1974.
11. FERNANDEZ RETAMAR, R. Caliban. *Casa de la Américas* (Havana), September-October 1971.
12. *Functional literacy in the context of adult education.* Berlin, German Foundation for International Development, 1973.
13. GILLETTE, A. *NGOs and Unesco.* Paris, Non-governmental Organization Standing Committee (Unesco), 1968.
14. —. *Youth and literacy: you've got a ticket to ride.* Paris/New York, Unesco/UNCESI, 1973.
15. *Guide for the preparation of pilot experimental work-oriented literacy projects.* Paris, Unesco, 1967. (ED/WS/1.)
16. HALL, B.; MHAIKI, P. *L'intégration de l'éducation des adultes en Tanzanie.* Dar es Salaam, University of Dar es Salaam, Institute of Adult Education, 1972.
17. HARMAN, D. *Community fundamental education.* Lexington, Mass., Lexington Books, 1974.
18. HENQUET, P. Lettre à la rédaction. *Opinion,* Paris, Unesco Staff Association, December 1973.
19. *Immunologie générale et immunologie médicale,* Paris, Heures de France, 1967.
20. *Intergovernmental Conference on Cultural Policies in Asia. Final report.* Paris, Unesco, 1974.
21. LADEJINSKI, W. The ironies of India's green revolution. *Foreign affairs.* New York, N.Y., July 1970.
22. LESTAGE, A. *Etude et questionnaire relatifs à l'orientation et au 'briefing' des nouveaux membres des secrétariats et des experts engagés dans les projets d'enseignement et de formation.* Paris, Unesco, 1974. (EHT/TEP-AL/SS, 21.)
23. LEWIS, O. *Village life in northern India.* Urbana, Ill., University of Illinois, 1958.
24. *Literacy as a factor in development.* Paris, Unesco, 1965. (Minedlit/3.)
25. M'BOW, A.-M. Unesco at the service of education in Africa. *Educafrica,* no. 1, 1974. Dakar, Unesco Regional Office for Education in Africa.
26. *Meeting on the Experimental World Literacy Programme. Final report.* Paris, Unesco, 1970. (ED/CONF. 53/9.)

27. *Meeting on the Experimental World Literacy Programme. Working document,* Paris Unesco, 1969. (SC/CONF. 53/2.)
28. MEISTER, A. *Alphabétisation et développement.* Paris, Anthropos, 1973.
29. NYERERE, J. Education for Liberation in Africa. *Prospects,* no. 1, 1975. Paris, Unesco.
30. *Operational evaluation: a basic guide for teacher-trainers,* Paris, Unesco, 1975. (ED/EHT/TCP/FLH/SS.)
31. OPLER, M. Factors of tradition and change in a local election in rural India. In: Park and Tinker (eds.), *Leadership and political institutions in India.* Princeton, N. J., Princeton University, 1959.
32. *The position as regards functional literacy pilot projects,* Paris, Unesco, 1968. (15C/52.)
33. *Practical guide to functional literacy,* Paris, Unesco, 1973.
34. *Report of the Secretary General on the World Campaign for Universal Literacy.* New York, N.Y., United Nations, 1964. (A/5830.)
35. *Reunión regional de jóvenes Latinoamericanos. Informe final.* Paris, Unesco, 1974.
36. ROCHIN. R. I. *The impact of dwarf wheats on farmers with small-holdings in West Pakistan. Excerpts from recent studies.* New York, N. Y., Ford Foundation, 1971.
37. RODNEY, W. African history and development planning. *Models of development.* London, Student Christian Movement, 1973.
38. ROGERS, E.; and HERZOG, W. Functional literacy among Colombian peasants. *Economic development and cultural change.* Chicago, Ill., January 1966.
39. RUDRA, A.; MAJID, A.; TALIB, B. Big farmers of the Punjab: some preliminary findings of a sample survey. *Economic and political weekly* (Bombay). September, 1969.
40. SALAME, N. *Le problème de l'alphabétisation.* Paris, Université de Paris I, 1973. (Thèse de doctorat d'Etat.)
41 SMYTH. J. Cost-effectiveness report on the work-oriented adult literacy pilot project in Iran. Synopsis. *Planning out-of-school education for development.* Paris, International Institute for Educational Planning, 1973.
42. THANT, U. *Proposals for action. The United Nations Development Decade.* New York, N.Y. United Nations, 1962. (62.II.B.2.)
43. *Third International Conference on Adult Education. Final report,* Paris, Unesco, 1972. (ED/MD/25.)
44. VARKEVISSER, C. M. *Socialization in a changing society. Sukuma childhood in rural and urban Mwanza, Tanzania.* The Hague, Centre for the Study of Education in Changing Societies, 1973.
45. *World Conference of Ministers of Education on the Eradication of Illiteracy. Final report.* Paris, Unesco, 1965.
46. *World literacy programme,* Paris, Unesco, 1964. (13C/PRG/14.)
47. *Young people and African cultural values.* Paris, Unesco, 1975. (SHC.75/WS/9.)